SOCIAL POLICY REVIEW 14

Developments and debates: 2001-2002

Edited by Robert Sykes, Catherine Bochel and Nick Ellison

The POLICY PRESS

First published in Great Britain in July 2002 by

The Policy Press
34 Tyndall's Park Road
Bristol BS8 1PY
UK

Tel +44 (0)117 954 6800
Fax +44 (0)117 973 7308
e-mail tpp@bristol.ac.uk
www.policypress.org.uk

British Library Cataloguing in Publication Data
A catalogue record for this book is available from the British Library

ISBN 1 86134 377 9 paperback
A hardback version of this book is also available

Robert Sykes is Principal Lecturer in Social Policy in the School of Social Sciences and Law, Sheffield Hallam University, **Catherine Bochel** is Senior Lecturer in Social Policy in the Department of Policy Studies, University of Lincolnshire and Humberside, and **Nick Ellison** is Senior Lecturer in the Department of Sociology and Social Policy, University of Durham.

Cover design by Qube Design Associates, Bristol.
Front cover: photograph of a biosphere roof, Eden Project, kindly supplied by Dawn Rushen

Printed and bound in Great Britain by Hobbs the Printers, Southampton

Contents

Notes on contributors

Peter Beresford is Professor of Social Policy and Director of the Centre for Citizen Participation, Department of Social Work, Brunel University.

Catherine Bochel is Senior Lecturer at the School of Policy Studies, University of Lincolnshire and Humberside.

David Byrne, Department of Sociology and Social Policy, University of Durham.

Caron Caldwell, Applied Social Studies, University of Luton.

Chris Crowther is Senior Lecturer in Social Policy, School of Social Sciences and Law, Sheffield Hallam University.

Nick Ellison is Senior Lecturer and Head of Department, Department of Sociology and Social Policy, University of Durham.

Caroline Glendinning is Professor Social Policy in the National Primary Care Research and Development Centre, University of Manchester.

Chris Holden, Department of Health and Social Care, Brunel University.

Martin Roche, Regional Research Institute, University of Wolverhampton.

Rosemary Sales is Reader in Social Policy, School of Social Science, Middlesex University.

Robert Sykes is Principal Lecturer in Social Policy, School of Social Sciences and Law, Sheffield Hallam University.

Monica Threlfall is Senior Lecturer in Politics, Department of European Studies, Loughborough University.

Mike Tomlinson, School of Sociology and Social Policy, Queen's University, Belfast.

Carol Walker, Policy Studies Research Centre, University of Lincoln.

David Wilkin is Professor of Health Services Research in the National Primary Care Research Centre, University of Manchester.

Nicola Yeates, School of Sociology and Social Policy, Queen's University, Belfast.

ONE

The year in social policy

Robert Sykes, Catherine Bochel and Nick Ellison

UK developments

As *Social Policy Review 13* went to press, the 2001 General Election had just been called, with Labour promising improvements in public services, including increases in the numbers of doctors, nurses and teachers, as a major part of its proposal for a second term. The editors' comments in this section at that time (Sykes et al, 2001) suggested that a re-elected New Labour government might need to be kept under pressure to deliver on all of its promises in the social policy field.

It is certainly the case that there has been pressure: excepting the attacks on the World Trade Centre in New York on 11 September and its aftermath, the debate over the future of public services has arguably been the dominant feature of the UK policy arena over the past year. In June 2001, as Labour romped home to a second landslide, there were fewer victory celebrations than had been the case in 1997. The government's approach was much about getting on with the tasks in hand, and prominent among these has been the condition and the future of public services, including the NHS, education and public transport. The NHS has remained in the headlines with a number of negative high profile cases being played out in the media. These included the occasion when Tony Blair and Iain Duncan-Smith became embroiled in a bitter row over a north London hospital's alleged neglect of a 94-year-old woman and the continued debate over waiting lists. In many instances the level of resourcing was an underlying theme of these concerns. At the same time, albeit with different causes, the government continued to struggle to allay growing public fears over the three-in-one injections against measles, mumps and rubella (MMR) and there was evidence that take-up of the MMR vaccine was falling below target levels in some areas.

Public transport has also remained a thorn in the government's side for a range of reasons, including rail strikes, delays for commuters, increasing congestion and the consequent impacts these have on business, industry and the economy. The Secretary of State for Transport gave the go-ahead for the part-privatisation of the London Underground, despite opposition from Ken Livingstone, the Mayor of London, commuters themselves and the House of Commons' Transport Select Committee. Added to this, the unseemly fracas within the Department for Transport, Local Government and the Regions, between the Secretary of State's special adviser, Jo Moore, and the Department's Head of Communications, Martin Sixsmith, played out in the media, did little to increase the public's confidence in those responsible for improving the public transport systems. Early in 2002 Ken Livingstone decided to push ahead with plans to charge drivers in central London £5 for each visit, despite concerns from parts of the media and the public.

For social services the inquiry into the death of Victoria Climbié seems certain to have far-reaching implications for children's services from both the public and voluntary sectors, and these, combined with some of the changes arising from the government's modernisation programmes, mean that the shape of large parts of the personal social services sector will be changed forever. The verdict in the Sarah Payne case led to renewed calls for a 'Sarah's law' that would require known paedophiles to be publicly identified. At the same time, arguments over the future of long-term care for older people rumble on, with continued pressure on the Westminster government to follow the line taken in Scotland and to accept that social care as well as health care should be provided free.

One of the common themes among the debates on the public sector has been the involvement of the private sector, whether it be through the use of private finance, private management, or merely the view of the private sector as an appropriate model for public provision. The involvement of the private sector has perhaps been particularly controversial for the trades unions, and 2001/02 have seen increasing displays of anger, including speeches by union leaders and calls for reductions or stoppages to funding for the Labour Party.

On the other hand, and concurrently with pressing ahead with initiatives involving the private sector, the government has appeared to be cautiously moving towards the view that if the public wishes to have better services then they will have to be paid for, with the clear implication that taxes, in one form or another, would have to rise in order for this to happen.

It is also worth noting the extent to which some issues from a year ago seem to have moved down the agenda. Fuel prices and genetically-modified (GM) foods have been much less in the news. In contrast, other issues, most notably racism, have retained their high profile, in part due to the trial of those accused of the murder of Damilola Taylor. In the eyes of some, this can be linked to the further clampdown on asylum seekers in the aftermath of 11 September, under the pretext of deterring terrorism (see 'International developments' later). However, on the issue of asylum seekers there was an acceptance by the government that the voucher system for payment for food and clothing has been unsatisfactory. In addition the 2001 Anti-terrorism, Crime and Security Act has been passed, bringing a variety of new powers to government, with 21 mainly Muslim organisations proscribed as 'terrorist'. An immediate reaction to the 'fear of terrorism' was a proposal mooted by the Home Secretary to introduce compulsory identification cards, although this later appeared to have fallen down the agenda.

While education has perhaps been somewhat less problematic for the government over recent years, there have remained a number of significant questions, including the recruitment and training of teachers, the appropriateness of judgements of standards and the development of appropriate skills, in addition to the inevitable issues over levels of resources. For higher education, the issue of student fees and loans remains, and there have been increasing signs from the government that it recognises that it may have to look again at funding, particularly given the stated desire to achieve its 50% student participation target by 2010.

The constitutional changes of Labour's first term have become increasingly embedded, with the Human Rights Act and devolution perhaps having the most obvious and immediate impact, although, as the chapters by Byrne (Chapter Three) and Tomlinson (Chapter Four) on devolution in the UK developments section of this book illustrate, some of the impacts have focused attention on issues of resource allocation, and public expenditure in particular, within the UK, and these are raising new and important questions for social and public policy. As devolution has progressed we have seen greater divergence in the component parts of the UK. Notably, in Scotland free long-term care for older people has been proposed and legislation banning foxhunting has been passed; in Wales the Assembly has made a limited change by freezing NHS prescription charges and reintroducing free school milk; and in Northern Ireland the Education Minister, Martin McGuinness, cancelled the publication of school-by-school league tables.

However, despite Labour's second landslide election victory, there are significant questions around democracy and political legitimacy. In the 2001 General Election the turnout was the lowest since 1914, with only 3 in 5 people voting and only 1 in 5 voting Labour, and at local government level turnout remains very low. Among the suggestions to reinvigorate democracy are proposals to make voting easier, such as Internet voting, greater use of postal voting and locating polling stations in supermarkets. For local government, the introduction of directly elected mayors has been suggested, in theory clearly identifiable and directly accountable to the electorate; only a handful of local authorities have succeeded in getting public support for this innovation through local referendums. However, despite its commitment to modernisation and reinvigorating democracy, the government's proposals for reform of the House of Lords are suggesting that only 20% of its members be elected.

It is perhaps appropriate at this stage to look ahead and to note that, reflecting both the passage of time and the apparent electoral dominance of New Labour, the party's second term has arguably, and perhaps inevitably, meant that attention has started to reflect less on the legacy of the Conservative years and has focused rather more on the extent to which Labour has been successful in achieving its aims and in fulfilling its electoral promises. It seems likely that the debates around social policy will also echo this across a range of issues, including the assessment of initiatives such as the National Child Care Strategy, the role of Tax Credits and concerns over pensions, as well as approaches such as the Private Finance Initiative, joint working and partnership. This suggests that future debates will continue to be interesting.

International developments

Widening our gaze to the international scene, there is surely one event which, in its original enormity and its aftermath, has dominated: the attack on the World Trade Centre in New York on 11 September and the subsequent 'war on terrorism'. Yet, despite the fact that various commentators and politicians have voiced the view that September 11 (as it has become known) has irrevocably changed the world, it is still rather difficult to establish quite how this change is to be characterised, let alone analysed. Clearly, there has been a massive military response involving the US and its allies, principally the UK, in seeking to destroy the Taliban and al-Qaeda forces in Afghanistan. While a new government has now been installed in Afghanistan, its future is still shaky and in need of both military and, probably, financial support. The military might of the US has been focused on destroying the al-Qaeda groups, but just when it may appear that the latter have been defeated, they mount retaliatory strikes against the US and, now, UK ground forces.

But what does all this mean for broader politics and policy making, particularly that which has social policy significance? Frankly, it is probably too soon to say, but we can begin to make some speculative suggestions for possible outcomes and developments. First, as ever, there is the issue of financial costs: leaving aside the massive costs to the US of rebuilding a major section of one of the foremost world cities, what of the costs to the US and other nations, such as the UK and other allies, of their military involvement in Afghanistan? Neither the US nor UK governments has so far put a price on the 'war on terrorism' but it does not take a financial wizard to work out that, in the medium to longer term, the massive costs of high technology equipment, armaments, personnel, transport and logistics will all have to be paid for. And where will the money come from? The two leading protagonists and thus the two countries with the highest costs are two of the leading lights of the neo-liberal school of government, and the notion that such governments will increase taxation to pay for their military activities is, to say the least, problematic. Perhaps the idea increasingly floated by the Labour government that in order to have better public services such as health and education the British taxpayer will need to pay more in taxes can be translated to paying for 'security' and 'the war on terrorism'. Yet this would constitute an enormous political risk for a government which has prided itself on its financial prudence, the more so as political opposition in the UK at last seems to be getting its act together, and the closer a general election approaches. The alternative, of course, is to reduce public expenditure elsewhere to counteract the increased defence/military costs, and social expenditure is, of course, in most Western capitalist states a key component of such expenditure. Perhaps in the US this course might be pursued by a government with less political, that is, electoral, reaction given the already attenuated character of federal welfare spending and the dominant liberal welfare ideology (but see below on the US steel tariffs). The notion, however, that a British or other European government could sell to its voters the idea of making cuts in welfare spending to pay for its anti-terrorist activities, however much publicly supported in the abstract, is far more dubious, especially at a time when such governments appear to be conceding that social and infrastructural spending on items such as transport might be increased, not decreased.

A second outcome would appear to be a hardening of official policy by certain European governments towards migrants and asylum seekers as fears over terrorist activities are translated into concerns, however ill-founded, that such terrorists are infiltrating the countries they are seeking to attack. These concerns have been fanned by a frankly xenophobic and even racist popular press and, as Rosemary Sales points out in her chapter in this review (Chapter Eight), even when asylum seekers do make it into countries such as Italy and the UK, they are commonly met with verbal and physical abuse from some sections of the indigenous population, coupled with official attitudes and policies which often appear to be designed to make life as difficult as possible for such people. As we have already suggested above, the UK government seems to be reconsidering its policies and their effects in this area. Notwithstanding such official shifts of position, however, as various refugee and ethnic minority pressure groups have pointed out, there appears to have been a rebirth of anti-Asian and anti-Muslim sentiment among various informal and semi-formal political groupings. This has expressed itself in verbal and physical attacks on people of 'Asian' appearance by vigilante groups and members of far-right political fringe groups in countries such as the UK, Germany and Italy. In response, it is noticeable, not least in the UK, that young Asians in particular have adopted a much more aggressive verbal and even physical stance against both racist attacks on their communities, and what they argue is their continuing unfair treatment in terms of jobs and access to public services.

So, in one very important sense, the global context for social policy making and development is likely to be affected in the longer term by the 11 September events and their aftermath. In all this the dominance of the US is crystal clear. Turning from the field of international politics to the international economy the dominance of the US is no less apparent. 'Anti-globalisers' continue to dog the meetings of the major capitalist countries and their leaders in various places around the world, even when, as in the choice of Kananaskis, Alberta for the G8 meeting in June 2002, venues are chosen more for their inaccessibility to protesters than for their suitability as meeting venues for the world's elites. As Nicola Yeates points out in her chapter (Chapter Seven), the 'anti-globalisers' now have well-developed communications and publicity systems (see, for example, www.protest.net) and are clearly planning to extend and develop their attempts to check and even reverse the activities of what they regard as the major institutions of neo-liberal globalisation, such as the International Monetary Fund (IMF) and the World Bank. Whether such protests are, in fact, having an impact on these international organisations and/or the leading capitalist governments is arguable. The World Bank continues to develop what, in comparison with previous pronouncements at least, appears to be a more socially conscious and welfare oriented approach: its 'strapline' on the World Bank website, for example, is 'Our dream is a world free of poverty'. Yet the commitment of all the various organisations such as the World Bank, the IMF, the World Trade Organisation (WTO), the Organisation for Economic Co-operation and Development (OECD), the EU and the governments of the leading capitalist countries voiced through the G8 organisation is to the neo-liberal path of deregulation, more flexible labour markets and economic growth as the only way to achieve poverty reduction. Leaving aside the more partisan political exchanges of the 'pro-' and 'anti-' globalisers, even apparently objective debate on the links between poverty and globalisation continues to be characterised by a clear divergence between those who argue that globalisation actually helps to reduce poverty on a world scale and those who argue that, at least in its unrestricted neo-liberal senses, it does not. A recent debate in *Prospect* magazine (March 2002) exemplifies the impasse which such arguments have reached. On the one hand, Martin Wolfe, chief economics editor of the *Financial Times*, argues that: (a) poverty and inequality on a world scale have fallen in the last 10 years; (b) that these falls are due to greater economic integration of the global economy; and (c) that the arguments of the 'anti-globalisers' are actually likely to increase rather than decrease poverty and inequality. On the other hand, Robert Wade, Professor of Political Economy at the London School of Economics and Political Science, contests Wolfe's reliance on World Bank and similar figures to support the first contention, and maintains that the distribution of income and poverty on a world scale continues, in any case, to be massively inequitable, and that inequality between nations and within some nations, especially China and India, continues to widen, at best, not helped by global economic integration and, at worst, exacerbated by it. The debate, which bears all the hallmarks of two advocates talking past each other, leaves those of us looking for an answer to the question 'Is (or isn't) globalisation making poverty better or worse?' without an answer, let alone a suggestion as to what can or should be done about world poverty reduction.

Perhaps, however, the very powers behind the 'Washington' consensus on economic strategy may be providing some of the most effective ammunition against pure neo-liberal economic and social policies themselves. President Bush's recent decision to impose tariffs on steel imports into the US has been met with a tirade of criticism, if somewhat hollow given their own previous protectionist activities, from other capitalist countries around the world. The EU member states (conveniently ignoring their own Common Agricultural Policy) has cried foul, sought the support of the WTO in reversing the US's actions, and threatened retaliatory tariff measures of its own. *The Economist* magazine, hardly a stalwart of the welfarist camp, has observed not only that the actions of the US government are, in its words 'disgraceful', but also suggested that the preferred course of action should have been for more, not less, federal welfare provision to support redundant US steelworkers. In what may prove to be something of a watershed in the rhetoric of at least the 'socially responsible' liberal camp (and increasingly echoed in the statements of the British Conservatives) *The Economist* argues that "... the principle should be 'protect the worker, not the industry'. The government should improve its assistance programmes for workers who lose their health-care benefits and pensions when firms fail, and it should look at new and more generous ways of helping workers find new jobs" (9 March 2002, p 13). This, of course, has been the line promoted by the EU in recent years. Are we about to see welfare reform measures now taking a westerly direction after so many years of American-influenced change?

Conceptual developments

Turning to theory, it is possible to observe a disjunction between two forms of theorising in social policy which may be becoming increasingly explicit. On the one side, the health of contemporary social democracy is an issue that continues to preoccupy social policy analysts, perhaps attracting additional interest due to the current obsession with attempts to theorise the impact of globalisation. Much of this work, implicitly or explicitly, deals with the state of the state and in so doing inevitably focuses on the role of public goods and services in welfare systems, which are widely recognised to be under pressure (Taylor-Gooby, 2001). On the other side, an equal amount of attention is being devoted to what might loosely be termed post-welfare theory. Work in this area is concerned with developing ideas that challenge traditional understandings of the welfare state and, by implication, social democratic solutions. The most obvious example here would be recent attempts to theorise a Green social policy (Fitzpatrick with Caldwell, 2001; Hoggett, 2001). Another case in point is the continuing effort to incorporate ideas of difference and recognition into thinking about contemporary welfare democracy and citizenship, possibly through forms of democratic deliberation (Lister, 2002), or through efforts to develop new ideas about democratic participation (see Beresford, Chapter Thirteen). Again, in a different manner, new thinking about geo-demographics is beginning to influence our conceptions of the post-welfare society, an approach that will briefly be considered below.

Of course, the suggestion that there is an implicit segregation between these different dimensions of theorising about social policy may be contested, not least by some of those involved in efforts to transcend them. There have, after all, been numerous attempts to recast the idea of the social democratic welfare state and the goods associated with it in terms better suited to changing times, just as there have been attempts to relate reformulated ideas of democracy, citizenship and so on to the central social policy concerns of poverty, equality and social justice. Perhaps there is a way through here, but such theoretical efforts are by their nature contested and, at the present time, may be unable to reconcile the different logics inherent in the social democracy/post-welfare division. Some examples will illustrate the point. Recent developments in thinking about globalisation and, at a rather different level, the current difficulties concerning pensions policies demonstrate the continuing case for a fairly traditional interpretation of social democracy. Conversely, efforts to apply Green thinking to the social policy arena and the emerging area of geo-demographics deny, explicitly or implicitly, the continuing relevance of social democratic solutions.

Taking globalisation first, current literature divides reasonably clearly into three perspectives. First, hyperglobalisers such as John Gray, Anthony Giddens and Ramesh Mishra argue that social democratic welfarism is effectively dead, national welfare states having had their capacity for domestic economic management, including their ability to decide levels of welfare spending, removed by a deadly combination of increasing trade openness and capital mobility. Second, others like Paul Pierson and Torben Iversen argue that globalisation is essentially a myth and that welfare state change can be more accurately ascribed to endogenous factors, particularly domestic sources of deindustrialisation. Finally, a middle way, typified in the work of Stephan Leibfried, Geoffrey Garret and others, suggests that the pressures arising from economic globalisation are indeed real, but that the welfare state can force limits to globalisation if suitably configured. The crucial variable here is the degree of embeddedness of social democratic institutions. Both the latter perspectives see a central role for the state as a provider of welfare, with commentators pointing out that social democratic policies continue to be pursued even in an age of welfare retrenchment. The third approach, in particular, regards state-based welfare democracy, best exemplified in the Nordic countries, as sufficiently powerful to offset the potentially damaging effects of global capitalism by preserving social protection and insulating vulnerable groups from the vagaries of the market. On this reading, then, comprehensive welfare provision remains associated with an active, interventionist state, the ultimate point being that social democracy is a system not only worth defending, but necessary to the preservation of equality and social justice in a globalised world.

The current difficulties concerning old age pensions also point to the need to retain comprehensive social provision. While the Nordic regimes and, in a less egalitarian manner, the Christian democratic welfare systems of Northern and Western Europe, have continued to fund their ageing populations generously, over a period of 20 years or so the UK and other liberal regimes have progressively reduced state involvement in pensions in favour of private alternatives. However, it now appears that private solutions have not worked. Falling stock markets have provoked a series of radical adjustments to many pension funds' payout arrangements, while the most recent irony is that the City is now advising individuals to re-enter the state pension system (SERPS). David Walker's (2002, p 23) comment that middle England believes passionately in the "welfare state for gran" aptly sums up the issue: there are certain elements of universal state welfare provision that voters want to preserve and may (once again) be willing to pay for in the form of higher taxes.

In contrast to this pro-state reasoning, post-welfare theories regard the traditional social democratic welfare paradigm with a degree of suspicion. Green theory is a case in point. Clearly Green thinking contains a number of different strands and its complexities cannot be discussed adequately here. Suffice to say, though, that certain elements of Green thought tend to be rejected by those interested in applying environmental thinking to social policy issues, what Dean (2001, p 498) refers to as the "discourse of deep ecology characterised by an anti-humanistic ecocentrism" being a good example. This leaves the rather more friendly variants of Green communitarianism and eco-socialism, which nevertheless stress the centrality of an anti-productivist ethic as a precondition for moves towards more ecologically sustainable ways of living. To anti-productivism should be added the prerequisite of democratic decentralisation and political participation, for, as Hoggett (2001, p 617) comments, the democratisation of political society at national and local levels is essential to the development of our moral and ethical capacities, his point being that governments have for too long tried to exclude citizens from participation in the complex ethical and moral questions that saturate collective everyday living. In the place of big government, then, comes local deliberative assemblies possessing certain executive and budgetary powers, and beyond that the thoroughgoing democratisation of local and national representative institutions themselves. Whatever the precise configuration of these institutions, it is plain that the centralised, social democratic welfare state, with its dependence on economic growth to provide a tax base sufficiently extensive to fund relatively generous transfer arrangements, in addition to a range of other collective goods and services, is the antithesis of the kind of welfare base Green theorists envisage.

A further, and different, example of contemporary post-welfare theorising comes in the form of new thinking about geo-demographics (Graham and Marvin, 2001). Arguments here are not anti-state as such, but regard collectivism, whether national or municipal, as increasingly redundant. On this view, the key institutional components of the post-war state are literally splintering in the face of the disruptive forces of privatisation and liberalisation. Of particular significance are the ways in which certain individuals and social groups are able to utilise resources, often electronic, in a manner that allows privileged access to a growing range of privatised information, goods and services. The result is the development of fractured identities, lifestyles and modes of belonging that are continually changed and reshaped, partly in the ongoing reflexive recreation of these personal resources themselves, partly in the physical transformation of the (urban) spaces in which these individuals live, and, partly, too, in the manner in which they choose to engage socially and politically in a changing public sphere. If the privileged circumstances of this growing urban professional class are contrasted with the levels of deprivation and exclusion experienced by more vulnerable groups, it is not difficult to see how the state's traditional role as a universal welfare provider and agent of social governance, could become focused increasingly narrowly on marginal and excluded groups. Once again, any process of this kind is plainly antithetical to traditional social democratic understandings of universalism and social justice.

So, here we have two very different paradigms of welfare theory, one seemingly convinced that the social democratic welfare state remains relevant in spite of, or perhaps because of, contemporary challenges to its existence; the other equally convinced that state welfare institutions are too dependent on economic growth, undemocratic or, at least for those able to enjoy the benefits of the privatised society, effectively outdated. There is obviously no space here to try to resolve the differences between these two theoretical dimensions of social policy, but of course the point is that there may be no policy-relevant means of achieving such a reconciliation. Instead we may have to make hard theoretical choices, not just about where each of us stands on the kind of issues raised here, but about the kind of theory contemporary social policy actually needs.

References

Economist, The (2002) 'George Bush, protectionist', 9 March, p 13.

Fitzpatrick, T. with Caldwell, C. (2001) 'Towards a theory of ecosocial welfare', *Environmental Politics*, vol 10, no 2, pp 43-67.

Graham, S. and Marvin, S. (2001) *Splintering urbanism*, London: Routledge.

Hoggett, P. (2001) 'Democracy, social relations and ecowelfare', *Social Policy and Administration*, vol 35, no 5, pp 608-26.

Lister, R. (2002) 'A politics of recognition and respect: involving people with experience of poverty in decision making that affects their lives', *Welfare and Society*, vol 1, no 1, pp 37-46.

Prospect (2002) 'Are global poverty and inequality getting worse?', March, pp 16-21.

Sykes, R., Bochel, C. and Ellison, N. (2001) *Social Policy Review 13: Developments and debates, 2000-2001*, Bristol: The Policy Press, in association with the SPA.

Taylor-Gooby, P. (ed) (2001) *Welfare states under pressure*, London: Sage Publications.

Walker, D. (2002) 'The return of universalism', *The Guardian*, 23 March, p 23.

Part One:
UK developments

After five years of Labour government it is not surprising that attention has now switched away from the Conservative years and has been replaced instead by assessments of the extent to which Labour has 'made a difference'. This, in a sense, provides something of a theme for the four chapters in this section. Given the centrality of constitutional and governmental reform to the agenda of the 1997-2001 Labour government, it is perhaps inevitable that devolution is starting to have an impact on social policy. While this has been immediately apparent in some of the policy decisions made by the devolved administrations, the concerns addressed in the chapters by Byrne and Tomlinson go beyond the immediate impact of individual policies to questions of resource distribution. Byrne, writing from the perspective of the North East of England, focuses on issues of sub-national resource distribution in the UK and the importance of these in determining policy opportunities, particularly at regional level. He considers ways in which we might understand public expenditure patterns and what this may mean for resource distribution in relation to issues of territorial justice. Tomlinson, focusing on Northern Ireland, considers the implications of the new constitutional arrangements for social policy. This is a geographical area frequently neglected in the literature, and as such this contribution is to be welcomed. He considers the issue of resource allocation between different components of the UK and examines arguments for changing conventions that have been in place for over 20 years. The impact of the 1998 Northern Ireland Act and the challenges presented by constitutional reform for social policy in Northern Ireland are also explored.

The chapter by Wilkin and Glendinning and that by Walker direct attention to some of the other concerns under Labour, such as reform of public services, service delivery, policy implementation, choice and inclusion. Wilkin and Glendinning consider the creation of Primary Care Groups and Trusts, the thinking behind these and their potential for reforming the NHS, as part of the government's 'modernisation' agenda. This chapter highlights the tensions between the demands of central government for tighter management and control, the rhetoric of devolved power, and the political challenge of meeting public expectations in this area.

The Labour government's Learning Disabilities Strategy is discussed by Walker. The White Paper on which this is based claims to put people with learning difficulties at the centre of future strategy and supports a lifelong approach to addressing people's needs. These are valiant objectives which, if successful, could be a significant example of joined-up government. The strategy is critically reviewed in the light of the goals set out in the White Paper and in doing so Walker raises broader issues around government policy, including resourcing, implementation, the use of consultation as a tool and the impact on the different agencies involved.

Overall, these four chapters serve to focus our attention not only on Labour's policies, but also on the deeper themes and implications of much of the government's thinking. As such they provide insight not only into the current developments but also to future challenges.

TWO

Modernising primary healthcare in England: the role of Primary Care Groups and Trusts

David Wilkin and Caroline Glendinning

> The National Health Service in Britain could not ensure that doctors
> … would choose overnight to be 'better' doctors; all it could do was to
> provide that particular framework of social resources within which
> potentially 'better' medicine might be more easily chosen and practiced.
> (Titmuss, quoted in Moon and North, 2000, p 72)

Introduction

This chapter discusses how, some 40 years after Titmuss wrote the above,
some of the last refuges of medical professional autonomy and individualism
are being challenged. It describes the latest 'framework of social resources'
– Primary Care Groups and Trusts (PCG/Ts) – and evaluates their
prospects for success in, among other things, generating 'better' doctors
(and nurses and other primary health professionals).

Historically, primary care – particularly the healthcare provided through
general practitioners (GPs) – has constituted both the cornerstone and
the Achilles heel of the National Health Service (NHS). Both as the
provider of easily accessible, low cost, first contact and continuing care
and as the gatekeeper to more expensive specialist health services, primary
care has played a major role in ensuring universal healthcare is available in
Great Britain, at relatively low cost. However, wide variations in the
levels and standards of primary care services, difficulties in containing
costs within a demand-led service, and the separation of primary care
from mainstream NHS management and planning have together prevented
the development of a service that is either of consistently high quality or
integrated with other community-based health services. For the past
50 years, general practice has remained a 'cottage industry' on the fringes

of the NHS, based on "individualistic, small shopkeeper principles" in which "the principles of free choice of doctors by patients and complete medical autonomy ... remain sacrosanct" (Klein, 1983, p 14).

The creation of PCG/Ts arguably represents one of the most radical reforms of the NHS since its inception. This chapter describes the reasons behind these reforms and their implementation; assesses the implications and the potential for transforming primary and community health services; and highlights some of the risks and threats which lie ahead. In particular, the chapter will assess the contributions (actual and potential) of PCG/ Ts to the 'modernisation' of the NHS. Broadly speaking, 'modernisation' is assumed here to refer to the high profile political objective of securing improvements in the delivery of public sector services. Within the context of the NHS, 'modernisation' also carries overtones of a challenge to traditional professional power, autonomy and practices, particularly on the part of the medical profession; and a degree of tension between this traditional power and newer, managerial influences. Within primary healthcare, improvements in the flexibility and responsiveness of services to patients, equity of access, quality, cost-effectiveness and collaborative capacity are key elements of the government's 'modernisation' enterprise.

However, in order for the full significance of these reforms to be appreciated, it is necessary first to describe the historical context of primary care and the challenges that faced the incoming Labour government in 1997 (fuller accounts of this history are provided in previous issues of the *Social Policy Review* by Petchey, 1996 and Glendinning, 1998).

From 1948 to 1997

Created in 1948, the NHS consisted of three separately managed services: hospitals, community health services and family practitioner services (GPs, dentists, opticians and pharmacists). Only hospitals and their staff were fully managed by the NHS. Community health services were largely administered by local authorities, while family practitioner services were provided by independent professionals, whose contracts to provide services to the NHS were administered by Local Executive Committees. The medical profession itself had rejected, during the 1940s, the option of a salaried GP service, choosing instead for GPs to contract individually with the NHS to provide services in exchange for a capitation payment for each of their registered patients.

Throughout the 1950s and early 1960s general practice remained a backwater of the NHS. Single-handed GPs practised in isolation, with little or no support and few incentives to improve services. However, the introduction in the mid-1960s of a new contract for GPs brought with it a new payment system, which aimed to reward improvements in the services GPs provided and offered financial support for GP premises, staff and equipment.

The mid-1960s to 1990 saw some significant, if patchy, developments in GP services. Single-handed practices declined, premises improved, nurses and administrative staff were appointed and the range of services provided by general practices increased. However, these developments were by no means universal. While the best practices took advantage of additional payments and support, many single-handed practices remained, and variations between the best and the worst practices probably increased (Jarman, 1981; London Health Planning Consortium, 1981; Wilkin et al, 1987).

A major reorganisation in 1974 transferred the management of community health services from local authorities to NHS District and Area Health Authorities, alongside hospitals. This removed one of the separate arms of the original tripartite NHS structure and allowed government to allocate a single budget for all hospital and community health services, which could more easily be controlled or capped where necessary. However, GP and the other family practitioner services (dentists, pharmacists, opticians) remained separately funded and administered by Family Practitioner Committees. GP services remained essentially demand-led, with expenditure levels (for example, on drug prescribing or requests for laboratory investigations) determined by a combination of demand by patients and GPs' patterns of professional decision making and behaviour.

The internal market reforms of the 1990s (Secretary of State for Health, 1989) were highly contentious and the object of considerable analysis and comment (see for example, Bain, 1994; Glennerster et al, 1994; NAO, 1994; Audit Commission, 1995; Coulter, 1995; Flynn et al, 1996; Petchey, 1996). For the purposes of this chapter, two aspects of the internal market need to be highlighted. First, these reforms focused on the funding and provision of hospital and community services, employing market mechanisms to tackle problems of quality and cost. The role of GPs in purchasing hospital and community health services, initially through standard GP fundholding and subsequently through a 'mosaic' (Smith et al, 1997) of alternative models (community fundholding, total purchasing pilots, multi-funds and locality commissioning groups) placed them in a powerful position to influence and shape the provision of hospital and community services. However, there is only limited evidence that GPs exploited this power to bring about changes in the costs or quality of hospital services (Glennerster et al, 1994; Mays et al, 2000). More apparent were improvements and extensions in the range of services provided in GPs' own practices, particularly in the first few years of fundholding (NHSE, 1994; Mays et al, 1998; Roland and Shapiro, 1998).

Second, the internal market did nothing to alter the independent status of GPs. Although a new GP contract, introduced in 1990, imposed new requirements on the profession (such as the obligation to offer an annual health check to all patients aged 75 plus) and introduced new financial incentives for GPs to take on more patients and provide new services, GPs' status as independent contractors to the NHS remained unchanged. Moreover, evidence on the implementation of the new contract suggests that a combination of resistance by GPs and scepticism on the part of managers may together have restricted its impact on GP behaviour and the services they provided (Glendinning et al, 1994). The new Family Health Service Authorities, which administered GPs contracts from 1990, remained separate from the health authorities that were responsible for hospital and community health services. In many areas, community health services were disaggregated from acute hospital services to form semi-autonomous NHS Community Health Services Trusts, but no attempt was made to integrate these with the primary care services provided by GPs and their practices. Moreover, apart from the allocation of fixed prescribing budgets to GP fundholders, expenditure on general practitioner services remained demand-led.

Towards the mid-1990s, the language and behaviour of the internal market shifted from purchasing and competition towards a greater emphasis on commissioning and collaboration. At the same time, the Department of Health began promoting the policy of developing a 'primary care-led NHS' (Petchey, 1996; Glendinning, 1998). Although subject to differing interpretations, this was generally understood to include a major role for GPs and other primary care professionals in shaping the development of the NHS as a whole. Two White Papers published just before the 1997 election (Secretary of State for Health, 1996a, 1996b) set out the government's plans for a more integrated health service, with primary care playing a central role.

New Labour, new NHS?

The Labour government that came to power in 1997 faced a number of challenges:

- GPs, and the services they provided within their practices, remained structurally and financially separate from mainstream NHS management and were not integrated with other community health or social care services.
- The GP contract had proved to be a blunt policy instrument for changing GP behaviour and practice.
- Although the internal market had succeeded in capping expenditure on hospital and community health services and on GPs' prescribing of drugs, the costs of the services provided by GPs remained demand-led.
- Substantial variations in the quality and coverage of primary care services remained. Such variations had particular salience for a Labour government committed to ending a 'two-tier' NHS, in which patients of GP fundholders were generally believed to enjoy speedier access to a wider range of better quality services than the patients of non-fundholders.

On the other hand, the internal market had drawn many GPs into planning, commissioning and purchasing services, particularly for their own patients, but also in some instances for the wider locality, through the variety of locality commissioning and fundholding arrangements. Moreover, within the internal market, this involvement arguably had a wider political significance: "without the involvement of fundholders and non-fundholding GPs, the legitimisation of purchasing strategies and priorities would have proved extremely difficult" (Moon and North, 2000, p 60).

The first Labour government was committed to recreating the NHS as a universal and equitable health service. This involved major reforms of the internal market and the abolition of GP fundholding in particular. The programme for reform was set out in the December 1997 White Paper, *New NHS: Modern, dependable* (DoH, 1997). Major policy themes in the White Paper included:

- improving health and reducing inequalities in the incidence of illness, morbidity and mortality;
- increasing equity in the availability of health services and treatments (including the end of the alleged two-tier provision associated with GP fundholding);
- improving the quality of health services;
- increasing the overall coherence and integration of services through closer collaboration, both within the NHS and between the NHS and other public and private sector providers of health and welfare services (for example, social services, housing and education).

Less explicit, but nevertheless important, underlying objectives were to exercise greater control over both the spending and the performance of healthcare professionals.

The organisational centrepiece of the reforms was the creation in England of Primary Care Groups and Trusts (slightly different arrangements were proposed for the other countries of the United Kingdom – see Rummery, 1998; Constitution Unit, 2001). These new organisations would retain the separation of purchasing and provision, at least for hospital services; but would replace the 'mosaic' of fundholding and commissioning models that had developed under the previous government. Each Primary Care Group (PCG) would cover all the GPs within a locality – typically about 50 GPs, serving around 100,000 registered patients. Dominated by primary care professionals, who were to constitute the majority of their governing Boards, PCGs were to be responsible for:

* improving the health of the local population and reducing health inequalities;
* developing primary and community health services;
* commissioning hospital services.

A highly significant development was to make PCGs responsible for managing a devolved, integrated budget made up from three formerly separate funding streams: the budget for purchasing hospital and community health services; funding for all GP drug prescribing; and the budget which had previously funded GP practice infrastructure – facilities such as premises, ancillary nursing and clerical staff and computing hardware.

PCGs were expected to draw on the previous experiences of GP fundholding and commissioning, at the same time as developing their own expertise and organisational capacity. This learning process was reflected in four levels of operation (Figure 2.1). At levels one and two, PCG/Ts would operate as sub-committees of their health authorities. At levels three and four they would become autonomous Primary Care Trusts (PCTs), having full responsibility for managing their budgets, commissioning and delivering services and accountable for their actions through mainstream NHS performance management arrangements.

In April 1999, 481 PCGs covering the whole of England went 'live'. Initially all PCGs began operating at levels one and two; by April 2000 the first 17 Trusts were created, with a further 23 in October 2000 and 124 in April 2001. Virtually all of these PCTs have moved directly to Level 4, becoming both providers of community services and

Figure 2.1: Levels of Primary Care Groups and Trusts

Level 1	Support and advise the health authority in commissioning care for its population.
Level 2	Take devolved responsibility for managing the budget for healthcare as a sub-committee of the health authority.
Level 3	Become established as a freestanding body (PCT) accountable to the health authority for commissioning care.
Level 4	Become established as a freestanding body (PCT) accountable to the health authority for commissioning care and *also* responsible for the provision of community health services.

commissioners of hospital services. The government subsequently announced (DoH, 2000) that all PCGs should become Trusts by April 2004; and that local health authorities would be abolished from April 2002. The very much smaller number of strategic health authorities which will replace local health authorities will have no direct role in providing or commissioning health services (DoH, 2001), but will be responsible for managing the performance of PCTs. Together, these changes mean that PCTs will be at the forefront of delivering the government's NHS modernisation targets and responsible for spending some 75% of the total NHS budget (DoH, 2001).

Thus for the first time since the founding of the NHS, primary and community health services are united within a single organisational framework, which is also responsible for commissioning hospital services. This new locality-wide framework for primary health services also provides unprecedented opportunities for more effective collaboration with other NHS organisations and with other public and private sector services, particularly local authority social services (Glendinning et al, 2001, 2002: forthcoming). The collaborative imperative is enshrined in the new 'duty of partnership', imposed on all NHS organisations by the 1999 Health Act. However, this chapter will discuss the role of PCG/Ts within the NHS, rather than their wider relationships and networks.

The remainder of this chapter reviews the evidence on the operation of PCG/Ts and their performance in three key areas: their organisation and governance arrangements; the creation and management of a unified healthcare budget; and their success in developing accessible and integrated primary and community services. Each of these elements will have a major impact on the capacity of PCG/Ts to deliver the 'modernising' improvements required by the government. Much of the evidence is drawn from the National Tracker Survey of PCG/Ts (Wilkin et al, 2000, 2001b). This longitudinal survey of a random sample of 15% of PCG/Ts aims to evaluate their development and performance during their first three years. It employs a combination of interviews and postal surveys of key individuals, including chief executives, chairs, social services representatives and clinical governance leads. The data presented in this chapter is based on the first two 'sweeps' of the Tracker Survey, carried out in 1999 and 2000, six months and 18 months respectively after PCG/Ts first went 'live'. Linked case studies are examining in more depth the implementation of clinical governance and the development of partnerships between PCG/Ts and local authorities.

Organisation and governance

As entirely new organisations, there is understandable interest in the internal structures and governance of PCG/Ts. Ultimately, PCG/Ts represent an attempt to unify the original tripartite structure of the NHS. They are also intended to be a 'Third Way' alternative to both the old hierarchical 'command and control' bureaucracy and the fragmentation of a market-led approach. Decisions about the strategic investment of considerable sums of money will be devolved directly to PCTs, thus enabling 'resources to be much more closely matched to the needs of local people'. As "primarily local organisations", PCTs are expected to take a "clear lead in developing local services and will be able to tailor services to local needs" (DoH, 2001, pp 14 and 22, passim). This devolution of resources and decision making is accompanied by a rhetoric of local democratic involvement, to "re-engage local communities to involve patients and the public in the design, delivery and development of local services" (DoH, 2001, p 12). How PCG/Ts discharge these responsibilities for major strategic and financial decisions and the involvement of local health professionals and communities respectively in these processes is therefore of considerable interest.

The devolution of strategic decision making and command over very substantial levels of resources to 'frontline' NHS professionals was not unconditional. The price for a position in the 'driving seat' of NHS modernisation was that, unlike GP fundholding, PCG/T membership is not optional. Furthermore, primary care professionals (GPs in particular) had to accept collective responsibility and accountability for service standards. GPs would retain their independent contractor status, but would be accountable to the PCG/T and *collectively* responsible for the services provided. Recognising the significance of these conditions, the British

Table 2.1: Percentages of PCG/T chairs rating stakeholder groups as 'well represented' in decision making (n=66, 2000 survey)

	%
GPs	91
Health authority	70
Social services	65
Primary and community nurses	64
Community Health Council	52
Local community	30
Voluntary organisations	19

Medical Association (BMA) set out its own terms for participation, the most important of which was that GPs should have the majority (seven out of 12) places on the decision-making Boards of PCG/Ts and have the right to decide who should chair the Board (usually a GP) (Sheaff et al, 2002: forthcoming). Other Board members are nurses (two), one social services representative, a lay representative, a health authority representative and the chief executive. This pattern of representation is broadly repeated in the Professional Executive Committee, the principle policy and decision-making body of PCTs.

Not surprisingly, given the terms negotiated by the BMA, GPs have quickly become the most influential constituency on PCG Boards and PCT Executive Committees. This was illustrated when PCG/T chairs were asked to rate the relative representation of different stakeholder groups in PCG/T decision making (Table 2.1).

Conversely, lay members consistently rated their own influence on decision making as lower than that of the chair, the chief officer or the GP Board members (Pickard et al, 2002: forthcoming). Majorities of both PCG/T Board chairs and lay representatives also considered that the interests of local communities were poorly represented. Although within their first few months 82% of PCG/Ts had consulted their local Community Health Councils and 47% had consulted organised patient groups, only 6% of lay representatives thought the interests of the general public were well represented (Wilkin et al, 2000; Alborz et al, 2002: forthcoming). This perception has persisted; a year later, 47% of Community Health Councils judged their local PCG/T's efforts at consultation with the wider community to be ineffective (Wilkin et al, 2001b).

The linked case studies have also revealed other consequences of the dominant position that GPs hold on PCG/T Boards. The traditional small business culture of general practice, with its long history of autonomy and independence and concern to optimise services for the patients of one practice, is difficult to integrate with a more strategic and locality-oriented perspective, or with the fundamental principles of collective responsibility which underpin the new demands on PCG/Ts (Marshall et al, 2002: forthcoming). The challenge for PCG/Ts is to change this traditional culture, through the acceptance of collective responsibility for improving the quality of primary and community health services; a willingness to share information about the quality of their services; and increased collaboration and sharing of resources between the GPs and practices covered by the PCG/T.

A further aspect of PCG/Ts' governance arrangements which is therefore of interest relates to their responsibilities for safeguarding and improving the quality of primary health services, including those services provided by self-employed, independent contractor GPs with their strong culture of individualism and even competition. 'Clinical governance' is the framework within which PCG/Ts are responsible for monitoring and improving the quality of clinical services. It includes activities such as audit; continuing professional education and training; and the use of guidelines to prescribe appropriate diagnostic and treatment measures. After only six months, 80% of PCG/Ts had already identified priorities for quality improvement and potential methods for monitoring the quality of clinical treatment, particularly in relation to GPs' prescribing behaviour and the management of chronic illnesses. Within the same timescale, a third of PCG/Ts were also developing financial incentive schemes to improve the quality of clinical decision making (other than in relation to prescribing). Most also reported developing methods for dealing with poorly performing GP practices, including clinical audit, benchmarking, redistributing resources to penalise or improve performance, informal discussions and formal disciplinary procedures. Moreover, almost half (47%) of PCG/Ts reported plans to make information available on the quality of their GP services. A year later, a wide range of quality improvement activities was reported (Campbell et al, 2001), including developing new opportunities for shared learning between GP practices, and between primary care teams, hospital staff and other community health services. Ninety per cent of PCG/T Boards or Executive Committees had access to information about the quality of care provided in their constituent general practices. More importantly, half of all PCG/Ts were sharing or planning to share information on quality of care between general practices. This will allow GPs and their staff to compare their own performance with that of other practices.

Similar progress towards a more open and collective approach to the provision of primary care was evident in initiatives to share and redistribute resources between practices. GP fundholding had encouraged general practices to improve services for their own patients, but there were no incentives to share resources or extend such initiatives to other practices. In contrast, many PCG/Ts have taken initiatives to extend and improve services, with the aim of reducing inequities and inequalities between GP practices. By 2000, 57% had introduced initiatives to share the services of counsellors between practices, 44% had extended access to practice-based minor surgery and 38% were sharing the services of specialist nurses. Almost two thirds (64%) were developing specialist GPs, to whom other local GPs could refer patients and thereby reduce the number of referrals to hospital specialists. Such redistributions were not always easy to achieve, particularly where they involved a diminution of the advantageous facilities secured by former GP fundholders. When asked about the most controversial issues dealt with by PCG/T Boards during their first six months, 32% of chief executives mentioned dealing with the legacies of GP fundholding and 26% cited dealing with the allocation of resources between practices.

In other areas of state welfare such developments would be unexceptional. However, in the context of English general practice they represent a fundamental change of culture. The independence, and often isolation, of general practice has been reflected until now in a lack of collective responsibility for standards of care and an unwillingness to share resources or information that might permit comparison of quality standards.

Unified budget for healthcare

The total budget available for the NHS, how it is allocated and the nature of decision making about funding services are all of enormous importance in shaping the services that patients receive. Moreover, the distribution of the NHS budget, both between and within PCG/Ts, is also linked to the government's overall objective of increasing equity within the NHS. As a mode of reimbursement for the services of independent contractors, the historical distribution of resources to fund the general medical services provided by GPs was highly inequitable. Rather than reflecting the characteristics and health needs of local populations, expenditure on general medical services was traditionally determined by a combination of the numbers of GPs; demand from patients; and the behaviours of individual GPs in prescribing, seeking diagnostic tests and referring patients to hospitals. Up to 1990, the budget for prescribing had also been entirely demand-led, although mechanisms to reduce the impact of demand on prescribing were gradually introduced during the 1990s.

The budgets allocated to PCG/Ts are intended to reflect the health needs of their populations through the application of a new 'weighted capitation' formula, which takes into account the demographic and socio-economic characteristics of the PCG/T population. However, in allocating budgets to PCG/Ts, health authorities have some flexibility in the speed with which they replace budgets determined on the basis of past expenditure with budgets determined by this more equitable resource allocation formula. Consequently, the budgets of most PCG/Ts are still determined by a combination of historic spending patterns and the new weighted capitation formula. There appears to be some inertia in adjusting PCG/T budgets to meet the new targets. Over half of PCG/Ts where discrepancies between historic and target budgets persist are not expected to complete the process of alignment until after 2004; and 23% of PCG/Ts expect never to have their budgets fully adjusted to the new, needs-led formula. The most common reason given by health authorities for setting the budgets of PCG/Ts at different levels from those indicated by the new resource allocation formula is in order to maintain the stability of services. Consequently, a considerable element of inequity is likely to remain in the allocation of resources to PCG/Ts, which will fail fully to reflect the demographic and socio-economic characteristics and needs of their populations.

Successive governments since 1948 have found it impossible to control spending on general practice. Replacing demand-led budgets by a weighted capitation formula of course also allows central government to predict and control expenditure. Moreover, it is intended eventually that all GP-related expenditure (that is, including the resources to reimburse GPs for the general medical services which they provide as independent contractors to the NHS) will also be included in the funding formula. For the first time this will provide an opportunity to predict and control the entire primary care budget – an enhanced responsibility that will of course be devolved down to PCG/Ts as they allocate their budgets between practices, community health, hospital services and prescribing – and, in future, between individual independent contractor GPs.

Another major feature of the budgets that PCG/Ts now manage is that they are unified; their total pot of money can be spent on any budget heading. This offers the flexibility to shift resources between areas of provision that were previously funded through entirely separate funding streams. In the first year of PCG/Ts, any such shifts were driven primarily by short-term budgetary problems (particularly an unanticipated increase

Figure 2.2: Numbers of PCG/Ts planning to reallocate resources between areas of expenditure (*n*=69, 2000 survey)

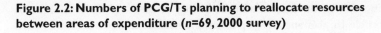

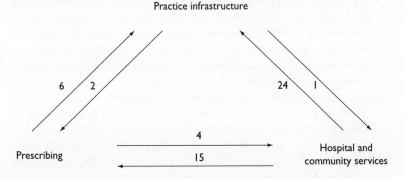

Practice infrastructure

6 / 2   24 / 1

4

Prescribing   15   Hospital and
                            community services

Notes:
a 16 PCG/Ts had no plans to shift expenditure between budget headings.
b 19 PCG/Ts who reported plans to reduce expenditure in one category and increase it in two
 (or vice versa) are counted as planning two shifts in expenditure.
c 12 PCG/Ts that reported plans to increase expenditure in one or more categories without
 reporting plans to decrease expenditure in any other are excluded from the total.
d the above figures represent numbers of PCG/Ts, not percentages.

in the prices of generic drugs). However, after 18 months, two thirds of PCG/Ts reported plans to make shifts in traditional expenditure patterns in line with their strategic priorities for developing services, and 43% were planning such shifts in order to finance specific service developments. The overall pattern appears to be one of moving resources away from hospital and community health services towards GP practice infrastructure and prescribing (Figure 2.2).

In organisations dominated by GPs, it is perhaps not surprising to find that planned shifts of resources are in general towards areas where GPs have direct control, namely prescribing and practice infrastructure. However, these shifts are only planned and it remains to be seen whether they are realised.

Developing primary and community services

So far this chapter has concentrated on the changes in organisational structures, funding and governance brought about by the creation of PCG/Ts. These changes are only of significance if they lead to improvements in services and, ultimately, the health and quality of life of patients. For the first time in the history of the NHS, PCG/Ts make it possible to plan and develop a comprehensive, coherent and integrated range of primary and community services, in response to identified patterns of need, with GP practice-based and other community health services complementing each other and with both providing coverage across the community as a whole. While it is too early to draw any conclusions about the impact on patient experiences and outcomes, it is already possible to detect changes in the services provided. Here the discussion will focus on two types of changes: those which aim to improve access to primary and community health services; and those aimed at integrating primary and community health services into a more coherent whole.

During the first round of the Tracker Survey, PCG/T Board chairs identified a number of problems for local people in accessing GP and practice-based services, in at least parts of their areas. Particularly common were long waiting times for GP appointments (29% of PCG/Ts), high list sizes (larger than average numbers of patients registered with individual GPs – 24% of PCG/Ts) and insufficient GPs (23%). A year later, PCG/Ts were undertaking a wide variety of initiatives to improve access to primary and community services (Wilkin et al, 2001a). These included extending GP surgery opening times (29% of PCG/Ts); improving GP appointments systems (41%); introducing new services in areas with inadequate GP provision (62%); introducing first contact primary care services run by nurses (42%) or pharmacists (38%); and healthy living centres (36%). Other initiatives to improve access were targeted at homeless people, refugees and asylum seekers and people living in remote rural areas. In the majority of instances, these developments were the result of interventions by the PCG/T itself. Altogether, 87% of PCG/Ts had at least one new scheme to improve access to primary care up and running by late 2000; only 13% had not initiated any such changes.

As Primary Care Groups make the transition to independent Trust status, they are able to integrate community nursing services with those provided by GP practice-based nurses and other allied staff. The work of practice nurses and community nurses (district nurses and health visitors) frequently overlap, but their different employment and management arrangements have made integrated provision difficult. However, PCTs can take over the provision of community nursing services and virtually all were planning to do so. Indeed, 77% of PCG chief executives identified the integration of primary and community health services as one of their three most important reasons for becoming a Trust, and 80% expected to achieve this integration as a result of moving to Trust status. By late 2000, almost half (49%) of PCG/Ts were already planning or introducing integrated teams of nurses and 59% had begun to introduce joint training for practice and community nurses. Not surprisingly, fewer PCG/Ts were yet ready to introduce more complex changes in nurses' employment, such as the introduction of common staff contracts or common management arrangements.

Conclusions: opportunities and threats

The creation of Primary Care Groups and their transition to Trust status is more than just the latest in a long history of NHS reorganisations. PCTs mark the end of the 1948 tripartite structure of hospitals, community services and family practitioner services, and their replacement by a single, integrated, managed healthcare organisation. Evidence from the first two years following the establishment of PCGs, including the first wave of Trusts, shows important changes occurring in the funding, governance and culture of primary care; and in patterns of investment and development in primary and community health services. As all PCGs make the transition to Trust status over the next couple of years, they will take on increased responsibilities for delivering high quality integrated services, reducing inequalities and improving the health of the local populations that they serve. To achieve this, they will have control over three quarters of NHS expenditure and will be able to manage directly many community and primary health services. Their performance will therefore be crucial to the delivery of the targets set out in the government's modernisation agenda and to improving the quality, equity and integration of primary and community health services.

Whether or not PCTs will succeed in bringing about the improvements in services and health which are expected of them will depend on a host of external factors, not least the overall levels of funding for the NHS and the tendency of government to make the NHS a victim of political 'hyperactivism' (Dunleavy, 1995). Two challenges in particular face PCG/Ts over the next few years. First, a growing gulf is appearing between political and public expectations of the transformative capacity of PCG/Ts and their ability to meet these expectations. Second, there are increasing tensions between the rhetoric of devolved power and responsibility on the one hand, and the demands of central government for close control and tight management of NHS performance as a whole, on the other.

Since PCGs were established in 1999, the pressure of expectations and pace of change have increased dramatically. Many new directives and service benchmarks have been introduced. All PCGs are expected to become Trusts by 2004; many are also in the process of merging with neighbouring PCG/Ts; and health authorities, whose role included supporting the development of PCG/Ts, were abolished in April 2002. Taken together, these demands are placing tremendous pressures on new organisations that are already trying to bring about major changes in services and, particularly challenging, traditional professional ways of working.

Furthermore, the ability of PCG/Ts to meet these demands is severely constrained by a shortage of managerial capacity. In its desire to control management costs, the government originally recommended that PCGs should be limited to an average management budget of £3 per head of population, based on the anticipated savings accruing from the abolition of GP fundholding. Unsurprisingly, more than two thirds of PCG/T chief executives in the Tracker Survey report that current staffing levels are inadequate and over half identify deficiencies in their organisational infrastructure, most commonly lack of management capacity, as obstacles to progress (Dowling et al, 2002: forthcoming). The few available estimates of the resources that PCG/Ts actually require to manage adequately their substantial organisational responsibilities put these at between £11 and £18 per head of population (Killoran et al, 1998; Place and Newbronner, 1999). Placed in an even wider perspective, it is estimated that the average administrative budget for US managed care organisations is £350 per head of population (Weiner et al, 2001). It is the combination of increasing expectations, tight timetables and insufficient capacity to meet these that gives cause for concern. One of the ways in which PCG/Ts have sought to deal with the problem of insufficient capacity is by merging with neighbouring PCG/Ts and combining their management budgets, with the expectation of achieving economies of scale in a larger organisation. The mergers that are currently planned would double the average size of the population served by PCG/Ts from around 100,000 to almost 200,000. Unfortunately, there is little evidence that increases in size beyond 100,000 population will yield the hoped for economies of scale (Bojke et al, 2001; Wilkin et al, 2002: forthcoming). On the other hand, there are good reasons to suppose that larger PCG/Ts may find it more difficult to maintain the support and engagement of either frontline health professionals or local communities.

The government's health service reforms have repeatedly emphasised the importance of devolving budgets and power to frontline staff and ensuring that services reflect the needs of local communities. PCG/Ts are at the forefront of this process. However, a further recurring theme in policy for the NHS is the commitment to equity, common standards of provision and quality across the country. This is reflected in the plethora of national standards contained in, for example, guidance from the National Institute for Clinical Excellence; inspections and standards set by the Commission for Health Improvement; care standards and service targets embodied in National Service Frameworks; and targets set out in the NHS Plan. These centralised prescriptions seriously limit the scope for local autonomy. PCG/Ts are performance managed against standards and targets that are set for them at national or regional level. Against these requirements, it is far from clear exactly what scope, if any, PCG/Ts will have to direct resources or organisational capacity to the priorities which their frontline professionals or local communities identify as most important. The importance of local priorities and their frequent divergence from national priorities and targets is reflected in the fact that 49% of PCG chief executives said in 2000 that one of the main reasons for wanting to become a Trust was to be able to focus on local priorities. If, as seems certain, the flow of national standards, targets and guidelines continues, the scope for local determination of priorities is likely to be even more limited than at present.

Together, the gap between expectations and capacity and the tensions between devolution and centralised management represent serious threats to the potential for PCTs to tackle some of the most enduring problems faced by the NHS. If PCTs are perceived to be little more than the recreation of the old centralised, 'command and control' health authorities, then it is unlikely that they will retain the engagement of frontline health professionals or succeed in involving local communities in setting priorities and making decisions. Rather, they require sufficient resources, including time and good management, to meet the expectations placed on them. They will also need to be allowed a degree of autonomy to determine their own priorities in the light of local needs and circumstances. PCTs represent the best opportunity for the NHS to deliver a more accessible, integrated and high quality primary health service. It is to be hoped that government can resist the temptation to micro-manage the service or to engage in yet another reorganisation.

Postscript: the 2002 Budget and the new GP contract

The substantial additional funding for the NHS announced in the 2002 budget and the simultaneous publication of a radically different contract for general practice, signal a new phase in the modernisation of primary health care. Stringent conditions will be attached to the extra funding including meeting national targets, reforming the organisation and funding of health services, and acceptance of new regulatory and performance mechanisms (DoH, 2002). In addition to service delivery targets (for example, access to primary care, waiting times for specialist treatment), PCG/Ts will be required to monitor the quality and quantity of their services and deliver this information to every household. A new integrated inspection body, the Commission for Healthcare Audit and Inspection will also be established to provide independent scrutiny of all healthcare providers. These measures will undoubtedly increase the tensions between devolution/local ownership and centralised policy/regulation. Moreover, by setting ambitious targets for improved performance and new regulatory mechanisms they risk increasing the gap between expectations and the capacity of PCG/Ts to deliver change.

The new draft GP contract published at the same time as the budget announcement of additional funding, is the most radical reform of the GP contract since it was drawn up in 1948 (NHS Confederation, 2002). The proposed shift from GPs as individual contractors to practice-based contracts represents a major change. Practices will be able to choose to provide different levels of service, including opting out of responsibility for the provision of 24-hour medical cover. Payments to practices will reflect the achievement of quality and performance targets, including measures of patient satisfaction. Contracts will be negotiated with, and managed by, PCG/Ts who will be responsible for allocating infrastructure resources to practices and ensuring that all patients have access to the full range of primary care services.

References

Alborz, A., Wilkin, D. and Smith, K. (2002) 'Are primary care groups and trusts consulting local communities?', *Health and Social Care in the Community*, vol 10, no 1, pp 20-7.

Audit Commission (1995) *Briefing on GP fundholding*, London: HMSO.

Bain, J. (1994) 'Fundholding: a two-tier system?', *British Medical Journal*, vol 309, pp 396-9.

Bojke, C., Gravelle, H. and Wilkin, D. (2001) 'Is bigger better for primary care groups and trusts?', *British Medical Journal*, vol 322, pp 599-602.

Campbell, S., Roland, M. and Wilkin, D. (2001) 'Primary Care Groups: improving quality through clinical governance', *British Medical Journal*, vol 322, pp 1580-2.

Constitution Unit (2001) *Devolution and health. Second annual report: Monitoring the impact of devolution on the United Kingdom's health services*, London: The Constitution Unit, School of Public Policy, University College.

Coulter, A. (1995) 'General practice fundholding: time for a cool appraisal', *British Journal of General Practice*, vol 45, pp 119-20.

DoH (Department of Health) (1997) *The new NHS: Modern, dependable*, Cm 3807, London: The Stationery Office.

DoH (2000) *The NHS Plan. A plan for investment, a plan for reform*, Cm 4818-I, London: DoH.

DoH (2001) *Shifting the balance of power within the NHS: Securing delivery*, London: DoH.

DoH (2002) *Delivering the NHS Plan*, Cm 5503, London: DoH

Dowling, B., Wilkin, D. and Coleman, A. (2002) 'Management in primary care groups and trusts', *British Journal of Health Care Management*, vol 8, no 1, pp 12-15.

Dunleavy, P. (1995) 'Policy disasters: explaining the UK's record', *Public Policy and Administration*, vol 10, no 2, pp 52-70.

Flynn, R., Williams, G. and Pickard, S. (1996) *Markets and networks: Contracting in community health services*, Buckingham: Open University Press.

Glendinning, C. (1998) 'From general practice to primary care: developments in primary health services 1990-1998', in E. Brunsdon, H. Dean and R. Woods (eds) *Social Policy Review 10*, London: Social Policy Association, pp 137-64.

Glendinning, C., Chew, C. and Wilkin, D. (1994) 'Professional power and managerial control: the case of GP assessments of the over-75s', *Social Policy and Administration*, vol 28, no 4, pp 317-32.

Glendinning, C., Coleman, A., Shipman, C. and Malbon, G. (2001) 'Progress in partnerships', *British Medical Journal*, vol 323, pp 28-31.

Glendinning, C., Coleman, A. and Rummery, K. (2002) 'Partnerships, performance and primary care: developing integrated services for older people in England', *Ageing and Society*, vol 22, no 2, pp 185-208.

Glennerster, H., Matsaganis, M. and Owens, P. (1994) *Implementing GP fundholding: Wild card or winning hand?*, Buckingham: Open University Press.

Jarman, B. (1981) *A survey of primary care in London*, Occasional Paper no 16, London: Royal College of General Practitioners.

Killoran, A., Griffiths, J., Posnett, J. and Mays, N. (1998) *What can we learn from the total purchasing pilots about the management costs of Primary Care Groups?*, London: King's Fund.

Klein, R. (1983) *The politics of the National Health Service*, London: Longman.

London Health Planning Consortium (1981) *Primary health care in inner London: Report of study group* (Chair: Sir Donald Acheson), London: DHSS.

Marshall, M., Sheaff, R., Rogers, A., Campbell, S., Halliwell, S., Pickard, S., Sibbald, B. and Roland, M. (2002: forthcoming) '"Creating the right culture": a qualitative study of the implementation of clinical governance in primary care groups and trusts', *British Journal of General Practice*.

Mays, N., Goodwin, N., Malbon, G., Leese, B., Mahon, A. and Wyke, S. (1998) *What were the achievements of the Total Purchasing Pilots in their first year and how can they be explained?*, National Evaluation of Total Purchasing Pilot Projects Working Paper, London: King's Fund.

Mays, N., Mulligan, J. and Goodwin, N. (2000) 'The British quasi-market in health care: a balance sheet of the evidence', *Journal of Health Services Research and Policy*, vol 5, no 1, pp 49-58.

Moon, G. and North, N. (2000) *Policy and place: General medical practice in the UK*, Basingstoke: Macmillan.

National Audit Office (1994) *General practitioner fundholding in England*, London: HMSO.

NHS Confederation (2002) *The new GMS contract – delivering the benefits for GPs and their patients*, London: NHS Confederation.

NHSE (1994) *Developing NHS purchasing and GP fundholding*, EL(94)79, Leeds: NHS Executive.

Petchey, R. (1996) 'From stable boys to jockeys? The prospects for a primary care led NHS', in M. May, E. Brunsdon and G. Craig (eds) *Social Policy Review 8*, London: Social Policy Association, pp 157-83.

Pickard, S., Marshall, M., Rogers, A., Roland, M., Sheaff, R., Sibbald, B., Campbell, S. and Halliwell, S. (2002: forthcoming) 'User involvement in clinical governance', *Health Expectations.*

Place, M. and Newbronner, E. (1999) *Roles, functions and costs of primary care trusts: The expected costs of managing a primary care trust,* York: Health Economics Consortium.

Roland, M. and Shapiro, J. (eds) (1998) *Specialist outreach clinics in general practice,* Manchester/Oxford: National Primary Care Research and Development Centre/Radcliffe Medical Press.

Rummery, K. (1998) 'Changes in primary health care policy: the implications for joint commissioning with social services', *Health and Social Care in the Community,* vol 6, no 6, pp 429-37.

Secretary of State for Health (1989) *Working for patients,* London: HMSO.

Secretary of State for Health (1996a) *Choice and opportunity. Primary care: The future,* London: The Stationery Office.

Secretary of State for Health (1996b) *Primary care: The future,* Leeds: NHS Executive.

Secretary of State for Health (1997) *The new NHS: Modern, dependable,* Cm 3807, London: The Stationery Office.

Sheaff, R., Smith, K. and Dickson, M. (2002: forthcoming) 'Is GP restratification beginning in England?', *Social Policy and Administration.*

Smith, J., Bamford, M., Ham, C. and Shapiro, J. (1997) *Beyond fundholding: A mosaic of primary care-led commissioning and provision in the West Midlands,* University of Birmingham: Health Services Management Centre/ University of Keele: Centre for Health Services Planning and Management.

Weiner, J., Lewis, R. and Gillam, S. (2001) *US Managed Care and PCTs: Lessons to a small island from a lost continent,* London: King's Fund.

Wilkin, D., Hallam, L., Leavey, R. and Metcalfe, D. (1987) *Anatomy of urban general practice,* London: Tavistock.

Wilkin, D., Gillam, S. and Leese, B. (2000) *The national tracker survey of primary care groups and trusts: Progress and challenges 1999/2000,* Manchester: National Primary Care Research and Development Centre, University of Manchester.

Wilkin, D., Dowswell, T. and Leese, B. (2001a) 'Primary Care Groups: modernising primary and community health services', *British Medical Journal*, vol 322, pp 1522-4.

Wilkin, D., Gillam, S. and Coleman, A. (2001b) *The national tracker survey of primary care groups and trusts 2000/2001: Modernising the NHS?*, Manchester: National Primary Care Research and Development Centre, University of Manchester.

Wilkin, D., Bojke, C., Coleman, A. and Gravelle, H. (2002: forthcoming) 'The relationship between size and performance in primary care organisations in England', *Journal of Health Services Research and Policy*.

THREE

Devolution in England: coping with post-industrial industrial regions – issues of territorial inequality

David Byrne

... the advocates of a new needs assessment are seeking technical solutions to *political* problems where none exist. (Midwinter, 1999, p 53; emphasis in the original)

Somebody should buy Midwinter a subscription to the North East's regional morning newspaper – *The (Newcastle) Journal*. The presence of at least one article or editorial a week comparing the massive advantages which higher levels of public spending offer to Scotland as compared with its adjacent region, might persuade him that there is indeed a political problem in a UK resource distribution pattern that massively advantages middle and upper class Scots (by residence) like himself against their neighbours, precisely through the political implications of the technicalities of the present funding formula. For example, the lead story in *The Journal* (6 November 2001) notes that per capita public expenditure in Scotland is £434 per annum more than in the North East, with £177 per head more on education and £181 more on health. It goes on to point out that GDP (Gross Domestic Product) per capita in the North East is 77% of the UK average, compared with Scotland's 96%. The scale of England in terms of population as against the other component 'nations' of the United Kingdom, and the very high degree of inter-regional inequality within England, is forcing the issue of regional level resource distribution onto the UK political and administrative agenda. The historical compromise embodied in the Barnett formula, so-called because it was introduced by Joel Barnett, Chief Secretary of the Treasury in the late 1970s as a method for allocating resources to the national departments delivering services, first in Scotland and then subsequently for Wales and

Northern Ireland, is clearly breaking down. This was part of the overall expenditure control mechanism of the Treasury in relation to spending departments and although the intention was that the operation of the formula would lead to a convergence of per capita spending among the UK's component nations over time, this has not proved to be the case. Rather the small 'nations' of the UK all have substantially higher per capita levels of expenditure in most service areas than is the case for England as a whole or for English regions, which are as, or substantially more, deprived than Scotland, although Wales and Northern Ireland remain deprived regions.

The usual justification advanced for this is that the smaller nations have substantially greater needs than England in terms both of social deprivation and in relation to geographically dispersed populations. However, the comparison between England as a whole and the much smaller other nations of the UK is essentially invalid. This is particularly the case given the severe impacts of deindustrialisation and the consequent reordering of the UK's space economy on England's own peripheral regions. It is comparisons between expenditure in English regions and expenditure in the small nations which is the contemporary issue. Indeed hostility to the financial consequences of Barnett[1] is now general in northern English regions and is provoking parliamentary discussion with Barnett himself initiating a House of Lords Debate (2001) calling for the scrapping of the formula.

Midwinter (1999) suggests that a simple per capita distribution of resources in the UK would advantage English residents only to the tune of £17 each per annum. This kind of approach is making the serious, and characteristically Scottish, mistake of equating England with the other 'nations' in the UK. This is an error of category and of scale in which scale differences generate the category error. The 'other nations' of the UK are merely regions if considered in terms of their population levels. Of the current English regions, all have populations larger than Northern Ireland's – the smallest, the North East, being two thirds as big again as Northern Ireland. Only the North East has a smaller population than Wales, at 90% of the Welsh level[2]. Five of the other English regions have larger populations than Scotland and all, except the North East, have populations of about the same size as Scotland except for London and the South East, which both have much larger populations.

Issues of sub-national resource distribution in the UK are in the first instance issues at this regional level. There are, of course, serious issues of resource distribution at the sub-regional level, among localities, and rather different issues of resource distribution affecting households and individuals. Indeed it is quite true to say that in any UK region intra-regional disparities among localities are far greater than inter-regional disparities. However, inter-regional disparities are of enormous importance because they determine one of the levels of context within which lives are lived. Le Grand (1991) argued that we have to understand equity in terms of equal choice sets. Choice sets – the domain of life chances for individuals – exist within specific spatial contexts and those contexts are more than just aggregates of individual conditions. They have a reality and determinant effect which is emergent – which is much more than just the sum of the elements composing them. This matters in terms of both policy possibilities and character of life experience at the levels of neighbourhood and locality. It matters most in relation to policy possibilities at the level of the region. In short, regions that are much better resourced in relation to needs can do things differently and better.

Understanding territorial inequality – the significance of emergence

Discussions of territorial inequality (Boyne and Powell, 1993; Hay, 1995) typically quote Davies (1968) as a baseline definition:

> ... in the services for which the most apparent appropriate distribution between individuals is 'to each according to his need', the most appropriate distribution between areas must be 'to each area according to the needs of the population of the area'. Since the former criterion is synonymous with social justice, we can call the latter 'territorial justice'.
> (1968, p 16)

In Davies' original text, and in almost all the studies that have followed his approach, 'the needs of the population of the area' has been understood as an aggregate of individual needs. This is somewhat surprising in discussions by geographers (or at least published in geography journals) after the 1980s given the considerable methodological debate about the emergent and real characteristics of the local which had developed by that time. The essential character of spatial units, both localities and regions, is now typically understood in terms of the emergent products of the factors interacting within those spatial units. When factors interact, we have to look at each context in detail because if there is interaction then things work differently for different cases. Analyses that focus on single factors cannot capture the character and consequences of interactions. Moreover interactive effects are multiplicative, not additive.

In other words, the needs of an area cannot be understood merely as the sum of individual needs. Concentrations of need define the type – the classification – of the area and such concentrations themselves constitute real sources of additional needs. This is exactly what emergence means. It is easy to grasp this in relation to health and deprivation at the neighbourhood level. Concentrated deprivation characterises – sets the type of – neighbourhoods and that type has a marked and measurable effect on the health states of individuals resident in the area. We are dealing with nested and intersecting complex systems here (see Reed and Harvey, 1992; Byrne, 1998). Two crucial points flow from this specification. The first, which is less significant for regions than for either neighbourhoods or localities, but by no means trivial even at the regional level, is that we must always recognise that where needs are concerned for an area the whole is greater than the sum of its parts. Here the parts are both sets of individual needs and specific characteristics of the area. We have interaction both among characteristics and among individual needs. This generates emergent properties in two senses. First, the actual needs of individuals and households are greater because of the compounding and multiplicative effect of the components of their deprivation. Second, the concentration of deprived individuals and households generates real area effects, which emerge at the levels of neighbourhood, locality, and even region. We all understand this intuitively. However, it is important to note that the linear models that underpin almost all statistical examination of these issues do not correspond with the way the real world works. This is bad enough in terms of social scientific understanding, but the same sort of linear models underpin important resource allocation processes among local authorities. These resources are allocated from the totals, which the Barnett formula accords to England, Scotland, Wales and Northern Ireland respectively. It seems as if things are going wrong at every stage.

This is the link to the second consequence of asserting that we are dealing with nested and complex systems. Typically people have tried to understand needs by using measures which appear to describe continuous variation. Often regression techniques have been used to amalgamate several continuous indices into a general index which is exactly a linear compound. However, if we are dealing with systems characterised by non-linearity, then our continuous measures and any system of ranks generated from them are not isomorphic with reality and do not constitute valid representations of difference. In non-linear systems changes in effects are not proportionate to changes in causes. What matters are not differences of degree but differences of kind[3]. Moreover (see Byrne, 2002), we should not try to ascertain causality by analysing out 'factors' that generate difference, but instead we need to explore the 'control parameters' that engender category change. We have to work with cases, not with variable attributes of cases, and what should interest us are the complex and interactive processes which change the relative location of particular cases. Again this is intuitively appealing. It reflects social science's constant interest in comparison – the comparative method – and what seems to be the innate human capacity for classifying things in our natural and social world in order to understand them (see Lakoff and Johnson, 1999).

This implies that we should not engage in statistical exercises which derive from the variable centred and inherently linear approaches which underpin the various manifestations of the general linear model – regression analysis, logistic regression, structural equation modelling, and such like. Instead we should work with classifications and explore the dynamics of classes over time. Dynamics is simply the study of change through time. 'Non-linear dynamics' deals with changes of kind rather than changes of degree. Here we have to think of two levels of dynamic transformation. The first is change in the actual classification structures themselves. If we use 'emergent' typologies, which are generated by comparisons among cases, then we should not be surprised if major socio-economic changes engender transformations in the actual types of objects of interest across the course of those transformations. In other words the set of types of UK regions in an industrial society will be different from the set of types of UK regions in a post-industrial society. Second, individual cases may move to different classes over a time period. A region may be in a relatively deprived class at one time and in a less deprived class at another or vice versa. What should be of particular interest to us is the complex interactive (and potentially multiple and varied) set of processes which engender such relative changes. Here the possibility of positive feedback engendering catastrophic transformation is important. Catastrophic changes are exactly changes of kind (qualitative changes) and may be either for the better or for the worse in terms of shifts in overall deprivation. Positive feedback means that perturbative changes become self-reinforcing and push change along even harder and further. The ideas of the multiplier and accelerator in macro-economics illustrate this well. The multiplier describes how in a recession general demand and especially consumer demand, falls, which makes the recession even deeper. The accelerator is the special fall in demand for capital goods, which is even steeper because producers postpone new investment until there is a sign of increasing demand for their products. The whole point of Keynesian methods in macro-economic policy is to introduce negative feedback through fiscal and social measures which maintain demand through government intervention and encourage investment through reducing the cost of borrowing. German regional policy has a similar intention in that resources are explicitly distributed to work to reduce long-term differences. The UK's resource allocation mechanisms for local authorities have a similar objective, but start from the base of national resource allocation under Barnett to the UK's four regions.

Now, given the number crunching capacities of digital computers in their present form, we have available a set of essentially exploratory tools for generating typologies and examining change in classifications and class memberships over time. Statistical exploration is the vital process of trying to see what the data are telling us about what the world is like and about how it is changing. These tools are the 'hierarchic fusion' approaches to numerical taxonomy generally described as 'cluster analyses' (see Everitt, 1993). Hierarchic fusion techniques work by constructing a 'dissimilarity matrix' across multiple dimensions for cases where each dimension is a particular variate measure of the case. The two least dissimilar cases are fused and treated at the next stage as a single case and the process is repeated. At each stage an 'error coefficient' is calculated which records differences between the present stage and the original data set. When there are large jumps in the value of the error coefficient we can conclude that very different types of things have been amalgamated into a single cluster and can so identify the immediately preceding level as representing a significant typology. We can represent this process graphically as a dendrogram, which maps out how the fusion process happens. Basically the bigger the distance between each level of fusion, the greater the error generated at that fusion and the more likely it is that two different categories have been put together at that point. We can see which levels matter – which is important when we have very large numbers of cases. With a small set of cases, as with UK regions, what we are focusing on is what regions are most like other regions. The dendrogram shows this by the pattern of fusion – by which cases join up at which stage to form a new cluster. We can see not only initial clusters but also the subsequent pattern of connection which indicates the degree of similarity among cases. More similar cases join up sooner. Establishing similarities is also always a process of establishing differences so we find cases which are alike and cases which are unlike. In other words we can differentiate and begin to think about what causes differences.

Changes in the classification of UK regions through the transition to post-industrialism

We can explore the dynamics of the UK's regions by comparing three sets of clusters generated using data derived from *Regional Statistics 14* (CSO, 1979), *Regional Trends 35* (ONS, 2000), and *Public expenditure: Statistical analyses 2000-01 and 2001-02* (HM Treasury, 2000, 2001). Data from the regional series can be used to categorise regions at the two time points by their social characteristics and the public expenditure data can be used to categorise by public expenditure volume and pattern. The method used in each case was hierarchical fusion by Ward's method using a dissimilarity coefficient. The first dendrogram shows the fusion pattern for the 1977 set and the second for the 1998 set of social characteristics based clusters (see Figure 3.1).

The dendrogram shows that there are five interesting clusters, which are evidently different and these are described in Table 3.1. Here we can see that the least prosperous areas of the UK were Northern Ireland, the industrial regions of England (North, North West, Yorkshire and Humberside and the East and West Midlands) – Cluster One, Wales and Scotland which make up Cluster Four, and Northern Ireland, on its own as Cluster Five. All these come together subsequently. East Anglia and

Figure 3.1: Cluster combine – social characteristics (1977)

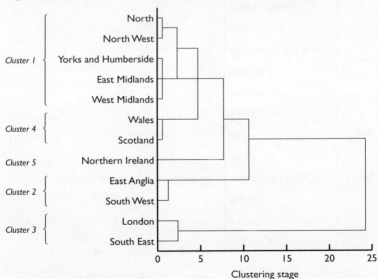

Table 3.1: Social character (1977)

Index	Cluster One*	Cluster Two*	Cluster Three*	Cluster Four*	Cluster Five*
SMR men	105	89	90	107	115
SMR women	105	94	92	106	114
Retention rate (education 16+)	21	22	34	33	23
Industrial employment: (males)	54	38	35	44	39
Industrial employment: (females)	29	21	19	22	26
Unemployment rate	7	6	5	8	11
Household income per week (£)	84	95	98	84	74
GDP per capita (UK 100)	95	92	113	94	78

*Regions:
Cluster One – North, North West, Yorks and Humberside, East Midlands, West Midlands
Cluster Two – East Anglia, South West
Cluster Three – London, South East
Cluster Four – Wales, Scotland
Cluster Five – Northern Ireland

Figure 3.2: Social characteristics (1997)

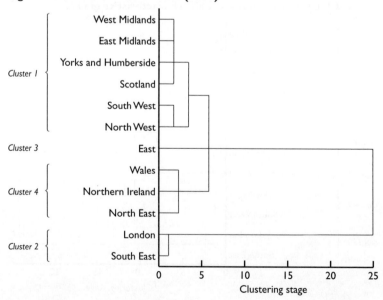

the South West – Cluster Two – were not prosperous but were much healthier (by standardised mortality rates [SMR]) and join up with the other regions at the next stage. London and the South East – Cluster Three – were healthy, prosperous and already radically different. Note that the greater South East – London and the South East – is the most distinctive set even at this date.

The dendrogram in Figure 3.2 shows that in 1997 we have four clusters, with again the radically different set comprising London and the South East – Cluster Two. The East[4], which on its own comprised Cluster Three, was somewhat more prosperous than the middle set of regions – including Scotland in Cluster One – and had a much lower SMR, but joined with them at the next stage. The poorest set now comprised Wales, the North East and Northern Ireland in Cluster Four and was closest to the middle set in Clusters One and Three with the London/ South East region being very different indeed. It is evident that the relative position of Wales and the North East has substantially worsened. Table 3.2 gives indicative figures for the four clusters. Ethnicity pattern was not used as a social characteristic because it always just produces London as a distinctive cluster, given London's uniquely varied ethnic

Table 3.2: Social character (1997)

Index	Cluster One*	Cluster Two*	Cluster Three*	Cluster Four*
Dependency ratio	110	99	97	134
All employment (industrial) (%)	29	19	26	27
Unemployment rate	6	6	5	8
GDP EU 100	96	128	99	83
Professional/managerial (%)	28	38	34	25
Semi- and unskilled (%)	21	15	18	21
Other than white (%)[†]	5	14	4	2
SMR	103	93	93	105
Adults working age employed (%)	74	78	76	67
Graduates	13	21	15	11
Mean household income per week (£)	400	517	451	354
Mean individual income per week (£)	167	221	190	145

*Regions:
Cluster One – West Midlands, Yorks and Humberside, Scotland, South West, East Midlands, North West
Cluster Two – London, South East
Cluster Three – East
Cluster Four – North East, Wales, Northern Ireland

[†] Not used to construct classification.

Figure 3.3: Combined public expenditure (1998)

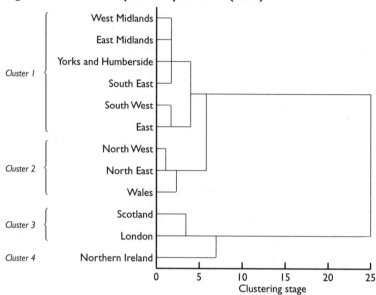

composition[5]. One thing that must also be noted is the massive extent of deindustrialisation in the UK as a whole and particularly in the English peripheral regions.

The expenditure clusters shown in Figure 3.3 give a very different picture from the social characteristic clusters for the same time point. Again we have four interesting clusters with a set of clusters with relatively low expenditure including all the English regions except the North East and North West, a set of somewhat higher expenditure clusters comprising the North East, North West and Wales, a set of much higher expenditure clusters comprising London and Scotland, and Northern Ireland on its own.

Social security expenditure was not used in constructing the expenditure clusters because it is a wholly national and uniform system throughout the UK in relation to levels of benefits and relates to individuals and households but not to any real base.

The per capita expenditure pattern is interesting (see Table 3.3). Northern Ireland merits high expenditure both because it is in the deprived set of regions and because a component of its high expenditure is the very high rate of spending on security. However, the UK's most prosperous region – London – and Scotland receive considerably more expenditure

Table 3.3: Public expenditure per capita (1998)

Index	Cluster One*	Cluster Two*	Cluster Three*	Cluster Four*
Dependency ratio	110	99	97	134
Education	639	686	800	935
Health	978	1,115	1,286	1,193
Transport and roads	123	140	174	123
Housing	18	50	123	166
Other environmental services	115	188	185	153
Law, police and public protection	270	316	378	649
Trade and industry	101	119	140	293
Agriculture	55	78	127	212
Culture	72	115	123	53
Social security†	1,621	1,988	1,766	2,069
Central administration	39	46	53	94
Total	4,031	4,841	5,155	5,940

*Regions:
Cluster One – West Midlands, Yorks and Humberside, South East, South West, East Midlands, East
Cluster Two – North East, Wales, North West
Cluster Three – London, Scotland
Cluster Four – Northern Ireland

† Not used to construct classification.

than much more deprived regions of the UK. In London's case a justification can be constructed because it is a severely polarised world city with areas of enormous deprivation and acute transport problems – although a return to the policy of regional dispersal might be a better way of solving issues of congestion than throwing money at roads and radial rail communications. Scotland has no such unique status. It is a rather more prosperous deindustrialised region than Wales or the North East and has no rationale other than political advantage for such high overall spending[6]. In terms of components, other than Northern Ireland's high public order spending, the most noticeable differences are in education, health and housing expenditure.

Plainly the existence of the Scottish National Party (SNP) in relation to the Westminster Parliament is a factor in Labour's reluctance to confront this mismatch of need and resources, but the proposed reduction in the number of Scottish MPs may modify this. There is the increasing pressure for both a regional level of government in England, strongest in the North East, but also now very real in the North West, and Yorkshire and Humberside. This is already leading to a demand for a recasting of resource allocation. It would also be very much in Wales' interest to demand a regional allocation of resources on a needs-based principle. Livingstone, as Mayor of London, has been demanding that London benefit from resources to the extent that it contributes to them, but this is a much less justifiable proposition given that much of the taxation collected in London reflects the location of both corporate headquarters and elites and derives from real earnings elsewhere in the UK.

Essentially the regional data demonstrate, particularly given that the East as a region includes areas such as Hertfordshire, Bedfordshire and Essex, which are plainly part of the South East, that there are two economic and social systems in the UK. One is the greater South East (London, the South East, and parts of the East), which is a services centred economy organised around a world city dominated in economic terms by trade in financial services and related activities. The other is the rest of the UK, which combines a declining manufacturing base, severely disadvantaged by macro-economic policies that serve the interests of trade in financial services, and adverse social conditions. What is interesting is that while London plainly bears the congestion costs of its economic structure and requires public expenditure to meet them, Scotland, which has no such costs, shares the London pattern of resourcing.

Within the peripheral UK there are clearly two different condition states. The majority state is represented by a set of regions that are disadvantaged but not severely so. Northern Ireland remains the severely disadvantaged place it has been since the 1930s. Wales and the North East have now joined it.

Emergence and internal variation revisited

Understanding social systems as complex means that traditional approaches to assessing inequality simply do not work. The UN's Human Development Index (HDI) is halfway move towards dealing with this issue by producing a weighted linear compound measure, but it still has the problem of trying to represent a world of ordered classes on a continuous scale. This is not simply a technical problem of measurement. Rather the technical problem is a manifestation of the emergent character of reality. In other words the effect on lives of living in a well resourced region with a high level of good public services is multiplicative rather than additive. Of course this is not the same for everybody. We have to return to the issues which derive from the existence of smaller scale area subsystems – in the case of regions we have to think about localities, and in particular city regions, and neighbourhoods within those local systems.

We need classificatory systems that operate at both of these levels. This is particularly the case in Scotland where additional resources often seem to have advantaged affluent people.

Higher education is a notable example, with four year courses and no tuition fees without accompanying progressive personal taxation (tax levels being nationally specified), as is the elimination of charges for social care. These examples indicate that high income recipients have their cake and eat it – good services and low taxation. Plainly there is serious need for careful internal examination of resource distribution within Scotland on a sub-regional basis. In effect Scotland's political elite whinge about the deprivation of the Scottish disadvantaged and utilise the resources gained thereby to the advantage of Scotland's prosperous – of people like and including themselves.

It should be reiterated that the general character of a system is a product of the interaction of all its internal components. In other words, emergence means that we have to consider whole system character. This is the advantage of using category membership. It demarcates in an immediately comprehensible way – one which accords with the innate human capacity to construct and interpret categories (see Lakoff and Johnson, 1999) – the actual nature of a system at a particular point in its trajectory.

Control parameters

One of the great advantages of understanding social systems as complex systems is that it offers the possibility of identifying control parameters – changes which may well involve complex interactions rather than shifts in a single component. This is the advantage of time ordered classifications. We can map changes between two times. These changes can be at either or both of two orders. First, we find that particular systems change their category membership. Second, we find that the category set itself may be transformed. If we compare the social characteristics typologies for regions in 1977 as compared with 1997, we find not so much a transformation in the typologies as a shift in relative position of components. The 'middle' regions have become more like the poor than the most affluent and two British regions are now in the same set as Northern Ireland. This is really quite dramatic because Northern Ireland's relatively bad position in the mid-1970s was in part due to the significance of an Irish pattern of farming – there were many small farms – in its economic structure, which meant that the west of the six counties was almost as poor as the Irish Republic was at that time. Although farming matters in both the North East and Wales, the reality for these two regions is that severe deindustrialisation is the transforming factor for both places, as it is in the east of Northern Ireland. However, it is not the only factor. We have to think about the interaction of economic change and patterns of governance, not just in relation to levels of public expenditure, but also in terms of policy autonomy and policy coherence. The situation in Wales has to be explored in relation to the failure of relative autonomy, but the North East has plainly been affected by being under policy regimes which are 'all England' in character and which have not taken any real account of the local emergent issues in this distinctive region. Here the much less substantial and more recent administrative autonomy of Wales is worth noting. Welsh administrative autonomy after the establishment of the Welsh Office in the 1960s was pretty ersatz compared with the administrative *and* legislative autonomy of Scotland.

Scotland has moved in the opposite direction to the North East and Wales. In the 1970s it was a peripheral disadvantaged region and was actually somewhat worse off than the industrial English regions and Wales. Now it is in the same set as the less disadvantaged English industrial regions, whereas Wales and the North East have joined Northern Ireland. We can at least postulate that Scotland's shift to a relatively better location is a product of the high public expenditure in that region in relation to the region's needs. Wales and the North East might have retained their category membership if they had received similar levels of expenditure in relation to need. In this sense we can suggest that public expenditure levels might be a control parameter that has operated to cancel out the effects of deindustrialisation. In contrast deindustrialisation without compensating high public expenditure has moved the north of England into the most deprived set of regions. We should also consider the relatively high degree of political autonomy in Scottish administration during this period and the long and real tradition of separate Scottish policy and legislation. It must be emphasised that we can merely explore possible causal processes by examining variate data patterns. We might attempt full retrodictive explanation by constructing simulations, but that is a technology we can anticipate rather than use as of now.

Reservations

The author has argued elsewhere (Byrne, 1999) that if there is a single control parameter for the general character of social orders, it is degrees of inequality. If we are going to examine spatial inequalities then we have to look not only at the regional level but also at the levels of localities and of neighbourhoods. We have reasonable approximations to both in terms of data resources, with local authority districts representing a workable operationalisation of the idea of locality and with wards being a less good approximation of neighbourhood[7].

On simple inspection if we look at SMRs – a simple but crude and literal measure of life chances – and examine only range, inter-quartile range and mean for SMR *for local authorities*[8] then we get Table 3.4. Range, a very crude measure of spread, is not widely different within UK regions. What is noticeable is that the extremes are often adjacent industrial cities or towns as highest, and suburban areas as lowest. Otherwise the lowest areas are generally deeply rural. In Northern Ireland, Derry is very much an outlier, whereas in former coalfield regions such high SMRs are quite general. The North-South effect on SMRs is very marked in this data pattern! Note that although the North East and Scotland have the same high mean SMR, the inter-quartile range for Scotland is much greater which shows that Scotland has more internal differentiation than the North East. The North East has a much more uniform pattern of deprivation. Glasgow and other central belt authorities have a profound effect on the Scottish figures, although figures for Argyll and the Western Isles are also high. Across the UK SMRs in former coalfield areas are markedly higher than the general norm.

Equity?

The idea of equity in resource distribution as being achieved if there is a good match between the pattern of existing needs and current resource allocation is simple and attractive. However, if we do think that the purpose of public policy is to achieve states for regional systems in the future, then this may be too simplistic. Rather we need to examine what makes a difference, what are the control parameters that engender a difference of state, and think about public expenditure as a means to achieve such phase shifts. Certainly in Britain we would need to consider how to shift the relative position of Wales and the North East until they were at least in the same category as Scotland and the other English provincial regions. Of course this may not be possible at the level of the specific regions without a transformation of the whole national space economy by addressing the implications of the South East for the rest of that space economy. This reflects, for example, the impact of national macro-economic policy dealing with exchange rates and consequent currency valuation for the remaining manufacturing base of peripheral Britain[9]. At the level of public expenditure it may well be that the crucial component is educational expenditure associated with regional investment

Table 3.4: Range of regional SMRs

Region	Inter-quartile range SMR	Mean SMR	SMR minimum	SMR maximum	Range
North East	5.8	114	90 Teesdale, Berwick	128 Derwentside	38
North West	18	112	90 South Lakeland, Fylde	127 Manchester	37
Yorkshire and Humberside	8	105	91 Ryedale	116 Doncaster	25
East Midlands	9.5	98	75 Rutland	119 Chesterfield	44
West Midlands	9	100	83 Solihull	112 Tamworth, Bromsgrove	29
East	9.5	96	75 Three Rivers	119 Watford	44
London	11	95	79 Richmond	105 Barking and Dagenham	26
South East	9	94	78 Epsom and Ewell	109 Dartford	31
South West	5	88	74 East Dorset	99 Swindon	25
Wales	13	101	91 Cardiff, Monmouthshire	127 Merthyr Tydfil	38
Scotland	15.5	114	97 East Dunbartonshire	139 Glasgow	42
Northern Ireland	6.3	101	86 Cookstown	117 Derry	31

support for industrial development, a lesson that the German *Länder* learned some 40 years ago, and which is the basis of the Republic of Ireland's success as 'the celtic tiger'. The clear implication of thinking about inequalities in terms of ordered states rather than as a continuous index is that we have to think about state shifts as the objective of policy in general.

The next stage in this research should be the building of simulation models, which allow us to retrodict the past trajectories of UK regions. Indeed there is no particular reason to confine this activity to the UK alone. There is sufficient European Union data for a larger set of European regions, which would enable the simulations to be made on a Europe-wide basis, although there should certainly be country-specific simulations. This is both a matter of the role of national policies and of the comparability of internal national accounting and social indicator data. We have quite enough data for initial state specifications in a UK simulation. Simulations are neither magic nor proof, but they are interesting as a way of exploring the possible effects of different policy options and expenditure patterns.

Notes

[1] Strictly speaking the Barnett formula, which allocates public spending increments/decrements around the 'nations' of the UK, is not the actual allocative mechanism which advantages 'other than England'. Rather it is that Barnett started from a baseline in which there was massive advantage given to Scotland and Northern Ireland in terms of per capita expenditure on services with rather less given to Wales.

[2] The old Northern region including Cumbria had 10% more people than Wales.

[3] This is a general point and means that tables of ranks – of schools, universities, hospitals, localities, neighbourhoods – are largely meaningless in terms of detail. We can certainly order, but what we should order are not the individual cases but the categories to which those cases belong.

[4] The East incorporates counties which had previously been part of the South East rather than East Anglia and are certainly in reality part of the greater South East region.

[5] If the people of Irish descent could be properly identified as a separate group, then using that trace would produce a very different patterning.

[6] Just to put the 'kibosh' on bleating about 'Scotland's oil' – it is necessary to note than under international law offshore territory is allocated according to the general tendency of the border between two countries. The Anglo-Scottish border runs at an angle of 60 degrees south to north and if extended into maritime waters puts many of the producing oil and gas sectors of the North Sea into English territory. An independent Scotland would have serious problems with this matter.

[7] The best way to operationalise neighbourhoods is by combining enumeration districts or postcodes, which are in the same classified group. Wards are too internally diverse and do not approximate to real social boundaries in many cases.

[8] These are not the figures for the region's population which are derived from micro-data. Rather they are the figures for the spatial aggregates of local authorities.

[9] It is worth noting that in a reunified Ireland there would be a new space economy dominated by Dublin in just the same way as Britain's space economy is dominated by the greater South East. This would have some very interesting and potentially negative implications for the North of Ireland in general and for greater Belfast in particular, although Derry is well placed to replicate Limerick's successful positioning within that space economy. Certainly the Irish space economy has no real place for a large manufacturing sector.

References

Boyne, G.A. and Powell, M. (1993) 'Territorial justice and Thatcherism', *Environment and Planning C: Government and Policy*, vol 11, pp 35-53.

Byrne, D.S. (1998) *Complexity theory and the social sciences*, London: Routledge.

Byrne, D.S. (1999) *Social exclusion*, Buckingham: Open University Press.

Byrne, D.S. (2002) *Interpreting quantitative data*, London: Sage Publications.

CSO (Central Statistical Office) (1979) *Regional Statistics 14*, London: HMSO.

Davies, B. (1968) *Social needs and resources in local services*, London: Michael Joseph.

Everitt, B.S. (1993) *Cluster analysis*, London: Edward Arnold.

Hay, A.M. (1995) 'Concepts of equity, fairness and justice in geographical studies', *Transactions of the Institute of British Geographers*, New Series 20, pp 500–8.

Heald, D. (1994) 'Territorial public expenditure in the UK', *Public Administration*, vol 72, pp 147–75.

HM Treasury (2000) *Public expenditure: Statistical analyses 2000-01*, Cm 4601, London: The Stationery Office.

HM Treasury (2001) *Public expenditure: Statistical analyses 2001-02*, Cm 5101, London: The Stationery Office.

House of Lords Debates (7 November 2001) *Hansard*, vol 628, part no 41, cols 225–31.

Lakoff, G. and Johnson, M. (1999) *Philosophy in the flesh*, New York, NY: Basic Books.

Le Grand, J. (1991) *Equity and choice*, London: Harper Collins.

Midwinter, A. (1999) 'The politics of needs assessment: the Treasury Select Committee and the Barnett formula', *Public Money and Management*, April-June, pp 51–4.

ONS (Office for National Statistics) (2000) *Regional Trends 35*, London: The Stationery Office.

Reed, M. and Harvey, D.L. (1992) 'The new science and the old: complexity and realism in the social sciences', *Journal for the Theory of Social Behaviour*, vol 22, pp 356–79.

The Newcastle Journal, 6 November 2001.

FOUR

Reconstituting social policy: the case of Northern Ireland

Mike Tomlinson[1]

I ... swear by Almighty God that I will be faithful and bear true allegiance to His Majesty, King George the Fifth, His Heirs and Successors, according to the law. (Oath of Allegiance in 1914)

We declare the right of the people of Ireland to the ownership of Ireland and to the unfettered control of Irish destinies, to be sovereign and indefeasible. The long usurpation of that right by a foreign people and government has not extinguished that right.... We hereby proclaim the Irish Republic as a sovereign independent state.... The Irish Republic is entitled to, and hereby claims, the allegiance of every Irishman and Irish woman. (Proclamation read out by Padraig Pearse in front of Dublin post office during the Easter Rising 1916, cited in Dummett and Nicol, 1990, p 113)

Introduction

Constitutional reform was a major theme of the first New Labour government. The scope of the 'constitutional crisis' facing the United Kingdom at the end of the 20th century had long been identified by Charter 88 as involving the lack of rights – political, civil and human – under the common law system. The organisation's original charter demanded a Bill of Rights, freedom of information, and a fair electoral system through proportional representation. It called for a radical overhaul of the parliamentary system to ensure the proper accountability of the Executive through Parliament, as well as the replacement of the non-elected and hereditary-based Upper House. Finally, the charter sought "an equitable distribution of power between the nations of the United

Kingdom and between local, regional and central government" (Charter 88, 1988). The mission was to guarantee all of these things, and more, by means of a written constitution. It stopped short of calling for the abolition of the monarchy.

Devolution of power away from Westminster was one of the more active areas of constitutional reform during the first New Labour government. In 1998, the Scotland Act, the Government of Wales Act and the Northern Ireland Act, all altered the constitutional relationships of the constituent 'countries' of the United Kingdom of Great Britain and Northern Ireland (to give the UK's full name). Northern Ireland (NI) has, of course, a rather special relationship to the UK devolution agenda. While there had been a devolved parliament in the North of Ireland since partition in the early 1920s, this was neither a consensual nor a democratic arrangement. The deep constitutional division between supporters of an Irish Republic and those with allegiance to the British Crown and the union with Great Britain, was not resolved by civil war in the South nor suppression of the republican forces in the North – although it certainly became more contained. After partition, government in NI rested in large part on the suspension and denial of civil and political rights for much of the period from 1921 to 1972, when the unworkable administration was finally suspended. For some 30 years following the introduction of 'direct rule', NI's own particular constitutional crisis has been only too obvious. The 1998 Northern Ireland Act, therefore, needs to be seen as reflecting both the broad movement towards UK devolution, as well as the unique political history of Ireland.

The main concern of this chapter is to consider the implications of the new constitutional arrangements for social policy. It begins with an argument that, as an academic subject, social policy is poorly prepared for the challenges raised by changing constitutional contexts. Then it looks at the key issue of resource allocation between the territories and associated arguments for changing conventions that have been in place since the late 1970s. Finally, and more speculatively, the potential and limitations of the 1998 Act are considered.

Social policy and the national question

While there has been no shortage of discussion of 'Third Wayism', communitarianism and citizenship in recent years, it is rare to find an academic social policy text that links these ideas explicitly to constitutional questions. The notion that *constitutional* reform has an important part to play in progress on social and economic rights, is not well established either in academic or political circles in Britain. As Klug (1997) suggests, this may be because of the current intellectual and political fashion of balancing rights with obligations. The 'Old Labour' discourse of rights and redistribution has come to be replaced by a New Labour one of 'social inclusion' coupled with social and moral conservatism (Levitas, 1998). While 18 years of Conservative governments – not to mention the fear of *permanent* Conservative rule – spurred on the cause of constitutional change, it seems to have seriously damaged positive notions of social rights. There is a consensus across the political spectrum that the individual right to compete in, and for, work is the primary social value which government seeks to promote and protect. For example, the UK government's report to the UN Recall Conference on social development (Geneva, June 2000) proclaimed that antipoverty strategy at the national level was rooted in tackling 'poverty of opportunity' (Foreign and Commonwealth Office, 1999).

A second general observation on social policy texts concerns how 'national' and 'country' issues are represented and handled. The word 'national' is one of the most casually used terms in the literature. In many instances the usage is simply empirically invalid. Similarly, there is an assumed integrity and homogeneity of the 'United Kingdom', which, from the standpoint of NI is distinctly 'unionist' in character[2]. Yet NI as such is very poorly located in the literature. Turn to any major British textbook on social policy and references to NI will be scarce, if not absent altogether (see Hill, 1997; Lavalette and Pratt, 1997; Leonard, 1997; Levin, 1997; Blakemore, 1998; O'Brien and Penna, 1998; Baldock et al, 1999; Pierson and Castles, 2000; May et al, 2001). This 'silence'[3] is most often manifest in the way the term 'UK' is used. Although NI is formally part of the UK, it is common practice to speak of the 'UK' but draw all examples and data from England and Wales, in other words Britain. 'British' and 'UK' are used interchangeably. The same point applies to Wales and Scotland: 'Britain' and 'Great Britain' are used when the author really means England (or even London!) (for an exception see Jones and McGregor, 1998).

In this way, the texts gloss over the specificity of the 'countries' and the problem of relations between them in terms of history, power, resource distribution and cultural formations. They thereby reproduce one of the core characteristics of much British social policy analysis – its assumed cosmopolitanism and belief in state welfare as socially (and nationally) integrative. Yet Fabianism and 'mainstream social administration' have long been shown to be nationalistic, imperialist, sexist and ethnocentric (Mishra, 1977; Williams, 1989). Social policy, especially in the context of

NI, may generate conflict and division (Birrell and Murie, 1975; Ditch, 1988). Nor is this a relatively recent issue – the ideological and political conflict over the constitution of the UK was experienced first hand by Beatrice Webb who, after spending her honeymoon in Belfast and Dublin, fell out with her best friend, Alice Stopford Green over Irish Home Rule (Seymour-Jones, 1993)[4]. In more recent times, challenging the Beveridge principle of 'national uniformity' has mainly been evident in the New Right's attempt to combine economic deregulation with the type of British nationalism which led Margaret Thatcher to assert that Northern Ireland was as much a part of the UK as her own constituency (House of Commons Debates, 1981). Only recently has social policy analysis in Britain come to be informed by a critique of British national identity as being constructed historically (in part) on the basis of anti-Irish racism and anti-Catholicism (Hickman, 1998), though such work remains rare and marginal. Issues of national identity, national aspiration and national democracy are at best reworked as second or third level questions of the division of responsibilities between tiers of government (Taylor-Gooby and Dale, 1981).

'Irish' social policy literature is also largely devoid of references to the North. This is surprising given that until 1999, the 1937 constitution described the national territory as "the whole island of Ireland, its islands and territorial seas"[5] (Bunreacht na h Éireann, 1992). One recent social policy text (Healy and Reynolds, 1998) refers in places to the United Kingdom, but there is not a single mention of Northern Ireland in 434 pages. The Anglo-Irish Agreement (British and Irish Governments, 1985) stimulated some explicitly North/South comparative work in the social policy field from the mid-1980s (for example, Cormack et al, 1985; McLaughlin and Fahy, 1999) and an all-Ireland social policy association was formed in 1997, but politicians rather than academics have led cross-border comparisons of government structures and policies.

Northern Ireland's invisibility remains the rule rather than the exception. While the Republic of Ireland is sometimes included in 'comparative' social policy, once again Northern Ireland misses out (see for example, Ginsburg, 1992; Cochrane and Clarke, 1993; Hill, 1996). It is typically neither the subject of mainstream 'UK' social policy discussion, nor a suitable case for comparative treatment: neither state nor nation, neither domestic nor international.

Within NI itself, the linkage between social and constitutional issues is strong. This is partly because of the fragility of the peace agreement and associated political institutions, but also because social policy issues are, more often than not, contested in terms of unionist and nationalist interests

(McLaughlin, 1998; Sheehan and Tomlinson, 1999). Under the Northern Ireland Peace Agreement[6], a Northern Ireland Human Rights Commission (NIHRC) was established with responsibility for developing a draft Bill of Rights to include provisions over and above the UK-wide Human Rights Act. There is currently a lively debate over the consultation document, which includes proposals for rights to national identity (British or Irish), to work, to an adequate standard of living, to healthcare and to housing (NIHRC, 2001). The draft NI Bill of Rights also covers women's rights and the rights of children, and it proposes a duty on public bodies "to develop and enforce programmatic responses to the social and economic rights" (2001, p 129). The interesting question is whether the institutionalisation of such rights will change current outcomes and distributions, and transform the dominant unionist/nationalist character of social policy debates.

'Differential devolution'

Speaking to the government's programme of constitutional reform in 1998, the Lord Chancellor set out a number of the issues in Charter 88's manifesto, but recognised that 'pragmatism based on principle' would not satisfy the most ardent supporters of constitutional change (Irvine, 1998). Critics, for example, have attacked the modernisation of the House of Lords (the second stage of which will only provide for a 20% elected chamber), and point out that under the 1848 Treason Felony Act a life sentence can still be given to anyone advocating the abolition of the monarchy, notwithstanding 'freedom of expression' under the Human Rights Act (see *The Guardian*, 2001)[7].

Regarding 'devolution schemes', Lord Irvine (1998) stated:

> The UK is an asymmetrical entity and the Government's approach reflects the different histories and contemporary circumstances of England, Scotland, Wales and Northern Ireland. We are not promoting a federal style uniform devolution of powers, but differential devolution to different parts of the United Kingdom.

The basic differences are that the Scottish Parliament and NI Assembly have the power to make 'primary' legislation, but the Welsh Assembly does not. This applies to any matters 'transferred' to the local parliaments and not 'reserved' by the Westminster government, or to any matters defined as 'excepted'. The legislation implies that reserved matters could be transferred in the future, while excepted matters could not. In NI's case, matters 'reserved' to Westminster cover criminal justice, public order, the National Minimum Wage, personal and occupational pension schemes, social security commissioners, data protection, intellectual property, consumer safety (goods), genetics, surrogacy, human fertilisation and embryology, telecommunications and "property belonging to Her Majesty in right of the Crown" (1998 Northern Ireland Act, schedule 3, para 2). Unlike in Scotland, policing is a reserved matter – although there are proposals to change this, and criminal justice, in a few years time. 'Excepted' matters in NI's case include taxes, national insurance contributions, control of the NI National Insurance Fund, national security, elections and registration of political parties, judicial appointments, titles and honours, the Crown and defence of the realm, treason, and the "regulation of activities in outer space"[8] (1998 Northern Ireland Act, schedule 2, para 20). Scotland has the so-called 'tartan tax' (the Scottish Variable Rate of Income Tax) which, under Treasury rules, is genuinely additional. Neither Wales nor NI has tax varying powers. NI's only taxation powers are the regional and district council rates which together amount to around 6% of all tax revenues attributable to NI. It is also worth noting that different systems of proportional representation are used in electing the devolved representative bodies.

Figures 4.1 to 4.3 illustrate how the political arrangements for the government of NI have changed as a result of the peace agreement and the 1998 Act. They include a new constitutional relationship between NI and the Irish Republic, embodied in the North South Ministerial Council (NSMC), a permanent 'conference' between the Irish and British governments, and a British-Irish Council linking all constituent parts of the UK with the Oireachtas.

The work of the NSMC, which has been badly disrupted by First Minister David Trimble's refusal to authorise the attendance of the two Sinn Féin ministers[9], is described in Table 4.1. The 1998 NI Act provides

Table 4.1: North South Ministerial Council activities

Implementation bodies	Matters for cooperation
Waterways Ireland	Transport
The Food Safety Promotion Board	Agriculture
The Trade and Business Development Body	Education
The Special EU Programmes Body	Health
The Language Body	Environment
The Foyle, Carlingford and Irish Lights Commission	Tourism

Figure 4.1: Pre-Agreement political structures

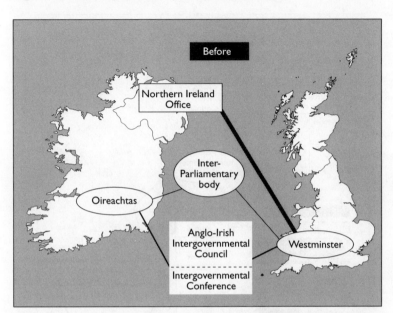

Figure 4.2: Political institutions after the 1998 Northern Ireland Act

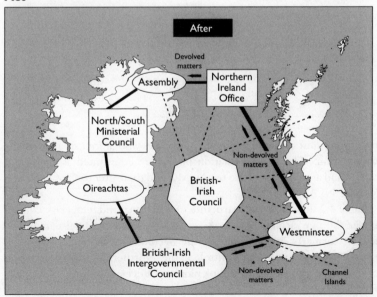

Figure 4.3: Post-Agreement political structures

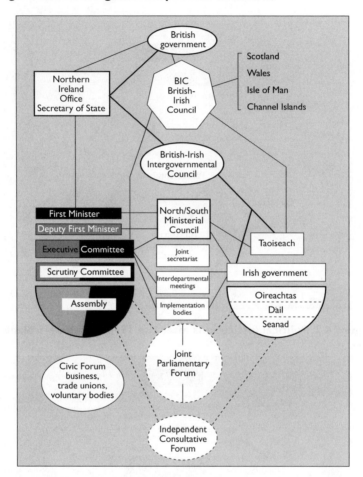

for a minimum of six 'implementation bodies' and *at least* six matters for
cooperation. The implementation bodies are constituted as all–Ireland
bodies and are accountable to the NSMC and thereafter to the Oireachtas
and the NI Assembly.

Table 4.2 shows the basic structure of functional and budgetary control
under the new arrangements. As can be seen, a substantial part of the
budget formerly in the hands of the Secretary of State for Northern
Ireland is now under the control of the Northern Ireland Executive,
covering ten ministerial portfolios, plus the Office of the First and Deputy
First Minister.

An inevitable consequence of budgetary devolution is to put the spotlight on what the different countries get from the Treasury and why. According to Travers (1999), it has had another 'unintended consequence', namely a growing awareness about English regional finances. Already, the North East of England, with a higher rate of unemployment, is demanding that resources be redistributed away from NI. There is a growing argument that "the Scots, the Welsh and, particularly, the population of Northern Ireland are feather-bedded by the Southern English" (Travers, 1999, p 2). In practical terms, this has begun to put pressure on the Barnett formula discussed in the next section. It is important to bear in mind at the outset (see Table 4.2) that not all NI expenditure is subject to the Barnett formula – it does not apply to the Secretary of State's Northern Ireland Office budget, and it applies to about 60% of the remaining NI public expenditure, most of the rest being social security payments.

The Barnett formula

It was David Heald who named the method for allocating resources to Scotland, Wales and NI in the late 1970s as the 'Barnett formula' after Joel Barnett who was Chief Secretary to the Treasury at the time (Twigger, 1998). The formula was first used in the 1978 Expenditure Survey and was designed to take the political heat out of public expenditure bargaining in anticipation of Scottish and Welsh devolution. The Treasury had conducted a needs assessment review, which showed, for instance, that for 1976-77, Scotland received 122% of the UK per capita spending when 116% would have been justified on the basis of need. It should be emphasised that the concept of 'need' involved here was very rudimentary. Nevertheless, the Barnett formula was adopted due to its simplicity and possibly for policy reasons (see later discussion). While devolution did not occur at the time, the Barnett formula was nevertheless applied to Scotland for 1979-80 and to Wales and NI two years later.

When first applied, the formula did nothing to change the historical baseline of allocations: it was only applied to proposed *changes* in English expenditure. If there is a decision to increase spending on health in England then NI, Scotland and Wales will get a Barnett formula-based increase. A second feature to note is that the formula applies to programmes that are directly comparable. Third, estimates of population are used as a crude measure of relative need. So the way the formula works is that the quantity of change is multiplied by the extent of comparability and then by a figure for the proportion of population in the territory, compared

Table 4.2: Components of public spending in Northern Ireland

Unit	Function	Resources	Source of funds
Northern Ireland Office	• The political process • Policing • Police reform • Security, including services in support of the security forces • Prison services • Payment of criminal damage and injuries compensation • Criminal justice, including juvenile justice centres and after-care • Criminal justice reform • Probation services • Information services • Grants to voluntary bodies concerned with the rehabilitation of offenders, crime • Prevention and victim support • Elections • Legal and forensic services • European Union Peace and Reconciliation projects • Northern Ireland Human Rights Commission • Equality Commission for Northern Ireland • Bloody Sunday Inquiry • Central (Northern Ireland Office)	2001-02 DEL = £1,138 million AME = £30 million Budget negotiated between Secretary of State for NI and Treasury Not subject to Barnett formula	Voted estimates as part of central UK government expenditure
Northern Ireland Executive (NIE)	• Agriculture, fisheries, forestry and rural development • Culture, arts and leisure • Education, schools, libraries and youth services • Industrial support and regeneration, and trade • Energy regulation • Environmental, planning, local government and other services • Roads, transport, water and sewerage services • Higher and further education, training and employment services • Health and personal social services • Social security benefits, social housing services and urban regeneration • European Union Structural Funds • Devolved administration finance and personnel services • Office of the First Minister and Deputy First Minister • Northern Ireland Assembly, Ombudsman and Commissioner for Complaints	2001-02 DEL = £6,311 million AME = £3,769 million (mainly social security benefits) According to the NI Programme for Government, the NIE controls £5,862 million of the budget in 2001-02 Only the NI Executive Programme for Government budget (above), subject to Barnett formula	Grant-in-aid National Insurance Fund transfers from Britain Regional and district rates Proportion of UK taxes raised in Northern Ireland
Lord Chancellor's Office	NI Court Service Public Record Office Land Registry	DEL = £70 million	Lord Chancellor's budget
Ministry of Defence Northern Ireland Commander of Land Forces	Army, Navy and RAF, support of policing	2001-02 planned total is £488 million, including £114 million AME and £46 million capital spending	Defence budget

DEL = Departmental Expenditure Limit; AME = Annual Managed Expenditure.

with England, Britain or Great Britain as appropriate. In the 1998 Spending Review, this meant using Great Britain as the population comparison in NI's case – a factor of 2.91% (based on 1996 population estimates). In the post-devolution 2000 Review, England was used as the comparison and the factor was 3.41%, a figure which applies to the three year planning period. The comparability proportions used for the spending review in 2000 are shown in Table 4.3, but it should be noted that a few items, such as water and sewerage services, cannot be compared at all because of privatisation of the service in England.

Clearly, this is not a needs-based system. It does not allow for the different demographic structures of the territories and does not attempt to build in measures of poverty, ill health or unemployment. But after 20 years of application, commentators have started to scrutinise the Barnett formula's long-term effects and raise questions about its fairness.

Table 4.4 looks at identifiable 'total managed expenditure'[10] for different parts of the UK as well as for the English regions. This covers about three quarters of all public spending so the analysis is by no means exhaustive (Treasury Committee, 1998). The figures have been calculated on a *per capita* basis and produce some striking variations. With UK values standardised at 100, NI has the highest total expenditure per head – 133% – while the South East (SE) has the lowest at 84%. The ratio of NI to SE expenditure is 1.67 for education and 1.31 for health and personal social services. NI has 2.75 times the law and order budget of the Eastern

Table 4.3: Comparability percentages used for 2000 spending review

	Scotland	Wales	Northern Ireland
Education/employment	93.3	82.0	99.7
Health	99.7	99.7	99.7
Transport	71.2	67.1	89.3
Housing and other environmental	96.5	94.9	99.4
Local government	56.4	99.9	42.6
Home Office	92.3	0.6	2.6
Trade and industry	20.2	19.5	25.7
Domestic agriculture	84.3	84.3	85.5
Culture, media and sport	95.3	87.5	100.0
Social security (administration)	0.0	0.0	100.0

Source: HM Treasury (2000) *Funding the Scottish Parliament, National Assembly for Wales and the Northern Ireland Assembly, A statement of funding policy*

region of England and 81.25 times the per capita spending on housing. NI is below the UK average in two programmes only, culture, media and sport (59% compared to the UK's 100%) and roads/transport (89%), but these two programmes make up a mere 5.1% of total UK expenditure per head.

The figures in Table 4.4 beg the question of territorial cross subsidisation, but they do not answer it in any way because of the absence of information on revenue. Territorial estimates of tax revenues are not routinely published by the Inland Revenue[11], although in NI's case they can be derived from the Northern Ireland Financial Statement. For 1997/98, for example, NI's attributed share of UK taxes was put at £4,413 million[12]. How that figure was arrived at is a mystery buried somewhere in the Treasury and the Statutory Instruments made under section 15 of the 1973 Northern Ireland Constitution Act. For the UK as a whole, £212,017 million was raised in central government taxation in 1997/98, so NI's attributed share amounted to 2.08%. These gross figures, however, give us no understanding of how the burden of different types of taxation varies by territory. This is important for any assessment of redistributive effects given that some taxes are more 'progressive' than others and that the degree of progression/regression has changed radically over the last quarter of a century.

Bearing these qualifications in mind, it is possible to estimate the notional value of territorial transfers using GDP data as a proxy for taxation revenues (see Travers, 1999). The National Statistics Office produces two measures of territorial GDP, one based on 'residence' and the other on 'workplace'. In the former, the income of commuters is allocated to where they live, rather than where they work. This makes a big difference to the figures for the territories in and around London, but is marginal elsewhere. For most of the 1990s, NI's residence-based GDP was measured at 2.2% or 2.3% of total UK GDP. Workplace GDP has been steady at 2.2% from 1993 to 1999 (the latest available figure at the time of writing). Given that the attributed share of taxes for NI was *lower* than this in the late 1990s, any calculations based on GDP may underestimate the degree of transfers involved.

One further point concerns the relationship of total spending to GDP. Since 1963-64 the proportion of GDP devoted to public spending has varied between a low of 37.9% and a high of 49.5%. The highest figures were recorded in the mid- to late 1970s and again in the early 1980s. The lowest figure during the period was for 1999-2000, the year used for territorial comparisons in the next table.

Table 4.5 presents a calculation designed to illustrate the difference between the public resources generated in a territory (using the GDP

Table 4.4: Per capita identifiable total managed expenditure (TME) 1999-2000

1999/2000	All	Social security	Health and personal social services	Education	Law, order and police service	Housing	Trade, industry, energy, employment services	Other environmental services	Agriculture	Culture, media, sport	Roads, transport
UK (£)	4,453	1,724	1,072	685	315	51	115	144	75	89	138
% of total	100	38.7	24.1	15.4	7.1	1.2	2.6	3.2	1.7	2.0	3.1
UK	100	100	100	100	100	100	100	100	100	100	100
Scotland	118	108	119	126	96	175	148	130	267	99	131
Wales	113	115	110	100	96	144	112	168	155	157	112
Northern Ireland	133	120	111	137	206	325	254	106	284	59	89
England	96	98	97	96	97	82	89	93	73	98	97
North East	109	119	102	100	104	57	103	117	75	143	96
North West	104	112	100	101	101	90	94	106	73	88	97
Yorkshire & Humberside	95	101	98	96	93	71	91	45	75	87	74
East Midlands	90	94	88	93	90	35	96	90	73	81	85
West Midlands	94	99	92	101	88	37	90	92	69	82	89
South West	92	97	91	92	85	35	87	79	75	83	88
East	88	89	92	96	75	4	86	76	73	75	95
London	113	97	121	108	144	304	94	126	72	176	122
South East	84	84	85	82	83	26	76	94	73	76	105

Source: Calculated from various tables in HM Treasury (2001) *Public expenditure: statistical analyses 2001-02*

Table 4.5: GDP, total managed expenditure and the notional value of territorial transfers per capita

	GDP (1999)	TME (1999/00)	Transfer	Notional value of transfer (£ pc)*	Actual TME received (£ pc)	Notional TME without transfer (£ pc)
UK value (£)	13,213	4,453	—	—	—	—
UK	100	100	0	—	—	—
Scotland	97	118	+21	935	5,255	4,320
Wales	81	113	+32	1,425	5,032	3,607
Northern Ireland	78	133	+55	2,449	5,923	3,474
England	102	96	−6	−267	4,275	4,542
North East	77	109	+32	1,425	4,854	3,429
North West	87	104	+17	757	4,631	3,874
Yorks, Humberside	88	95	+7	312	4,230	3,918
East Midlands	94	90	−4	178	4,008	3,830
West Midlands	92	94	+2	89	4,186	4,097
South West	91	92	+1	45	4,097	4,052
East	116	88	−28	−1,247	3,919	5,166
London	130	113	−17	−757	5,032	5,789
South East	116	84	−32	−1,425	3,741	5,166

Source: Notional transfer value based on UK TME value (£4,453)
* Transfer %, using data from HM Treasury (2001) *Public expenditure: statistical analyses 2001-02*

proxy) and territorial public expenditure. The fourth column of data provides a measure of the notional value of the transfer per capita between the territories at the end of the last decade. The last two columns respectively show; a) what the actual public spending per capita was; and b) what the spending would have been without transfer (that is, matched to GDP). The table shows that at the end of the 1990s the North East had a lower GDP per capita than NI, yet was receiving a notional transfer of about £1,000 less per capita per year, providing prima facie evidence in support of the claims mentioned previously.

There is, however, a danger in reading Tables 4.4 and 4.5 uncritically. Implicit in the Treasury territorial data is the idea that we are comparing like with like, socially, economically and politically. The territories are not equivalent entities in these respects and the programmes themselves are treated differently according to both constitutional and Treasury regimes. In addition, Table 4.5 in particular encourages the idea that 'fairness' and 'equity' depend on matching inputs and outputs – that territorial units should get what they deserve in terms of taxation paid. A 'national' framework for redistribution, in contrast, suggests that other principles come into play around which there is consensus and which include agreement about allegiance to the nation itself. The Treasury's 1970s needs assessment exercise, referred to previously, stated that the principle of allocation was to achieve the same standards of public service provision throughout the UK (Treasury Committee, 1998). In NI's case, this was said to be the principle behind the Social Services Agreement Act of 1949 (Birrell and Murie, 1980; Tomlinson, 1995).

Where national allegiance is under threat, most obviously in Scotland and NI, then it is likely that English nationalism and regionalism will popularise arguments for the withdrawal of subsidies from the reluctant members[13]. This is especially the case once any 'special circumstances' (of whatever nature) justifying the subsidies disappear.

Awareness of the transfers within English regional politics is recent, but in NI's case the transfers have been visible and the subject of a longstanding debate about the feasibility or otherwise of NI leaving the UK (Tomlinson, 1994). There is also a well-developed politics of 'special case-ism' characterised by using the conflict and its effects as the basis for justifying extra resources, especially for the security industry, which enjoyed a 'blank cheque' for much of the last 20 years. Because of the system of financing NI established at partition, the 'subvention' received from the Treasury is readily identifiable. At the end of the 1970s the subvention was £944 million (1979/80), with a further £96 million spent on the 'extra costs' of the British Army's role. By 1996/97 it had climbed to £3,448 million (plus £505 million military expenditure). That year, £1,047 million was spent by the Northern Ireland Office (on policing, prisons and such like), leaving £2,401 million of the subvention for social and other expenditures. Social security expenditure, not subject to the Barnett formula or under the NI Executive's budget, amounted to £3,152 million in the same year. Had the Executive been in existence in 1996/97, it would have had responsibility for 54% of the total NI public spend – a corresponding figure applies to the latest public expenditure estimates.

NI appears to have held on to relatively high levels of overall public spending. At first sight this is surprising because in theory the application of the Barnett formula should lead to a convergence of spending levels between the territories through the so-called 'Barnett squeeze', according to some commentators. Bell (2001) has simulated the application of the formula to Scotland, Wales and NI and demonstrated that convergence would be most rapid in a situation of strong growth in public spending (see also Kay, 1998; McCrone, 1999). Midwinter (1999) challenges the view that one intention of the formula was to deliver convergence in per capita funding, although the Treasury has acknowledged this is one of the features of the formula (Treasury Committee, 1998)[14].

In practice, as Heald (1994) has shown, convergence was very minor in the 1980s, largely due to cutbacks or slow public spending growth, the fact that a large proportion of public spending (nearly half in NI's case) bypasses the Barnett formula, and finally, because of the way the population ratios have been applied. The rounding up of 1976-based population ratios for Scotland (from 9.57% to 10% of GB population) and the rounding down for England (85.31% to 85%) and for Wales (5.12% to 5%), benefited Scotland but disadvantaged Wales. NI was also rounded down at the time, but retained a figure with two decimal places (2.79% was rounded to 2.75%). The Barnett formula has been subject to a lag in the population factor because ratios were not updated until 1992 and again in 1998. In the 1992 revision, the NI figure was revised upwards to 2.87%. Scotland, with its declining population relative to England, gained from this process in the 1980s, while NI lost out. Another problem is that in some years the Treasury simply cut the baseline figures before applying the formula.

In 1998, the Treasury Committee expressed disappointment that "no Government studies have been made in relation to the appropriateness of the Barnett Formula and how it relates to needs" (Treasury Committee, 1998, para 12). It went on to state that a new needs assessment "would help to show whether the Barnett Formula remains the appropriate method of allocating annual expenditure increases (or savings) to the four nations of the Union.... It is important there should be maximum possible agreement on this in all parts of the UK" (Treasury Committee, 1998, para 12).

The most recent concern about the Barnett formula, from NI's point of view, is the likely adverse effects of the change to resource-based accounting for public expenditure purposes. In a position paper for the Northern Ireland Assembly (Northern Ireland Executive, 2001), the Executive argued that

> convergence [to English per capita expenditure levels] would be accelerated very significantly under the new resource budgeting regime if the Barnett formula were applied to the calculation of changes in the capital charges that apply to capital assets in the public sector. This is because our public asset base is proportionately much larger than our population share relative to England. (section 2, para 40)

The new accounting system effectively puts pressure on public bodies to dispose of unused assets or to put them to use.

The idea that NI does very well out of public spending and that this is due to the workings of the Barnett formula does not stand up to scrutiny. The large programmes, which invite direct comparison and which *are* subject to Barnett, are health and education, both of which are 99.7% comparable to England. NI per capita spending on education is the highest in the UK (at 137%) followed by Scotland (126%), but Scotland's programme is less comparable (93.3%). The division of schools between Catholic, Protestant, integrated and Irish language sectors, the historic consequences of retaining the grammar/secondary school structure, and the relatively large proportion of rural schools, are clearly factors which create higher operating costs in NI[15]. But NI's spending may not be so out of line in any case – it has 3.88% of the UK education budget and 3.40% of the UK's school-age population. Regarding health (for which the UK average spend in 1999/2000 was £1,072 per capita), NI spending (£1,193) is lower than London (£1,301) (where special factors relating to UK-wide service provision apply) and Scotland (£1,271), and about the same as Wales. Within the English regions, the North East comes out on top (at £1,090) and the South East is the lowest (at £914). A cursory examination of health data suggests that NI ranks the worst on a number of indicators, including the reporting of good health, age standardised mortality rates for respiratory diseases, smoking rates, perinatal mortality, and deaths from road accidents. Twenty-two per cent of patients wait 12 months or longer for hospital admission compared to 4.2% in England and 0.6% in the North East (Northern and Yorkshire NHS Regional Office Area)[16]. The only major indicator for which England stands out as being worse off is notification rates of tuberculosis. Rates per 100,000 have increased from 10.4% to 12.8% between 1990 and 2000, whereas in NI they have declined from 8.2% to 3.4% over the same period (McGinty and Williams, 2001).

Repositioning Northern Ireland

This chapter has focused on *what* is spent on social policy, rather than *how* it is spent. From the previous discussion, it is clear that devolution obviously gives more scope to the latter than the former – in NI's case, there is very little autonomy in the new financial arrangements under the 1998 Act. This is not to underestimate the value of being able to spend money differently (when allowed!) or to shift resources around within and between programmes. But the Treasury determines NI's taxation, negotiates with the Secretary of State the law and order budget, decides on the overall level of subvention and then makes increases to key social programmes such as health and education dependent on what it decides to do for England. Furthermore it determines the level of increase using the Barnett formula which is squeezing programme budgets towards English per capita levels with no regard to levels of need or differences in the structure of provision. To make matters worse, the introduction of the Resource Budgeting regime in public expenditure accounting will, if the Barnett formula is applied to changes in capital charges, further disadvantage NI. NI is also being pushed into the Private Finance Initiative[17].

Although the focus of this chapter has been largely on finance and associated intra-UK political tensions, there is also the politics of social policy to consider. While NI's core social policy provisions have always replicated British law and practice, there are nonetheless significant differences, some unique and some organisational. The distinctive character of NI's social policies reflect the different historical periods of constitutional relationship with Britain. Prior to direct rule, unionist governments moulded the post-war welfare state, not into a replica of labourist universalism, but into a somewhat precarious 'Orange state'. This was based largely on the marginalisation of the nationalist minority and the policy areas most affected were economic development (including industrial location), housing and public sector employment. Private sector employment was also highly segmented. With the agreement of the Catholic Church (which at the time was hostile to state-based social provision), the education system was divided on the basis of religion and differentially funded. The absence of universal suffrage and the presence of draconian special powers to deal with political dissent provided the final ingredients to this exclusivist policy culture.

Direct rule from 1972 produced its own peculiarities. Some of these were directly related to the issues of discrimination and Catholic/Protestant community differentials, while others were specifically and explicitly concerned with conflict management and containment (Ruane and Todd, 1996; Tomlinson, 1998). The lack of political institutions and working relationships between the main political parties meant that local government was emasculated and that key social services became centralised under non-elected boards. The NI civil service was expanded and its function changed from being a direct agent of unionist government to one of providing permanence and stability as Westminster governments came and went.

It is against this background that the potential impact of the 1998 Northern Ireland Act needs to be assessed. Much has already been done to challenge the policy culture of exclusivism referred to previously and there is much in the Agreement and new structures that institutionalise 'equality'. But structures and safeguards have to be worked at if a new culture of equality and human rights is to secure a proper foothold and grow. Unquestionably, the Assembly has the capacity to democratise policy making and to shake up the power of the civil service established under direct rule. But it is also fragile for as long as unionists of various shades threaten to collapse it.

One of the arguments associated with the peace process is that resources formerly devoted to conflict containment could now be transferred to other programmes – around 10% of the total resources devoted to NI could be redistributed in this way to underpin social, economic and political development. There are many barriers to such a process, not least the vested interests within the security industry and the continuing instability of the political institutions, coupled with both loyalist and republican opposition to the current settlement. Prior to devolution, for instance, the Secretary of State was in a position to switch post-ceasefire savings on property compensation to other budget headings, but it is less clear how such a redistribution might occur now. Security savings, when they occur, are more than likely to revert to the Treasury.

Another consequence of the division of budgets between the Secretary of State and the NI Executive is that when the English regional debate hots up, this is likely to impact more strongly on the Executive's budget than on security. Past experience shows that, irrespective of the security situation, security budgets are less vulnerable to retrenchment than social spending.

In defence of its budget and responsibilities, the NI Executive will rightly argue against the continued use of the Barnett formula during the next spending review. A needs-based formula is preferable to one based on population estimates, notwithstanding the difficulties of agreeing this with the Treasury and the probable resistance of Scotland to changing the present regime. Besides, unlike NI, Scotland has (as yet unused) tax varying powers. There has been some debate within NI about acquiring such powers and the creative use to which they might be put. One obvious candidate is North-South cooperation, which could extend existing NSMC work on health, education, economic development, transport and communications infrastructure. Any funding from the North could be matched by funding from the South.

The prospect of NI acquiring taxation powers will inevitably be shaped by unionist and nationalist calculations regarding NI's future within the UK. Unionists and nationalists may agree on seeking the best deal possible from the Treasury, but nationalists will be instinctively less content with Treasury conservatism and control. They are not impressed by the regionalist arguments of English nationalists that NI is a pampered part of the UK, and will seek ways of maximising economies of scale and policy cooperation with the Dublin government.

Reconstituting social policy

UK constitutional reform presents new challenges for social policy analysis. While there have been welcome developments in the discipline in terms of comparative and international analyses over the last decade, there has been a relative neglect of constitutional issues within the UK.

The analysis of territorial resource distribution presented here supports the case for a more thorough and considered basis for allocation than currently provided by the Barnett formula. A 'needs-based' formula is instinctively more attractive to social policy analysts than one based on gross population comparisons, but this is much easier to say than to agree. The Treasury, however, will be increasingly challenged to produce a fairer mechanism.

Devolution phase one has stirred up the debate on the Barnett formula. The new arrangements foster a politics of distribution, not redistribution, both within NI and between NI and Great Britain. Devolution phase two (involving the English regions) will further sharpen the politics of territorial distribution between the territories of the UK, whether considered as 'countries' or a mix of countries and the English regions. The current practice of the Treasury in presenting territorial spending data is fanning a debate that needs to be better informed by the specificities of the different parts of the UK and their historical relations with the Westminster government. In particular, both sides of the redistributive equation need to be considered – the variable burdens and effects of different types of *taxation* as well as spending. No such data are published at present.

We may be encouraged to put the English regions and NI on the same spreadsheet but there the similarities end. English regional devolution is not comparable to NI's new constitutional framework under the peace agreement for at least four reasons. Firstly, a key element of the agreement is the developing range of activities between the North and South of Ireland – albeit very small in budgetary terms at present. Secondly, although England has been involved in the NI conflict in a number of ways, it has not experienced indigenous conflict of a similar nature and extent. Thirdly, no English region will be constituted in such a way that if it so chooses it may leave the UK. Fourthly, no area of the UK has experienced such a long history of conservative government as NI. Of the 80 years since partition, NI was ruled by the unionist section of the Conservative and Unionist Party for 50 years and by Conservative direct rulers for a further 23 years. That legacy requires compensation, whatever NI's future destination.

Notes

[1] The author wishes to thank Paddy Hillyard and Eithne McLaughlin for their comments on the first draft of this paper.

[2] The Quality Assurance Agency's benchmarking statement for social policy, for example, refers to 'the UK welfare system' and 'UK welfare institutions'.

[3] Paddy Hillyard (1995) has described the silence on Northern Ireland among British criminologists and other academics as 'the silence of the lambs'.

[4] Green was part of a group of Protestant women in London who, with Cumann na mBan, organised a shipment of arms to the Irish Volunteers in 1914 – herself putting up £1,500 (Taillon, 1996).

[5] Under the NI Peace Agreement (Irish Government, 1998), the following amendments to Articles 2 and 3 of Bunreacht na h Éireann (the Irish constitution) were put to a referendum:

Article 2:
It is the entitlement and birthright of every person born in the island of Ireland, which includes its islands and seas, to be part of the Irish nation. That is also the entitlement of all persons otherwise qualified in accordance with law to be citizens of Ireland. Furthermore, the Irish nation cherishes its special affinity with people of Irish ancestry living abroad who share its cultural identity and heritage.

Article 3:
1. It is the firm will of the Irish nation, in harmony and friendship, to unite all the people who share the territory of the island of Ireland, in all the diversity of their identities and traditions, recognising that a united Ireland shall be brought about only by peaceful means with the consent

of a majority of the people, democratically expressed, in both jurisdictions in the island. Until then, the laws enacted by the Parliament established by this Constitution shall have the like area and extent of application as the laws enacted by the Parliament that existed immediately before the coming into operation of this Constitution.

2. Institutions with executive powers and functions that are shared between those jurisdictions may be established by their respective responsible authorities for stated purposes and may exercise powers and functions in respect of all or any part of the island.

[6] One of the ironies of the Agreement is that there is no agreement on what to call it. The British government and unionists tend to refer to the 'Belfast Agreement', while nationalists call it the 'Good Friday Agreement'. The 'Northern Ireland Peace Agreement' is the label given by the Irish government.

[7] While the 1848 Treason Felony Act was principally used against newspaper editors in Ireland (notably John Mitchell) during the Great Famine, it nevertheless had a dampening effect on the development and expression of republican ideals elsewhere.

[8] This does not seem to have prevented three retired police officers paying 48 dollars to have a distant star in the Hercules constellation named after the 'Royal Ulster Constabulary', (now the Police Service of Northern Ireland) (*The Observer*, 2 December 2001).

[9] The two Sinn Féin ministers, Bairbre de Brun and Martin McGuinness, are responsible for the two largest programmes in the Executive, health and education respectively. The grounds for the refusal have been declared illegal by the NI courts on two occasions.

[10] Total Managed Expenditure is defined as the sum of the Departmental Expenditure Limit and the Annually Managed Expenditure.

[11] However, see Twigger (1998) who cites an internal Treasury paper on the 'Principles to govern determination of the block budgets for the Scottish Parliament and National Assembly for Wales'.

[12] This includes Inland Revenue taxes (income tax, corporation tax, and so on) Customs and Excise taxes (VAT, excise duties, and so on) and vehicle excise duties. Social security contributions are credited to the Northern Ireland National Insurance Fund and the health service.

[13] The right to Irish reunification is explicitly recognised in Section 1 (2) of the 1998 Northern Ireland Act. The Secretary of State may periodically hold a poll on the issue and "if the wish expressed by a majority in such a poll is that Northern Ireland should cease to be part of the United Kingdom and form part of a united Ireland, the Secretary of State shall lay before Parliament such proposals to give effect to that wish as may be agreed between Her Majesty's Government in the United Kingdom and the Government of Ireland".

[14] Midwinter is quoted in *The Observer* (4 March 2001) as describing the idea of the Barnett squeeze as "extremely silly".

[15] On the differential funding of Catholic and Protestant schools, see Gallagher (1989).

[16] These figures come with a warning that they are not strictly comparable between the 'countries'.

[17] Resource Budgeting is supposed to increase the 'productivity' of public assets. It effectively penalises the 'non-use' of assets and is likely to act as a further incentive for public bodies to asset-strip and engage in Private Finance Initiative (PFI) for the development of capital programmes.

References

Baldock, J., Manning, N., Miller, S. and Vickerstaff, S. (eds) (1999) *Social policy*, Oxford: Oxford University Press.

Bell, D. (2001) *The Barnett formula*, Stirling: Stirling University.

Birrell, W.D. and Murie, A. (1975) 'Ideology and social conflict', *Journal of Social Policy*, vol 4, no 3, pp 243-58.

Birrell, W.D. and Murie, A. (1980) *Policy and government in Northern Ireland: Lessons of devolution*, Dublin: Gill and Macmillan.

Blakemore, K. (1998) *Social policy: An introduction*, Buckingham: Open University Press.

British and Irish Governments (1985) *Agreement between the Government of the United Kingdom of Great Britain and Northern Ireland and the Government of the Republic of Ireland*, Hillsborough.

Bunreacht na h Éireann (The Irish Constitution) (1992) Dublin: Stationery Office.

Charter 88 (1988) *The Charter*, London: Charter 88.

Cochrane, A. and Clarke, J. (1993) *Comparing welfare states: Britain in international context*, London: Sage Publications.

Cormack, R., Osborne, R.D. and McCashin, A. (1985) 'Social policy in Northern Ireland and the Republic of Ireland', *Administration*, vol 33, no 3, pp 271-3.

Ditch, J. (1988) *Social policy in Northern Ireland between 1939-1950*, Aldershot: Avebury.

Dummett, A. and Nicol, A. (1990) *Subjects, citizens, aliens and others*, London: Weidenfeld and Nicolson.

Foreign and Commonwealth Office (1999) *UK national report: Implementation of the Copenhagen declaration and programme of action*, London: Foreign and Commonwealth Office.

Gallagher, A.M. (1989) 'Education and religion in Northern Ireland', *Majority Minority Review*, no 1, Coleraine: University of Ulster.

Ginsburg, N. (1992) *Divisions of welfare: A critical introduction to comparative social policy*, London: Sage Publications.

Heald, D. (1994) 'Territorial public expenditure in the United Kingdom', *Public Administration*, vol 72, pp 147-75.

Healy, S. and Reynolds, B. (eds) (1998) *Social policy in Ireland: Principles, practice and problems*, Dublin: Oak Tree Press.

Hickman, M. (1998) 'Education for "minorities": Irish Catholics in Britain', in G. Lewis (ed) *Forming nation, framing welfare*, London: Routledge/ Buckingham: Open University Press.

Hill, M. (1996) *Social policy: A comparative analysis*, Hemel Hempstead: Prentice Hall.

Hill, M. (1997) *The policy process in the modern state* (3rd edn), London: Prentice Hall/Harvester Wheatsheaf.

Hillyard, P. (1995) 'The silence of the lambs: British academics and the Northern Ireland problem', Paper presented to the biennial conference of the British Association for Irish Studies, Newcastle University, September.

HM Treasury (2000) *Funding the Scottish Parliament, National Assembly for Wales and the Northern Ireland Assembly, A statement of funding policy*, London: HM Treasury.

HM Treasury (2001) *Public expenditure: Statistical analyses 2001-02*, Cm 5101, London: The Stationery Office.

House of Commons Debates (10 November 1981) *Hansard*, col 427.

Irish Government (1998) *The Northern Ireland Peace Agreement: The agreement reached in multi-party negotiations*, 10 April, Dublin.

Irvine, Lord (1998) 'Government's programme of constitutional reform', Lecture to the Constitution Unit, Westminster, 8 December.

Jones, H. and McGregor, S. (eds) (1998) *Social issues and party politics*, London: Routledge.

Kay, N. (1998) 'The Scottish Parliament and the Barnett formula', *Fraser of Allander Quarterly Economic Commentary*, vol 24, no 1, pp 32-48.

Klug, F. (1997) *Reinventing community: The rights and responsibilities debate*, London: Charter 88.

Lavalette, M. and Pratt, A. (eds) (1997) *Social policy: A conceptual and theoretical introduction*, London: Sage Publications.

Leonard, P. (1997) *Postmodern welfare: Reconstructing an emancipatory project*, London: Sage Publications.

Levin, P. (1997) *Making social policy: The mechanisms of government and politics, and how to Investigate them*, Buckingham: Open University Press.

Levitas, R. (1998) *The inclusive society? Social exclusion and New Labour*, Basingstoke: Macmillan.

May, M., Page, R. and Brunson, E. (eds) (2001) *Understanding social problems: Issues in social policy*, Oxford: Blackwell.

McCrone, G. (1999) 'Scotland's public finances from Goschen to Barnett', *Fraser of Allander Quarterly Economic Commentary*, vol 24, no 2, pp 30-46.

McGinty, J. and Williams, T. (eds) (2001) *Regional trends no 36*, London: The Stationery Office.

McLaughlin, E. (1998) 'The view from Northern Ireland', in H. Jones and S. McGregor (eds) *Social issues and party politics*, London: Routledge.

McLaughlin, E. and Fahy, T. (1999) 'The family and the state in Ireland, North and South', in A. Heath, R. Breen and C. Whelan (eds) *Ireland North and South: Perspectives from the social sciences*, Oxford: Oxford University Press.

Midwinter, A. (1999) 'The Barnett formula and public spending in Scotland: policy and practice', *Scottish Affairs*, no 28, Summer, pp 83-92.

Mishra, R. (1977) *Society and social policy: Theoretical perspectives on welfare*, Basingstoke: Macmillan.

Northern Ireland Executive (2001) *Preparing for 2002-03: The executive's position report to the Assembly*, Belfast: Northern Ireland Assembly.

NIHRC (Northern Ireland Human Rights Commission) (2001) *Making a Bill of Rights for Northern Ireland: A consultation by the Northern Ireland Human Rights Commission*, Belfast: NIHRC.

Northern Ireland Act (1998) (c. 47) London: The Stationery Office.

O'Brien, M. and Penna, S. (1998) *Theorising welfare: Enlightenment and modern society*, London: Sage Publications.

Pierson, C. and Castles, F. (eds) (2000) *The welfare state reader*, Cambridge: Polity Press.

Ruane, J. and Todd, J. (1996) *The dynamics of conflict in Northern Ireland: Power, conflict and emancipation*, Cambridge: Cambridge University Press.

Seymour-Jones, C. (1993) *Beatrice Webb: Woman of conflict*, London: Pandora.

Sheehan, M. and Tomlinson, M. (1999) *The unequal unemployed: Discrimination, unemployment and state policy in Northern Ireland*, Aldershot: Ashgate.

Taillon, R. (1996) *When history was made: The women of 1916*, Belfast: Beyond the Pale Publications.

Taylor-Gooby, P. and Dale, J. (1981) *Social theory and social welfare*, London: Edward Arnold.

The Guardian (2001) 'Victorian act that killed the press', 23 June.

The Observer (2001) 'RUC lives on in deepest space', 25 November.

Tomlinson, M. (1994) *Twenty-Five years on: The costs of war and the dividends of peace*, Belfast: West Belfast Economic Forum.

Tomlinson, M. (1995) 'The British subvention and the Irish peace process', *International Policy Review*, vol 5, no 1, pp 69-74.

Tomlinson, M. (1998) 'Walking backwards into the sunset: British policy and the insecurity of Northern Ireland', in D. Miller (ed) *Rethinking Northern Ireland: Culture, ideology and colonialism*, London: Longman.

Travers, T. (1999) 'Will England put up with it?', *The Guardian*, Society section, 21 April, pp 2-3.

Treasury Committee (1998) Second Report, *The Barnett formula*, 1997/8 HC 341.

Twigger, R. (1998) *The Barnett formula*, House of Commons Library Research Paper, 98/8.

Williams, F. (1989) *Social policy: A critical introduction*, Cambridge: Polity Press.

FIVE

'Revolutionising' care for people with learning difficulties? The Labour government's Learning Disabilities Strategy[1]

Carol Walker

In March 2001 the Secretary of State for Health, Alan Milburn, launched the first major strategy aimed at "radically improving the life chances of people with learning disabilities for 30 years" (DoH, 2001a, p 1). The White Paper, *Valuing people: A new strategy for learning disability for the 21st century* (DoH, 2001b), was launched following a consultation with a range of professionals, service users and family carers and drew on the work of a number of sub-committees which had produced recommendations for the government. At its launch the Secretary of State claimed that "A revolution in care is needed to increase opportunities for thousands of people, their carers and families.... Our ambition as a government is to create a society where there genuinely are opportunities for all" (DoH, 2001a, p 1).

The White Paper sets out a clear philosophy on which service provision for this group of service users and their family carers is based. This represents a consolidation of recent thinking in this field and is a marked advance on the last White Paper published 30 years ago (DHSS/Welsh Office, 1972), the main goal of which was the de-institutionalisation of people with learning difficulties from long-stay institutions. The new White Paper claims to put people with learning difficulties at the centre of future strategy and is based on the four key principles of civil rights, independence, choice and inclusion. It supports a lifelong approach to addressing people's needs. It aims to impact on a large number of agencies, several of which have given scant regard to this group in the past: social services, health, education, housing, employment, the Benefits Agency and the independent and voluntary sector. If successful it would be a significant example of 'joined-up' government.

The ambitious goals of the government have received widespread support from those working in the field. However, there are major issues relating to implementation. The learning disabilities strategy is being introduced at a time of major change within both health and social care services. How well will the new structures be able to respond to the many demands being put on them? Still more significant is the level of new resources available for this area of policy, which the government has recognised has been grossly under-resourced. In the press release launching the new strategy, the headline read: "New learning disabilities strategy aims to increase opportunities: £100m fund to revolutionise care" (DoH, 2001a, p 1).

This chapter critically reviews the new learning disabilities strategy. It looks at the process of consultation and involvement of people with learning difficulties and others, which preceded publication. It examines the goals which the strategy sets, both in terms of the extent to which they address the major issues facing people with learning difficulties and their family carers, and service providers. Finally, it considers how practicable the goals are in the light of major structural upheaval in key services and the amount of resources available.

The process

In the White Paper, *Valuing people*, reference is made to the "extensive consultation (which took place) over more than a year" with a range of people with key interests in the learning difficulty field (DoH, 2001b, p 10). In the White Paper the extent of consultation is presented as follows:

- the Department of Health's National Learning Disability Advisory Group and the Service Users Advisory Group, who were consulted on emerging issues;
- six working groups (on children, family carers, health, supporting independence, workforce planning and training, and building partnerships) which brought together people with learning difficulties, family carers, local authority, NHS and voluntary sector representatives, and researchers, as well as personnel from the key government departments;
- seven regional workshops across the country attended by almost one thousand people, including people with learning difficulties and family carers;

- seminars on particular themes, such as parents with learning difficulties, and consultation with disabled children, to produce ideas for improving services;
- contributions from a dedicated website (www.doh.gov.uk/learningdisabilities).

Despite the undoubted commitment of people closely involved in the development of the strategy, true consultation – that is, that which affects outcomes – was inevitably limited. The most influential were, no doubt, the six working groups. These looked at six key areas and had a wide membership. With the exception of the group on Supporting Independence they did not include people with learning difficulties, whose consultation was separate, and did not include family carers in their own right. However, many 'professionals' and 'experts' were also the family carer of a child or adult with learning difficulties. It would have been appropriate to involve family carers who did not also have a professional role in the field. However, it is surprising and depressing how many experts and others who, despite being key movers and shakers in the policy field, still struggle to get appropriate service provision for their own family member. Their experiences could not fail to impress that it would be even harder for other family carers to secure the necessary support. The Department of Health provided the largest numbers of members and the chairs for all the groups except the Family Carers and Supporting Independence Groups. Representation of voluntary organisations was smaller than might have been expected given the range and size of organisations working in this field. There were also relatively few researchers and academics. The composition of the Family Carers Group, which was set up after the others, was quite different from the others. A working group on this theme was introduced after the process had started and the other groups set up following internal and external pressure. An independent consultant, who is also the mother of a man with learning difficulties, chaired the group and its membership was mainly drawn from the voluntary sector. A significant shortcoming in the working group structure was the lack of consultation between them. There was no resource – financial or in time – to allow joint meetings to ensure that the different groups took into account significant issues outside of their remit. The Family Carers Working Group met with several groups of carers and made a video with one group of family carers in Sheffield, which was submitted to the Minister of Health.

The level of participation in the seven workshops held regionally across the country may appear impressive on paper, but unfortunately the impact of these on the final strategy was negligible, if there was any impact at all, as they were held at the very end of the process when the working group reports were all but completed. Certainly, in the regional meeting which I attended there was considerable anger at the timing of the meetings. There was also very considerable scepticism, widespread among practitioners and families, that the new strategy would provide any concrete change on the ground in the form of more and better services.

The attempts to include people with learning difficulties and family carers in the development process were very welcome. The Service Users Advisory Group, with representatives from a number of advocacy and self-advocacy groups, including *People First, Mencap, Change* and *Speaking Up*, met several times during the year and visited five different parts of the country to consult with other people with learning difficulties. They produced their own report which was fed into the main Advisory Group discussions and was published in an accessible version alongside the White Paper. The title of their report is *Nothing about us without us* (DoH, 2001c). Given this emphasis on user involvement, it is disappointing that the White Paper retains use of the term 'learning disabilities' even though it is acknowledged that 'learning difficulties' is "the preferred term among user organisations and disability writers" (DoH, 2001b, p 11, fn 3). The preface to the main White Paper similarly and briefly dismisses the preferences with regards to the terminology to be used for family carers:

> The carers who helped us develop the new strategy prefer to describe themselves as 'family carer' because this emphasises the family relationship. The Department of Health uses the term 'carer' to describe people who are not paid for caring and 'care worker' for people who are paid to work as carers (DoH, 2001b, p 10, fn 2).

The label attached to this group of service users has often been changed – most notably from 'lunatics' and then 'mentally handicapped' to 'learning disabilities' and 'learning difficulties'. It can provoke fierce discussions. However, given that the government heralded a 'revolution' in provision in this area and given the alleged high priority given to putting service users themselves at the heart of the strategy, would it have been too much to ask that they could, at the very least, choose the label by which they would be called 'after the revolution'?

Contrary to the quiet slinking out of government documents in the 1980s, publication of this, and other White Papers, under the New Labour government has been refreshingly accessible. Alongside the White Paper, which was available from the government website, the government published an accessible printed version, a CD ROM and a tape for people with learning difficulties. The reports of the Services Users Advisory Group (DoH, 2001c), the Family Carers Working Group (DoH, 2001d), and a report on learning difficulties and ethnicity commissioned as a background paper for the White Paper (Mir et al, 2001) were published and distributed alongside the main document. Altogether there were seven documents totalling over 360 pages of glossy paper with illustrations and photographs, which together with the other outputs, were packaged in a perspex folder over three-and-a-half centimetres thick. This contrasts with the 66 A5 pages of the previous White Paper, *Better services for the mentally handicapped* (DHSS/Welsh Office, 1972). The question is, whether the content is any better and will it lead to any real change?

The road from 1972 to 2001

Between the two White Papers, published in 1972 and 2001, a sea change occurred in the philosophy and practice regarding people with learning difficulties. There were three broad major changes in policy. First was the shift from segregated institutional provision towards more inclusive community-based forms of care. This reflected a shift in philosophy towards the type of care most appropriate for people with learning difficulties which was based on inclusion and independence rather than segregation and dependence and was a key goal of the 1972 White Paper. However, this very principled shift gained an economic and political momentum in the early 1980s when the then Conservative government announced steps to speed up the closure of the long-stay hospitals, including those for people with learning difficulties. While this huge shift in service philosophy and delivery has not been without difficulties (see, for example, Collins, 1993), the advantages for individual people with learning difficulties living within the community are well established (Booth et al, 1990; Walker et al, 1993). This trend helped to focus more attention on the (in)adequacy of community provision for people with learning difficulties. However, the very significant ramifications that this policy change had on people with learning difficulties already living in the community, especially on the majority who lived with family carers, received little attention.

While the closure programme and prioritisation of effort and resources towards resettling people into more ordinary settings within the community dominated the policy agenda, the needs of people living with their families and the needs of their family carers who had received little priority in the past, continued to get scant attention by the formal paid service sector (Grant, 1986; Heller and Factor, 1993; Prosser and Moss, 1996;Todd and Shearn, 1996). For example, a review of community care plans in the mid-1990s revealed that less than one third made reference to people living with family carers despite the fact that the majority of people with learning difficulties do so (Turner et al, 1995).

Alongside the de-institutionalisation of people with learning difficulties, there have also been very important changes in the service philosophy and practice with respect to this group. The widespread international debate on normalisation (Brown and Smith, 1992) and 'ordinary life' models of support (King's Fund, 1980) led service provision for people with learning difficulties in the UK to move away from the goals of segregation and containment, towards models of care that facilitate inclusion and participation. People with learning difficulties were seen as individuals in their own right, not as passive recipients of, largely medical, services. Learning difficulty services in the UK have increasingly focused on the model of independence, not dependence. There is evidence to show that, even for people with the most profound and complex learning difficulties, it is possible to create a package of support, which is based on their abilities, not disabilities, on their own preferences, not on service constraints, and based on inclusion rather than exclusion. There are many important respects in which learning difficulty services have failed to meet these agreed aspirations but they remained fundamental to thinking in the field of learning difficulties in the UK.

A second policy issue has been the quality of care and support available in the community for people living with their families. Indeed the wide-scale de-institutionalisation policies of the 1980s led to accusations of service users in the community receiving a two-tier service, with those who had moved out of the long-stay hospitals getting a 'Rolls Royce service' supported by funds which accompanied them in their move, compared to those who were already living in the community – either in hostels or with families. Such fears proved to be justified (Walker et al, 1996). Community care policy and practice in Britain has increasingly operated in a casualty mode, stepping in as a last resort when the family care system breaks down (Qureshi and Walker, 1989; Walker 1989, 1997). Sufficient resources were never allocated to enable an effective preventive system to operate, where paid service providers work in partnership with family carers. Community care policy was founded on the assumption of family care but family carers themselves were never treated as citizens in their own right, nor as experts on the care of a particular person. In the past 10 years the role of carers has been highlighted by such organisations as *Carers UK* (previously the *Carers' National Association*) and legislation recognising their role and needs was introduced in the 1995 Carers (Recognition and Services) Act. In 1999, the UK government published the National Carers' Strategy (DoH, 1999). However, it was acknowledged that the needs of family carers of people with learning difficulties had not been addressed either in the preparatory work for this or in its findings. The need to address the circumstances of people with learning difficulties living in the family home has been made more urgent by the ageing of the population. An increasing number are surviving to older age and are surviving to the point that their family carers can no longer continue to care, and an increasing number are outliving their family carers (Walker and Walker, 1998). This presents a major challenge to services which is going to grow in the future (Audit Commission, 1989).

The shift away from institutional care to community care towards more independent, participatory models of support, has been accompanied by a third but unwelcome trend: privatisation of welfare services and public expenditure contraction. The quasi-market system, introduced under the Conservative governments of the 1980s and continued under New Labour, provided strong incentives for local authorities to ration the amount of care they provide more and more tightly, for example, by disputing responsibility with local NHS trusts; purchasing residential care, whether or not it was appropriate, if cost recovery was more likely than from domiciliary care; targeting resources only on people with the highest levels of disability, thereby further excluding the possibility of preventative work; capping the costs of care; and concentrating provision on those without relatives to provide care. All of these rationing devices have made it particularly difficult for family carers but also jeopardised services going to those living in dispersed, supported housing in the community. Funding for this kind of care was much more vulnerable than the funding which had previously gone into the long-stay hospitals. Although the New Labour government belatedly began to put extra investment into public services, no new money was put into learning difficulty services either in social services or health. Thus the pressure on resources continued to be extremely tight.

As well as increased rationing, from the 1980s onwards there has also been a massive increase in charges for community care services. This put particular pressure on family carers but of course also impacted on people living in other community settings who had to pay more. It created a substantial barrier to the integration of health and social services provision, reinforcing what Frank Dobson, then Secretary of State for Health, called the 'Berlin Wall' between the two (Walker and Walker, 1998). The main reason for levying charges from the 1980s onwards stemmed from inadequate funding (Chetwynd et al, 1996). This policy has continued under New Labour, with many local authorities increasing and extending charging policies for services for people with learning difficulties.

Valuing people: another 'British revolution'

Too often governments and ministers try to show their macho credentials by claiming that their policies are radical, even revolutionary. So the terms in which the Secretary of State for Health announced new proposals in the area of learning difficulties were not new; they did, however, suggest that something very real and different might happen in this field:

> People with learning disabilities have too long had their needs ignored. For 30 years forgotten generations of people with learning disabilities have lost out. That must change.
>
> A revolution in care is needed to increase opportunities for thousands of people, their carers and families. Alongside better services there will be a new drive to improve education and employment opportunities. Our ambition as a government is to create a society where there genuinely are opportunities for all. (DoH, 2001a, p 1)

Of course, if that revolution is to be successful then the beneficiaries would be people with learning difficulties themselves and the family carers who still provide the vast majority of care and support. That a dramatic change in this field is essential is not in doubt. Despite the very major changes which have occurred over the past 30 years, in particular the closure of most, although by no means all, the large, long-stay mental handicap hospitals, the experience of most people with learning difficulties, including those living in the community, is of a life with limited opportunity, restricted participation, and for family carers of worry of how to cope with the present and more worry about what will happen in the future (Magrill, 1997).

Valuing people (DoH, 2001b) sets out a clear philosophy on which policy and service provision for people with learning difficulties and their family carers will be based, and provides a clear framework within which the paid service sector will work. The White Paper represents a consolidation of recent thinking in this field and is a marked advance on the previous White Paper published 30 years ago, the main goal of which was the de-institutionalisation of people with learning difficulties from long-stay mental handicap hospitals. The new White Paper claims to put people with learning difficulties at the centre of future strategy and provide a lifelong approach to people's needs. It aims to do so by influencing a large number of agencies, several of which may previously have had little regard for this group. If successful, it would be a significant example of joined-up government.

The White Paper is based on four key principles: civil rights, independence, choice and inclusion, which reflect recent service philosophy and practice in the UK which draw on 'ordinary life' models (King's Fund, 1980), the normalisation debates (Brown and Smith, 1992) and O'Brien's five accomplishments (O'Brien, 1985). The White Paper suggests that legislation such as the 1998 Human Rights Act and the 1995 Disability Discrimination Act can be used to secure these goals.

Civil rights: the White Paper states that "the Government is committed to enforceable civil rights for disabled people in order to eradicate discrimination" (DoH, 2001b, p 23). As such, people with learning difficulties should have rights to a decent education, to vote, to marry and to express their opinions. The White Paper further states that: "All public services will treat people with learning disabilities with respect for their dignity, and challenge discrimination on all grounds including disability" (DoH, 2001b, p 23).

Independence: promoting independence is said to be part of the government's modernisation agenda: "while people's individual needs will differ, the starting presumption should be one of independence, rather than dependence, with public services providing the support needed to maximise this. Independence in this context does not mean doing everything unaided" (DoH, 2001b, p 23).

Choice: "Like other people, people with learning disabilities want a real say in where they live, what work they should do and who looks after them. But for too many people with learning disabilities, these are currently unattainable goals. We believe that everyone should be able to make choices. This includes people with severe and profound disabilities who, with the right help and support, can make important choices and express preferences about their day to day lives" (DoH, 2001b, p 24).

Inclusion: "Being part of the mainstream is something most of us take for granted. We go to work, look after our families, visit our GP, use transport, go to the swimming pool or cinema. Inclusion means enabling people with learning disabilities to do those ordinary things, make use of mainstream services and be fully included in the local community" (DoH, 2001b, p 24).

In Part Two of *Valuing people*, 'Better life chances for people with learning disabilities', the proposals are divided into six areas, which reflect the main working groups: for disabled children and young people; more choice and control for people with learning disabilities; supporting (family) carers; improving health for people with learning disabilities; housing, fulfilling lives and employment; and quality services. As with Part One, there is very little in Part Two that anyone can disagree with; it is motherhood and apple pie, and reflects much mainstream thinking in services, which is at least aspired to if not fully achieved. Part Three, 'Delivering change', is probably more important. How to achieve the change and genuinely make a difference to people is what is crucial if the White Paper is to become a success.

The main priorities identified in Part Two, 'Better life chances for people with learning difficulties' can be summarised as follows (from DoH, 2001b pp 4-9):

Disabled children and young people

- maximising life chances through equal access to educational opportunities, health and social care whether living with families or other settings;
- including children with learning difficulties in other government social protection measures for children, such as the Quality Protects programme, the Special Educational Needs Programme of Action and the ConneXions service;
- improving services at the point of transition from children to adult services to provide continuity of care as they move into adult life. This area was highlighted as being a major problem for young people and their family carers.

More choice and control for people with learning disabilities

- to enable people with learning difficulties to have as much choice and control over their lives as possible and the services and support they receive;
- £1.3 million a year for three years to develop advocacy services, direct payments to be extended and a national forum for people with learning disabilities to be created;

• person-centred planning is seen to be essential to deliver real change and to create a single, multi-agency mechanism for achieving it. Guidance to be provided on this and funds to be available through the newly created Learning Disability Development Fund.

Supporting carers

• the role of family carers is seen as a lifelong commitment which should be supported throughout by all local agencies;
• £750,000 allocated to develop with Mencap over three years a 'national learning disability information centre and helpline'. Councils to be 'encouraged' to identify all family carers over the age of 70 and those from minority ethnic communities, both of whom had been identified as being in greatest need by the Family Carers Working Group. Family carers to be represented on the Learning Disability Task Force;
• some changes in social security legislation, particularly changes in the Invalid Care Allowance, will benefit family carers, according to the White Paper, to the tune of £500 million over three years.

Improving health for people with learning disabilities

• to improve access to health services to reflect the extra health needs of many people with learning difficulties;
• "We will ensure that people with learning disabilities, including those from minority ethnic communities, have *the same right of access to mainstream health services* as the rest of the population" (DoH, 2001b, p 6; their emphasis). The NHS to promote equality for people with learning difficulties from minority ethnic communities in line with the 2000 Race Relations (Amendment) Act. Health facilitators to work with all learning disability teams to promote better healthcare and each individual to have their own Health Action Plan.

Housing, fulfilling lives, and employment

• housing: to improve housing choices and control for people with learning difficulties and their family carers. The Department of Health and the Department for the Environment, Transport and the Regions to work together to provide guidance on housing care and support options. Everyone should have been moved out of long-stay hospitals into accommodation in the community by 2004;

- fulfilling lives: "To enable people with learning disabilities to lead full and purposeful lives in their communities and develop a range of activities including leisure interests, friendships and relationships" (DoH, 2001b, p 7). The mechanisms proposed are a five-year modernisation programme for local authority day services; involvement of the Learning and Skills Council to ensure equal access to education; discrimination on transport to be outlawed; services for parents to be improved; Department of Social Security (now Department for Education and Employment) staff to receive disability awareness training;
- employment: to improve on the 10% of people with learning difficulties who currently have jobs. Targets to be developed to facilitate this. A study of the links between supported employment and day services to be undertaken; the DfEE to "ensure careful assessment of entitlement to Disability Living Allowance" (DoH, 2001b, p 7) and job brokers under the New Deal for Disabled People to be trained to work with people with learning disabilities.

Quality services

- raising standards and quality of services for people with learning difficulties to promote independence, choice and inclusion. Local quality assurance frameworks for learning disability to be in place by April 2002. Action to be taken to assist vulnerable or intimidated witnesses to give evidence in Court;
- replace the largely unqualified learning disability workforce with one that is appropriately trained and qualified;
- provide good quality services for people with additional or complex needs, such as older people, people with severe and profound disabilities, people with learning disabilities who also have epilepsy/autism/ challenging behaviour.

As the above summary of proposals shows, there is very little with which to disagree. It reflects a rights-based rather than a needs-based approach; it offers a whole life approach; it puts people with learning difficulties and their families at the centre; it acknowledges that they suffer from exclusion and discrimination in our society. It also promotes greater involvement of service users at all stages of the planning and delivery of services; greater inter-agency working; and greater use of mainstream initiatives to promote the rights of and positive outcomes for people with learning disabilities. The problems stem from how achievable these goals are without continued political priority and extra resources being given to this area. In his Foreword to the White Paper, the Prime Minister wrote:

> I know the publication of a White Paper, how ever good its proposals, does not itself solve problems. The challenge for us all is to deliver the vision set out in this document so the lives of many thousands of people with learning disabilities will be brighter and more fulfilling. It is a challenge I am determined this government will meet. (DoH, 2001b, p 1)

The White Paper offers the following proposals to turn *Valuing people*'s worthy aspirations into reality under the heading, 'Delivering change':

- "Effective partnership working by all agencies is the key to achieving social inclusion for people with learning disabilities" (DoH, 2001b, p 8). Learning Disability Partnership Boards to be established to promote stronger local partnerships;
- "Making change happen ... will take time and requires a long-term implementation programme. At national level, we will be investing new resources in 2001/2002 to support implementation. We will:
  - set up a Learning Disability Task Force to advise ... on implementation;
  - establish an Implementation Support Team to promote change at regional and local level;
  - fund a £2 million learning disability research initiative ...;
  - at a local level, Learning Disability Partnership Boards will have lead responsibility for ensuring implementation ... to develop local action plans by 31 January 2002 ...;
  - the Social Services Inspectorate will carry out a national inspection of learning disability services in 2001/2002" (DoH, 2001b, p 9).

The main focus of implementation, therefore, is on the creation of new structures – some would argue 'talking shops'. While people with learning difficulties and family carers will be represented, what guarantees are there that their voices will be heard and their views acted on? Furthermore, individual participation can merely reflect, not represent, the views of the wider community of people with learning difficulties and may certainly not reflect the wide range of abilities therein. In the past representation has focused on the 1.2 million people with mild to moderate learning disabilities; little attention has been addressed on ensuring that the views and needs of those with more profound disabilities – which may be different – are taken into account.

The strategy organises the proposals discussed above into 11 main objectives: maximising opportunities for disabled children; transition into adult life; enabling people to have more control over their own lives; support for carers; good health; housing; fulfilling lives; moving into employment; quality; workforce training and planning; and partnership working. The 11 core objectives are then subdivided into 42 sub-objectives, some of which have performance indicators attached to them. There is a list of 73 'key actions' to be pursued nationally and locally, many of which require the involvement of mainstream services (Towell, 2001). A very ambitious timetable was attached to some of the targets, not least the recruitment of the Implementation Support Team and the Learning Disability Task Force within months of publication. The Learning Disability Partnership Boards were to be up and running by October 2001 and submitting revised Joint Investment Plans by 31 January 2002 to act as local action plans. Thus the fundamental bases of local strategies were to be submitted within eight months of publication, during which time the Boards had to be created and policies discussed. This is a very tight timetable for the establishment of a new type of participatory organisation to produce proposals on an innovatory strategy. While most areas formally met the timetable, it does beg the question about the way members were recruited and the level of consultation which took place.

In the Implementation Guidance issued on 31 August 2001, the number of action points had been reduced to 19, of which 11 had a target date. The creation of the Learning Disability Partnership Boards, and the submission of revised Joint Investment Plans, have already been mentioned. Other targets included:

- a review by autumn 2002 of the role and function of community learning disability teams;
- production of a framework for introducing a person-centred approach to planning services by spring 2002;
- production of an inter-agency quality assurance framework by spring 2002;
- a workforce and training plan by summer 2002;
- a local housing strategy for people with learning disabilities and related plans for commissioning care and support packages by winter 2002/03;
- a programme for modernising day services by winter 2002/03;
- a local employment strategy and local targets for increasing the employment rates of people with learning disabilities by winter 2002/03.

This is a remarkable programme of work for already overstretched services. Furthermore, most of the work in 2002 is required at a time when responsibility for learning difficulty services in all areas is under review and in many areas will shift from local community health trusts to social services, Primary Care Trusts or other health-related organisations. This enormous structural change will severely challenge and possibly undermine the ability to deliver the plans let alone the services. There are unlikely to be any Learning Disability/Difficulty Trusts; this work will therefore be subsumed under other Trusts – sometimes Mental Health (to which many family carers object); to Primary Care Trusts who have limited or no experience of service provision to this group, let alone understanding of the debates around independence, person-centred planning and choice and so on; or to social services departments (of which families in many areas have very little positive experience).

A second criticism which could be levied at the White Paper, is the lack of clarity on some key issues. *Valuing people* inevitably offers limited detail on what is meant by some key terms and how they may be achieved. The British Institute of Learning Disabilities (BILD) argues that the White Paper has not spelt out what the key principles of civil rights, inclusion, choice and independence mean in practice (BILD, 2001). Williams (2001) argues that:

> … the concepts of independence and inclusion are rather more powerful in the social model [of disability] than they are presented in the White Paper. In the social model, independence is not defined as not being dependent (on other people or aids and equipment). It is defined as having enough supports to enable you to have the same freedom as everyone else in society. A good policy discussion of independence for people with learning difficulties thus requires an analysis of areas of restriction for those people, and a commitment to resources which will remove those restrictions. (p 5)

Finally, delivery of the rhetoric of inclusion, independence, choice and rights is rather more straightforward than the reality. How to actually achieve these goals, which involves both a massive change in attitude by the general public, by practitioners, by other service professionals and often by family carers, as well as a huge change in service provision and practice, is less obvious. Furthermore, how extensive can rights be, especially when resources and services are strictly rationed? Giving people rights implies entitlement to services but the White Paper makes no such promises.

The weaknesses of the 'Delivering change' strategy hinges, of course, on the lack of new money and lack of some key targets. The £100 million initially promised for the first two years to support the new strategy cannot really begin to address any of the key ambitions for the White Paper and certainly is not sufficient to "revolutionise care" as claimed in the press release which accompanied its publication. Just meeting the 'Quality services' objectives would require more, especially given the pressure on both health and social services budgets at present. Learning difficulty services remain a low, perhaps the lowest priority, for both. The earmarked Learning Disability Development Fund (£20 million for capital spending and revenue spending announced as £30 million in the White Paper published in March 2001 but reduced to £22 million in the Implementation Guidance published in August 2001, HSC/LAC 2001) beginning in 2002 is expected to meet the costs of developing integrated facilities for children with severe disabilities and complex needs; of moving the remaining people out of long-stay hospitals; modernising day services; developing specialist local services for people with severe challenging behaviour; and developing supported living opportunities for people living with older carers. While this is a welcome addition to the £3 billion already spent on services for this group of service users, it is questionable whether it is sufficient, given the pressure under which so many local authorities are working. The MLD Alliance, which promotes the concerns of people with mild and moderate learning difficulties, share this concern (Schwabenland, 2001):

> We have very little criticism to make of the rhetoric of the paper. It is excellent. Our concerns are primarily about implementation.... The reality is that all over the country local authorities are tightening their eligibility criteria resulting in thousands of people being denied any services at all. The finer points about how to deliver services rather pale into insignificance against this serious problem which is not addressed in the White Paper.... (p 4)

She continues to express her concern that, in a continued environment of limited resources and inevitable rationing, people with mild to moderate learning difficulties will lose out, as priority focuses, as in the White Paper, on those with greater levels of dependence and disability.

As David Towell (2001) has pointed out:

> ... the resource assumptions on which this ambitious strategy are based remain opaque. Unlike the 1971 version, it does not seek to define

necessary levels of provision even though tackling the 'post code lottery' is a major objective. Nevertheless it does point to the need for substantial investment ... to provide support to the predicted 1% a year growth in the number of people with severe disabilities, meet the requirements of currently under-served groups ..., address large geographical variations ..., improve staffing (does better trained mean better paid?) and challenge the poor quality of much provision. (p 3)

Obviously there may well be room for improvement and greater efficiency for spending the current £3 billion per year allocated to this service. However, mere publication of the White Paper raises expectations – it is well known that many services are grossly inadequate both in terms of quality and availability, and the White Paper claims to be committed to meeting the needs of previously neglected groups. All these factors will increase the need for extra resources. Similarly, greater independence does not come cheap. The lives of people with learning difficulties are restricted and family carers neglected *because* it is cheaper for services to ignore those not in crisis than to intervene (Walker et al, 1996; Walker and Walker, 1998).

And after the 'revolution'?

In *Valuing people*, Prime Minister Tony Blair and the Secretary of State for Health, Alan Milburn, both promised that the implementation of this White Paper would lead to dramatic improvements in service provision for people with learning difficulties and their families. It promises cradle to grave provision, with people with learning difficulties, and their family carers, at the centre, both in terms of planning services and in terms of the individual support each will receive. It promises to give higher priority to the needs of family carers and to produce a better-qualified and well-trained workforce. It promises to facilitate better inter-agency working and to integrate the needs of people with learning difficulties into the mainstream provision of other services such as education, housing, transport and health. It has incorporated into mainstream official thinking important principles, which are essential if people with learning difficulties are to be equal members of society with equal opportunities and choices. It promises to promote the rights of people with learning difficulties and to end discrimination in services to people from minority ethnic communities, who have been particularly badly served up to now (Mir et al, 2001).

The rhetoric is unimpeachable. But there are serious worries about implementation and delivery. This 'revolutionary change' is being introduced at a time when social services departments are already at risk of sinking under numerous new initiatives, when community-based health services are being radically reorganised and when the main health priorities for governments are hospital based. It is expected to do this on £100 million extra over two years, which was reduced by £18 million within five months of publication. Calls to offer genuine participation to people with learning difficulties and their families are being implemented at such a speed that it is unlikely that, at least in the early formative months, they will have any significant influence.

People with learning difficulties and their families deserve a revolution in care in the 21st century. *Valuing people* offers a strategy for beginning to do that. But government cannot keep ducking the funding issue. The worthy and desirable goals of *Valuing people* do not come cheap. The more successful the strategy is, the more expensive it will become as more people will want to exercise their rights to independence, integration and choice. Despite 30 or more years of cynicism, *Valuing people* has succeeded in raising many people's expectations. It is likely that, for some, services will improve. However, without a very substantial injection of extra money – as well as the reorganisation of current spending – *Valuing people* will not come anywhere near offering adequate services, let alone real opportunities, for all people with learning difficulties.

Note

[1] The use of the two terms, 'learning disabilities' and 'learning difficulties', is deliberate. The former is favoured by government, the latter by people with learning difficulties themselves.

References

Audit Commission (1989) *Developing community care for adults with a mental handicap*, London: HMSO.

BILD (British Institute of Learning Disabilities) (2001) 'Comment on White Paper implementation guidance' (www.bild.org.uk).

Booth, T., Simons, K. and Booth, W. (1990) *Outward bound: Relocation and community care for people with learning difficulties*, Buckingham: Open University Press.

Brown, H. and Smith, H. (1992) *Normalisation: A reader for the nineties*, London: Routledge.

Chetwynd, M., Ritchie, J., Reith, L. and Howard, M. (1996) *The cost of care*, York: Joseph Rowntree Foundation.

Collins, J. (1993) *The resettlement game: Policy and procrastination in the closure of mental handicap hospitals*, London: Values into Action.

DoH (Department of Health) (1999) *Caring about carers: A national strategy for carers*, London: DoH.

DoH (2001a) Press release, 2001/0140.

DoH (2001b) *Valuing people: A new strategy for learning disability for the 21st century*, Cm 5086, London: DoH.

DoH (2001c) *Nothing about us without us*, London: DoH.

DoH (2001d) *Family matters: Counting families in*, London: DoH.

DHSS (Department for Health and Social Security)/Welsh Office (1972) *Better services for the mentally handicapped*, Cmnd 4683, London: HMSO.

Grant, G. (1986) 'Older carers, interdependence and the care of mentally handicapped adults', *Ageing and Society*, vol 6, pp 333-51.

Heller, T. and Factor, A. (1993) 'Aging family caregivers: support resources and changes in burden and placement desire', *American Journal on Mental Retardation*, vol 98, no 3, pp 417-26.

HSC/LAC (2001) *Valuing people: A new strategy for learning disability for the 21st century: Implementation*, HSC 2001/016, LAC (2001) 23.

King's Fund (1980) *An ordinary life: Comprehensive locally-based residential services for mentally handicapped people*, London: King's Fund.

Magrill, D., Handley, P., Gleeson, S., Charles, D and the SCP Steering Group (1997) *Crisis approaching: The situation facing Sheffield's elderly carers of people with learning disabilities*, Sheffield: Sharing Caring Project.

Mir, G., Nocon, A. and Ahmed, W. with Jones, L. (2001) *Learning difficulties and ethnicity*, London: DoH.

O'Brien, J. (1985) *A guide to personal futures planning*, Atlanta: Responsive Systems Associates.

Prosser, H. and Moss, S. (1996) 'Informal care networks of older adults with an intellectual disability', *Journal of Applied Research in Intellectual Disabilities*, vol 9, no 1, pp 17-30.

Qureshi, H. and Walker, A. (1989) *The caring relationship: Elderly people and their families*, London: Macmillan.

Schwabenland, C. (2001) Social Policy Forum, Institute for Applied Health and Social Policy (www.hsj.co.uk/socialpolicy/forum.htm).

Towell, D. (2001) Social Policy Forum, Institute for Applied Health and Social Policy (www.hsj.co.uk/socialpolicy/forum.htm).

Todd, S. and Shearn, G. (1996) 'Time and the person: the impact of support services on the lives of parents of adults with intellectual disabilities', *Journal of Applied Research in Intellectual Disabilities*, vol 9, no 1, pp 40-60.

Turner, S., Sweeney, D. and Hayes, L. (1995) *Developments in community care for adults with learning disabilities: A review of 1993/4 community care plans*, London: HMSO.

Walker, A. (1989) 'Community care', in M. McCarthy (ed) *The new politics of welfare*, London: Macmillan, pp 205-25.

Walker, A. (1997) 'Community care policy: from consensus to conflict', in C. Pereira, D. Pilgrim and F. Williams (eds) *Community care: A reader*, London: Macmillan.

Walker, C. and Walker, A. (1998) *Uncertain futures: People with learning difficulties and their ageing family carers*, Brighton: Pavilion Publishing.

Walker, C., Ryan, T. and Walker, A. (1996) *Fair shares for all: Disparities in service provision for different groups of people with learning difficulties living in the community*, Brighton: Pavilion Publishing.

Walker, C., Ryan, T. and Walker, A. (1993) *Quality of life after resettlement for people with learning disabilities*, Manchester: North West Regional Health Authority.

Williams, P. (2001) Social Policy Forum, Institute for Applied Health and Social Policy (www.hsj.co.uk/socialpolicy/forum.htm).

Part Two:
International developments

There is a strong flavour of globalisation running through this section this year. Two of the chapters, by Chris Holden and Nicola Yeates, focus specifically on the significance of globalisation as a process affecting social policy development, while Rosemary Sales' chapter on European migration and Monica Threlfall's on the EU's developing social policy agenda set their discussions in an increasingly globalised policy context.

The section begins with Holden's chapter which discusses the impact of globalisation on the welfare state as the leading actor in social policy development and, essentially, seeks to rebut the cruder versions of the globalisation thesis which argue for the loss of state autonomy and policy-making power. He draws our attention to what he calls the meso-level of analysis rather than macro-debates about globalisation. After outlining and discussing some of the key approaches to globalisation and social policy, he focuses his analysis on a case study of the relationship between major international private providers of long-term care operating in the UK, and three other key actors: the state, staff and unions, and older people themselves. What his chapter illustrates is that deterministic claims about the loss of state power, at least in this field of social policy provision, are simply not borne out: the state continues to be the key actor in shaping the long-term care sector.

Nicola Yeates' chapter focuses less on the detailed relationship between globalisation and social policy in specific countries or policy areas, and draws attention more to the growing significance of the 'anti-globalisation' movements around the world. In recent years, these movements have become very visible at the various meetings of international organisations when they have discussed economic and social policy. Yeates provides a fascinating examination of these protests and the responses to them and moves on to suggest what the implications of globalisation for social policy are in this context. The chapter reviews recent 'anti-globalisation' campaigns and examines the composition and methodologies of the 'anti-globalisation' movement. Yeates then focuses on the impact of the movement on social policy through a consideration of state responses to the protests. In the light of both examinations Yeates then suggests what the implications of these popular protests may be for social policy analysis by outlining a new 'internationalist' agenda which, she argues, should structure future academic analysis in this area.

Rosemary Sales' chapter is based on a research project which looked at migration and citizenship rights in Europe. The research examined the processes of exclusion facing two migrant groups: those from Turkey (including Kurds) and those from ex-Yugoslavia, and focused on London, Paris and Rome, although in this chapter she focuses primarily on London and Rome. Both Italy and the UK have recently experienced new dimensions to their immigration experiences, following first the break-up of Yugoslavia and the increase in asylum seekers of both countries, then the 11 September events in New York and the subsequent 'war on terrorism'. Sales provides a cool and incisive account of experiences which both asylum seekers and 'economic migrants' have been having in Italy and the UK, and the policies which governments have been making and remaking as they have been caught up in the various ideological, economic and political cross-pressures which characterise this area of policy making. Sales concludes that current developments in migration policy are producing a growing gap between long-term residents, those with various kinds of temporary residence or protection, asylum seekers and undocumented migrants. Social exclusion appears to be the common prospect for many migrants to both countries, but for the latter two groups in particular it seems likely to worsen in the foreseeable future.

The final chapter in this section, by Monica Threlfall, provides a much-needed summary and analysis of where EU social policy is going, especially for those students and academics who are struggling to keep up with the confusing array of legal instruments and statements issuing from this body. In the past social policy analysts have had to cope with the fact that social policy in the context of European integration has had the meaning of labour policy more than broader social welfare policy. Therefore EU 'social policy' developments have tended to be phrased more in terms of 'the needs of workers', both female and male, and on employment-related problems than on identifiable social policy topics such as healthcare, housing or personal social services. What Threlfall manages to illustrate with admirable clarity is both how these developments have occurred in the past, and also how they may now be taking on a somewhat different character. She asks the question, 'Is EU social policy moving from its "labourist" origins to a more "welfarist" character?', and provides some fascinating analyses of recent trends such as the adoption of a new Social Agenda by heads of state at the Nice Summit in 2000, the inclusion of chapters in the latest EU Charter entitled 'Equality' and 'Solidarity', and the EU Declaration on Fundamental Rights.

SIX

Globalisation and welfare: a meso-level analysis

Chris Holden

Introduction

Globalisation and its potential impact upon welfare states has been debated frequently in recent years. The core of this debate has been about the extent to which changes in the world market have placed new constraints on national governments in terms of the economic and social policies they may implement. Deterministic claims that globalisation effectively robs governments of policy autonomy, spelling the end of social democratic arrangements based on closed national economies, have been countered by those arguing that the globalisation of the world economy has been exaggerated, or that states retain substantial room for manoeuvre. This is an important debate that is briefly surveyed in the first section of this chapter. However, what most of these accounts have in common is that they are focused at the level of the nation state and the impact upon it of the world market in general. This chapter shows how debates about welfare and globalisation may be focused at other levels of analysis, concentrating particularly on a meso-level of analysis. The framework developed by Ruigrok and van Tulder (1995) is adapted to an analysis of the relationship between internationalised private providers of long-term care operating in the UK and three other key actors: the state, staff and unions, and older people themselves. The chapter contests deterministic claims about the loss of state power by concluding that the state is the key actor in shaping the long-term care sector. However, the outcome of state policies is likely to be a trend towards greater concentration and internationalisation in the sector, an outcome in the long-term interests of those providers that are already large and internationalised.

Welfare and the globalisation debate

The 'globalisation' of the world market is usually seen as resulting from the growing extent and intensity of international trade, investment and financial flows, facilitated by advances in transport and communications technologies. There is disagreement about the significance of these changes, with the 'hyper-globalists' (for example, Ohmae, 1990; Reich, 1991) on one side, arguing with the 'sceptics' (for example, Ruigrok and van Tulder, 1995; Hirst and Thompson, 1999) on the other. There is not room here to assess these debates fully, but this chapter broadly takes the view of Held et al (1999, p 27) and Perraton et al (1997) that globalisation is best regarded as a contested *process*, rather than a fully realised end point. Within social policy literature there are various assessments of the impact of globalisation on the welfare state, which reflect the positions taken in the wider literature. Palier and Sykes (2001) have identified three broad approaches. Firstly, there are those accounts which argue that globalisation is pushing all states in broadly the same direction, that is welfare retrenchment and the dominance of neo-liberal policies. Mishra (1999) is the best example of this view, and his work will be discussed later. Secondly, there are those, such as Pierson (1998), who argue that contemporary changes in welfare states have not been caused by globalisation, but by other factors. Thirdly, there are those accounts (for example, Esping-Andersen, 1996) which argue that globalisation is having effects on welfare states, but that these effects vary between different types of welfare state, and that these states retain a degree of autonomy in terms of how they respond to external pressures.

This chapter is primarily concerned with the first of these views. This dominant, deterministic thesis has become a new paradigm that promotes the inevitability of welfare retrenchment, what Held et al (1999, p 31) call 'political fatalism'. Despite inconsistencies and ambiguities in his account, Mishra (1999, p 6) sums up this view well:

> Put simply, by providing capital with an 'exit' option, globalization has strengthened the bargaining power of capital very considerably against government as well as labour.... Thus money and investment capital can vote with their feet if they do not like government policies.... Indeed globalization virtually sounds the death-knell of the classical social democratic strategy of full employment, high levels of public expenditure and progressive taxation.

George (1998, p 34) makes a similar claim when he argues that globalisation "is a good example of structural forces overriding ideological influences", and offers globalisation as "the central explanatory notion" in approaching welfare developments in advanced industrial societies today.

In this view, the only active policies states can pursue are in the areas of education and labour market efficiency (Reich, 1991). Investing in education and increasing labour supply through active labour market policies, such as the British 'New Deal', increases national competitiveness as countries compete for investment from internationally mobile firms (for a critique of these policies see Jordan, 1998; Holden, 1999). Such policies are ultimately those advocated by Esping-Andersen (1996, p 256), who argues that a strategy based on education and training can be the basis for a "positive-sum solution", which avoids the "trade-off between jobs and equality". 'Lifelong learning' and 'social investment' strategies can eliminate the surplus of unskilled workers and ensure that inferior low-paid jobs do not become lifecycle traps, but merely stopgaps or first entry jobs.

While Esping-Andersen (1996) emphasises the differences between welfare states, he shares with the deterministic thesis the assumption that exogenous developments in the world market have placed constraints on states that push them in a particular direction. Yet deterministic claims of a perfectly integrated world market have been questioned for a variety of reasons. Firstly, the extent of globalisation may be exaggerated in such accounts (Ruigrok and van Tulder, 1995; Hirst and Thompson, 1999). Secondly, the same authors have pointed out that the majority of investment flows have come from *and gone to* other industrialised countries, casting doubt on the claim that unemployment in the advanced economies is a result of transnational corporations (TNCs) seeking cheaper labour in less developed countries. Furthermore, most foreign direct investment (FDI) is also regionally based. So the world economy is actually bound together by threads of investment between the three dominant economies of the US, Europe (of which Germany is the core) and Japan – what Ohmae (1990, p 6) calls the "'interlinked economy" of the "Triad". The evidence therefore suggests that although there is a significant trend towards internationalisation in the world economy, this falls short of the claims of the more deterministic globalisation theorists.

This trend towards internationalisation need not lead us to the conclusion that the state has become powerless. In fact, the state itself has often been a powerful *agent* of change. This is an argument advanced most forcefully by Weiss (1997, 1998). She argues (1998, p 204) that, "states may at times be facilitators (even perhaps perpetrators) rather than mere victims of so-called 'globalization'". She presents evidence that states such as Japan, Singapore, Korea and Taiwan are increasingly acting as 'catalysts' for the internationalisation strategies of corporate actors. Neo-liberal states such as Britain can also be seen to have acted to facilitate globalisation. Dominelli and Hoogvelt (1996, p 48) argue that in Britain the central government has played a crucial role in "transmitting the global market discipline throughout the economy". This has been possible because even today the state has direct control over 40% of gross domestic product (GDP). Thus privatisation has seen huge transfers of money from the public sector to the private sector in the form of subsidies and tax cuts to business, and has created an infrastructure for the private sector to trade with through various forms of contracting out.

The most important point, however, is that rather than withdrawing, states may be changing the *form* of their intervention. Weiss (1998, p 196) refers to this as state 'adaptivity'. Held et al (1999, p 431) argue that, "different historical forms of globalization may be associated with quite different state forms". Contemporary globalisation may even, therefore, dramatically expand the scope for state initiatives. According to Held et al states in advanced capitalist societies (SIACS):

> ... are undergoing a profound transformation as their powers, roles and functions are rearticulated, reconstituted and re-embedded at the intersection of globalising and regionalising networks and systems. The metaphors of the loss, diminution or erosion of state power can misrepresent this reconfiguration or transformation.... For while globalization is engendering a reconfiguration of state-market relations in the economic domain, SIACS and multilateral agencies are deeply implicated in that very process. (1999, p 440)

As Taylor-Gooby (1997, p 186) puts it "government is becoming more rather than less significant", although the increased use of the private sector in welfare shifts the emphasis of state intervention to regulation rather than provision. This issue of regulation is particularly important, and will be returned to later.

Levels of analysis

Deterministic accounts of globalisation and social policy are thus open to a number of criticisms. However, other accounts point to national specificities and the mediating effects of different levels of policy making in determining how states adapt to external pressures. Comparative approaches, such as that used by Esping-Andersen (1990, 1996), have been particularly good at recognising the importance of national institutions and practices. A more sophisticated approach, therefore, might conclude that the influence of globalisation has to work its way through several 'layers' of national institutions and practices, leading to different results in different countries. Yet this still assumes a one-way flow from the world market 'downwards' through the different levels (each having its own mediating effect), finally ending at the actual delivery of welfare services 'on the ground'. The chain of causation is not usually seen as being able to work in the opposite direction (however, see Sykes et al, 2001).

One way of attempting to deal with this problem is to utilise the concept of 'structuration'. This concept has been theorised by Giddens (1981, 1984) and involves a two-way concept of agency and structure where each impacts on the other. As Held et al (1999, p 27) put it: "globalization is akin to a process of 'structuration' in so far as it is a product of both the individual actions of, and the cumulative interactions between, countless agencies and institutions across the globe". Utilised in this context, structuration could acknowledge the potential for national institutions and practices to modify the working of the world economy: that is for the chain of causation to work 'upwards' as well as 'downwards'. A good example of this is the way in which the decisions taken by some governments on financial liberalisation (Thatcher's being the obvious example) encouraged others to do the same to remain competitive. Thus decisions taken by conscious agents produce a new structure (in this case an open world financial market), which is difficult to reverse – actors are constrained by their own past decisions (Cerny, 1990, 1996).

This acknowledgement of different levels of policy making and activity is related to the 'level of analysis problem'. This was identified by Singer (1961) in the discipline of international relations (IR). He argued that in IR, as in any science, "the observer may choose to focus on the parts or on the whole, upon the components or upon the system" (1961, p 77). This means we may "choose between the flowers or the garden, the rocks or the quarry, the trees or the forest, the houses or the neighborhood, the cars or the traffic jam, the delinquents or the gang", and so on (Singer, 1961, p 77). The complexity and significance of these levels of analysis decisions are indicated by the longstanding controversies between, for example, social psychology and sociology or micro- and macro-economics. According to Singer, in IR, authors had:

> ... roamed up and down the ladder of organisational complexity with remarkable abandon, focusing upon the total system, international organisations, regions, coalitions, extra-national associations, nations, domestic pressure groups, social classes, elites, and individuals as the needs of the moment required. And though most of us have tended to settle upon the nation as our most comfortable resting place, we have retained our propensity for vertical drift, failing to appreciate the value of a stable point of focus. (1961, p 78)

Each level of analysis will have its own strengths and weaknesses. So, for example, in IR the two most commonly used levels of analysis were the international system, usually conceived as a system of nation states, and the level of the individual nation states themselves. The systemic (international) level of analysis allows for comprehensive study of "international relations in the whole", although it tends to "lead the observer into a position which exaggerates the impact of the system upon the national actors and, conversely, discounts the impact of the actors on the system" (1961, p 80). It also requires the postulation of "a high degree of uniformity in the foreign policy operational codes of our national actors" (p 80). This is a similar criticism to that which has been made previously of deterministic accounts of globalisation and social policy. The national state level of analysis, on the other hand, allows for differentiation among the actors in the system, but may lead to an exaggeration of the differences between them.

The comparative approach favoured by many social policy analysts has usually been pitched at the national level. This involves comparing the social policies of different countries and changes in them so as to detect common trends and differences. Yet little work has been done on globalisation and social policy that is pitched at other levels of analysis. Deacon (1997) is one exception to this, having argued for a shift to 'global social policy' analysis through a focus on supranational and transnational institutions. Mohan (1996) is another exception, having surveyed accounts of change in the NHS at three levels of analysis[1]. In Mohan's account the 'macro' level of analysis sees welfare states as converging on a common set of solutions, as in the grip of forces beyond their control, and/or as grappling with common dilemmas that leave them with very little scope for manoeuvre, just as the crude version of the globalisation thesis does. For Mohan, 'meso' level analyses are pitched at the level of national state policies, which may arise from the character of governments' ideological predispositions and political strategies. Finally, 'micro' level accounts focus on the processes operating either internally within the NHS or within British society. According to Mohan, all of these three levels of analysis offer important insights into the nature of change in the NHS, but none of them alone is sufficient. He thus concludes that a degree of 'eclecticism' is required if a comprehensive account of NHS reforms is to be constructed.

This chapter utilises another form of the meso level of analysis adapted from that developed by Ruigrok and van Tulder (1995) to study industrial restructuring in the world economy, and applies it to internationalised private providers in the UK long-term care market. Ruigrok and van Tulder's analysis is based on the concept of an 'industrial complex'. An industrial complex is a 'bargaining arena' composed of six actors: the *core firm*; its *supplying firms*; its *dealers and distributors*; its *workers*, who may or may not be represented by a union; its *financiers*; and its local, regional and national (and even supranational) home and host *governments*. Each core firm will have a series of bargaining relationships with each of the other actors in its industrial complex. Ruigrok and van Tulder therefore provide a framework for the meso-level analysis of the relationships between internationalised firms and a range of other actors (including the state), which is distinct from those approaches based on analyses of the interaction of the state with the world market in general. Resting as it does upon the concept of a core firm at the heart of an industrial complex, such an approach is particularly suited to analyses of areas of welfare where provision is undertaken by private companies.

This chapter employs an adapted version of this meso level of analysis in relation to the UK long-term care sector, where the majority of provision is undertaken by independent organisations. Some of the leading for-profit organisations in this sector are highly internationalised (Holden, 2002b), and can thus form the basis for a meso-level analysis of this type. However, a number of modifications need to be made to the analytical framework in applying it to the concerns of social policy. While internationalised private providers of a welfare service are placed at the centre of the analysis, the other actors have also been selected to reflect the concerns of social policy. The state is therefore retained as a key actor, as are the staff working for the firms. Suppliers, financiers and distributors are excluded from the analysis, given the social rather than purely economic concerns of the chapter. However, an extra set of actors are included in the form of older people and care home residents themselves. Thus internationalised firms in the long-term care sector are, in this perspective, deemed to have a set of relationships with each of the other three actors: the state, staff and unions, and older people and their organisations. The evidence for the following analysis is based on both interview and documentary research.

The key factor affecting the relationship between the firms and each of the other actors will be the form and extent of organisation of the non-firm actors. These are the general conditions that affect the 'balance of power' between the firms and each of the other actors (although it is not assumed that these relationships are necessarily ones of conflict). At any given moment in time, the existing form and extent of organisation of each of the non-firm actors will enable, constrain and set limits to their capacity to influence the firms, and of the firms to influence them. It will also provide the basis for any attempt to *change* the form and/or extent of that organisation. This is the element of 'structuration' in the analysis. As Giddens (1984) points out, this reflects Marx's famous statement that, "Men make their own history, but not in circumstances of their own choosing" (quoted in Giddens, 1984, p xxi).

In general, the greater the *extent* of their organisation, the more powerful the non-firm actors will be. For example, a union with more members is, other things being equal, more powerful than one with fewer members. However, the *form* of their organisation may also affect their capacity to act and the precise way in which they pursue their goals. The same is true for the extent of their *internationalisation*, which Ruigrok and van Tulder (1995) identify as a key factor affecting the bargaining position of other actors in relation to internationalised firms. They argue that, in general, the more internationalised other actors are, the more bargaining power they will have vis-à-vis the firm. However, in practice this depends on the nature of the actor's international organisation. A union, to extend the example, may belong to an international federation, but this may not be an effective instrument for action (Ruigrok and van Tulder, 1995, p 85). Hence, an analysis of the *form* of organisation is as important as that of the *extent* of organisation.

The remainder of this chapter applies this analytical framework to the three actors of the state, staff and unions, and older people, before drawing its conclusions.

The state

The state may intervene in the provision of welfare services through three principal means: direct provision, tax and subsidy, and regulation (Le Grand and Robinson, 1984; Le Grand et al, 1992). In the UK long-term care sector, the state has been steadily withdrawing from direct provision since the early 1980s. However, this process has also entailed a concomitant increase in subsidies to private providers, first through social security funding for residents, and then through the community care system, which since 1993 has given local authorities the responsibility for purchasing packages of care (Bradshaw, 1988; Ebrahim et al, 1993; Harrington and Pollock, 1998). The shift from direct state provision to subsidy has also entailed the creation of a system of regulation in order to enforce minimum standards in a market where profit making has become the key goal of the largest private providers (Wistow et al, 1996; Knapp et al, 2001). The shape, nature and effects of the regulatory system are thus key elements in an analysis of the relationship between the state and internationalised providers.

Up until April 2002, the regulatory system had been organised in a decentralised fashion, with local authorities responsible for residential homes and health authorities responsible for nursing homes. However, from April 2002 all private providers of long-term care will be regulated by a new National Care Standards Commission (NCSC), which will be responsible for enforcing a new set of national minimum standards (DoH, 2001). These regulatory changes are inconsistent with the notion of a 'powerless state', since the state is clearly increasing and centralising its regulatory powers here. The new national minimum standards (NMS) caused controversy from early on, since they were likely to impose heavy costs on providers as a result of the physical input standards (for example, minimum room sizes) and the staffing standards, which initially demanded that a third of staff in nursing homes should be qualified nurses. Provider associations argued that the proposals would force many operators out of business. Although some concessions were made in the final standards, notably the dilution of the requirement for one third nursing staff in nursing homes, the standards have now been adopted without radical revision.

It is clear that the state has been able to centralise and significantly increase its regulatory powers, despite protests from providers. These changes will affect all providers in terms of the extra costs they will impose, including large and internationalised ones. However, it is the largest providers that will best be able to absorb these increased costs, because they are able to make use of substantial economies of scale, both through building larger homes and through the purchasing of bulk supplies (Holden, 2002b). Large providers are also able to raise funds for expansion through borrowing or sale and leaseback deals. Thus, the ultimate outcome of the reforms is likely to be an increase in the level of concentration in the sector.

Government policies in a number of areas affecting the sector are likely to have similar effects, simultaneously squeezing the profit margins of all providers, yet ultimately benefiting those that are already large and internationalised (Holden, 2002a). Where funding is concerned, the position of local authorities as primary purchasers gives them significant power in local markets. According to the consultancy Laing & Buisson (1997, p A189): "Outside small and isolated communities there is no area in the UK where supply side concentration begins to match the concentration of purchasing power in the hands of local authorities, which now account for about 75% of all new care home placements". Local authorities' near-monopoly (monopsony) purchasing position has thus allowed them to hold fee rates at artificially low levels, while central government funding restrictions have resulted in unsustainable levels of overcapacity across the sector, thus facilitating the concentration process.

At the international level, and like most other states, Britain is involved in a series of supranational institutions and agreements, which may have some bearing on trade and investment in care services. The two principal ones are the European Union (EU) and the General Agreement on Trade in Services (GATS), which is administered by the World Trade Organisation (WTO). As a member of the EU, the British government is bound by the European Public Procurement Directive (EPPD) (EU, 1992), which seeks to increase cross-border competition between providers of public services within the single market. The EPPD stipulates that governments should not discriminate against foreign providers and that no 'non-commercial' considerations should be used when procuring public services. GATS operates on the basis of general principles, such as national treatment for foreign operators and 'most favoured nation' treatment (that is, all foreign firms must be treated alike), as well as on the basis of specific negotiated obligations which countries have to opt into or 'schedule' (Hoekman and Primo Braga, 1997). Although GATS is at a fairly early stage, the WTO has continued to promote the cause of services liberalisation, with potentially far-reaching implications for health and social services (WTO, 1998; Deacon, 2000, 2001; Ruane, 2001).

The British state thus has significant involvement in international agreements and supranational institutions. Reflecting the political climate in developed nations, these tend to commit governments to liberalising measures rather than imposing supranational regulation upon *firms*, although the EU does affect the regulation of firms through directives aimed at protecting working conditions. An example of this is the Working Time Directive (EU, 1993), discussed later. Although the national state has increased its regulatory powers in this sector, it may thus be argued that there are significant institutional constraints on the policies of the

British government (as opposed to constraints imposed by the world market itself or by multinational firms). However, the attitude of British governments in the post-war period has been an extremely liberal one in relation to FDI generally (Held et al, 1999, p 257), and, insofar as it is privately provided, healthcare has been no exception. Liberalising supranational agreements do not therefore conflict with the approach of British governments, but rather have been voluntarily entered into in line with their worldview.

Staff and unions

The range of unions with the potential to organise in the long-term care sector is fairly large, and includes UNISON, the General Municipal and Boilermakers union (GMB), the Royal College of Nursing (RCN), the Transport and General Workers Union (TGWU) and Manufacturing, Science, Finance (MSF). However, union membership is generally low, and the TGWU and MSF currently have no real presence in the sector. Of the other three unions, although to some extent they organise different groups of workers, there is considerable overlap in the types of workers who might be their members. UNISON organises the lower part of the occupational hierarchy, from cleaners through care assistants to nurses. GMB organises all workers in the sector through its Association of Professional and Executive Staffs (APEX) wing, but has launched a bid for the organisation of managers (see Edmonds, 1998). The RCN organises nurses only, but this includes a number who are also small owners or managers.

The RCN has the largest individual membership, given that most nurses belong to it. However, this does not mean that it has been able to organise as a functioning body on a branch level, and it has traditionally acted more as a professional association than other unions in the health sector. Both UNISON and GMB have made significant gains in recent years, both in terms of individual membership and in terms of a small number of company level recognition deals. Yet most of the largest and most internationalised firms in the sector remain hostile to union recognition, and both these unions have met significant problems arising from the overall structure of the sector. Despite concentration and corporatisation at the top end, the sector as a whole remains primarily composed of small providers. Even in large firms, the workforce is scattered across a number of workplaces, making functional organisation in proper branches difficult.

All of the unions belong to international federations of various kinds.

One of these, the International Federation of Commercial, Clerical, Professional and Technical Employees, which has since merged with other federations to form the Union Network International, was formed specifically to combine different service unions under one umbrella in response to privatisation and the increasing involvement of multinationals. It has had some success in coordinating union organisation in some areas, including the care sector. Yet the value of these international federations to date has primarily been in providing a means of information exchange and of lobbying supranational governmental institutions such as the European Union, rather than in increasing bargaining power. Both UNISON and GMB also have direct links with the American Service Employees International Union (SEIU), which has been very successful in pursuing a militant campaign of recruitment and recognition among corporate care providers in the USA. In particular, the SEIU was able to secure recognition from one of the US firms with operations in the UK. However, this seems to have made no difference to UNISON's attempt to gain recognition from the firm's UK subsidiary, and the SEIU remains a source of inspiration and information rather than an international bargaining partner.

The difficulty of organising in the sector has therefore meant that the unions have had to evaluate carefully the resources they commit to it. They are thus faced with the dilemma of wanting to organise those workers who are perhaps most in need of them as a result of low wages, long working hours, flexible contracts and organisational isolation, but knowing that resources put into this sector may not result in large membership increases. UNISON, for example, has had much more success in organising workers in contracted out NHS ancillary services that have been taken over by multinationals, signing recognition deals with a number of large companies. The union thus faces a tough decision about where its resources are most effectively employed. The solution adopted by all of the unions active in the sector has been to use government legislation as the primary means of both building membership and improving working conditions.

Legislation has been used as a basis for building membership in two ways. First, most of the existing membership has come from transfers of local authority or health authority homes into the private sector. The 'Transfer of Undertakings (Protection of Employment)' Regulations (TUPE, 1981), known as 'TUPE', implement the provisions of the European Acquired Rights Directive (EU, 1977). Thus operations transferring to the private sector must guarantee the existing working conditions of staff, and in many cases the unions have been able to both retain existing members as well as recruit new ones prior to the transfer. The second means for building membership relates to the more recent 1999 Employment Relations Act, which implemented the proposals of the *Fairness at work* White Paper (Cm 3968, 1998). This provides for union recognition where 50% of the workforce are members, or where a majority (of at least 40% of the workforce) vote for it in a ballot. This then provides the basis for unions to force employers to sign recognition deals where they can gain a critical mass of membership. Ironically, it may thus prove to be the large corporations that are more susceptible to recognition deals, since the unions may strategically target certain large employers for recruitment drives and recognition negotiations under the provisions of the act. There have already been signs that some corporate employers may reverse their open hostility to union recognition and negotiate deals as a result of this legislation.

There are also two major pieces of legislation that have improved pay and working conditions in the sector. First, the National Minimum Wage (NMW) legislation, introduced in April 1999, will have a significant impact on the long-term care sector. Although its impact has been uneven geographically, reflecting differing wage rates in local labour markets, it has already raised the wages of significant numbers of care workers (Cm 4571, 2000, para 4.34), including those working for internationalised corporations. Laing & Buisson (1999-2000, p 171) estimated that the total cost to private and voluntary care homes would be over £90 million per annum. The NMW thus not only provides for a means of raising employees' wages which the unions have been unable to achieve through their own direct pressure, but it will also add to regulatory changes in imposing new costs on providers (Holden, 2002a).

The second means by which legislation has improved working conditions in the sector has been the introduction of the European Working Time Directive (WTD) through the Working Time Regulations (DTI, 1998). Implemented in October 1998, these set a working time limit of an average of 48 hours per week for all workers in the UK, which applies to casual and agency staff as well as those on more permanent contracts. The unions can thus afford workers in the sector some protection by ensuring the WTD is implemented properly. However, the WTD will also impose extra costs on providers, primarily as a result of the entitlement to three weeks paid annual leave (which rose to four weeks after November 1999) (PWR, 1999).

Analysis of the form and extent of union organisation in the sector actually indicates the central role of *the state*. The relative weakness of the unions has led them to rely on government initiatives both to build their own membership and to improve the working conditions of staff. Yet, once again, the intervention of the state through the imposition of the NMW and the WTD will significantly raise costs for all providers, without concomitant increases in local authority fee rates. While this demonstrates the state's role as the most powerful actor in the sector, it is important to note that these costs will be borne more easily by large and internationalised firms as a result of their capacity for economies of scale. Inadvertently or otherwise, state intervention is thus promoting further concentration in the sector, an outcome that is in the long-term interests of those providers that are already large and internationalised.

Residents and older people's organisations

Including residents and older people themselves in the analysis is both important and problematic. It is important because the well being of the residents is the very raison d'être of these services. It is problematic because residents are the group least likely to organise themselves independently. Many (although by no means all) users in residential and nursing homes require high levels of support, mentally and emotionally, as well as physically. A relative increase in those aged 85 or over has increased 'dependency' levels still further. Residents will wish to receive good quality care and support, but will not necessarily want the responsibility of monitoring that, or have the capacity to do so. This is, of course, why the state regulation system exists. Consequently, where residents are organised in any collective sense, this tends to take the form of residents' committees or meetings at the care home level. While these can be an effective means of residents providing some input into the organisation of the regime within which they live, the staff rather than the residents themselves usually initiate them. This may be wholly appropriate, however, it does not represent an independent form of organisation by residents, but rather a means of quality control and consultation by providers themselves. For example, many large providers of care services have a policy of organising such meetings, and this may be written into their internal quality assurance programme.

There are organisations that campaign on behalf of residents, such as *Counsel and Care* and the *Relatives and Residents Association*, and there are also organisations formed by, or which campaign on behalf of, older people more generally. The *National Pensioners' Convention*, for example, was formed by older people to campaign in their interests, and has strong links with the trades union movement. Charities such as *Help the Aged* and *Age Concern* have also become very influential, and often have substantial networks of local groups. However, such organisations rarely negotiate directly with providers of services to older people, although they may work alongside them in industry bodies such as the *Continuing Care Conference*. Rather, their activities are generally divided into information and advice services for older people on the one hand, and campaigning or lobbying activities on the other. The latter are generally aimed at improving the lives of older people by influencing government policy, either through direct lobbying or more general campaigning aimed at influencing public opinion. These activities are also strengthened by research programmes carried out by the organisations.

Campaigns run by these organisations often have a great deal of bearing on the long-term care sector, and all of them have been fully involved in the debate surrounding the regulatory changes discussed previously. *Counsel and Care*, for example, has argued for an 'industry' regulator for long-term care of the type set up to monitor and control the privatised utilities. However, what all these campaigns have in common is that they are focused on influencing *government policy* rather than influencing the behaviour of providers directly. The activities of older people's organisations thus confirm the central role of the state in shaping the sector and setting the parameters within which privately owned organisations operate. Furthermore, although most of these organisations are affiliated to international associations, such associations tend to replicate the activities of their national affiliates at the supranational level, lobbying and providing research findings to bodies such as the United Nations and the European Union. As argued earlier, while these organisations impose restrictions on national governments, and may in time come to assume some of their functions, they are the creations of nation states themselves.

Conclusion

Applying a meso-level analysis to the long-term care sector demonstrates the continued centrality of the state in this area. Although many of the largest private firms in the sector are highly internationalised, the state has managed to increase and centralise its regulatory powers without conceding substantial increases in subsidy. The other two actors included in the analysis were unable to exert the same level of influence over providers. Rather, the activities of unions and older people's organisations in focusing their efforts on influencing government policy confirms the importance of the state in shaping the sector as a whole and setting the parameters within which private firms must operate.

The deterministic globalisation thesis relies heavily on the possibility of 'exit' by internationalised firms (Weiss, 1998, p 184), and this is the basis of Mishra's argument (1999, p 6). Such arguments would assume that internationalised long-term care firms would seek to shift their investment out of the UK in response to the imposition of stricter regulatory criteria by the state, especially as the new regulations will raise costs while state funding continues to be restricted. Yet there was no evidence of this in the research discussed here. On the contrary, large and internationalised firms have generally welcomed the regulatory changes, largely because they will increase consistency and thereby make it easier than the previous arrangements for large firms to homogenise the quality of care in their outlets across the country. It may be argued that these particular firms are less mobile in being able to take advantage of exit opportunities, since as service firms they must invest where the service is consumed (Holden, 2002b). It is therefore not possible for them to produce in low cost countries and then export to developed countries. Yet this simply strengthens the case against determinism, since services are not an irrelevant part of the world economy, but account for the majority of output in developed countries and form a large and growing part of international trade and FDI (Hoekman and Primo Braga, 1997). Research that investigates the internationalisation of services in relation to the globalisation debate is therefore likely to become increasingly important.

The findings from the analysis in this chapter do not necessarily apply to all sectors of the economy, and do not tell us all we need to know about the relationship between the welfare state and the world market in general. Neither can they be extrapolated unconditionally to other areas of welfare provision. For example, the government has restricted funding in long-term care (an area where private provision is well established), thus imposing a form of economic 'rationalisation' on the sector, which will lead to a further 'maturing' as the parallel processes of concentration and internationalisation increase. However, private provision in other areas of welfare is fairly limited in the UK. In those areas there is evidence that, rather than restricting funding, the government is willing to pay over the odds to attract private providers (Pollock et al, 2001). The analysis given here does, however, clearly contradict deterministic claims about the loss of state power: the state is an active and powerful agent shaping the market.

The outcome of government policy is likely to be an increasing concentration of provision in long-term care, and a deepening of internationalisation as existing large firms utilise their advantages. This indicates that the common practice of assuming an antinomy of interests between nation states and TNCs is misleading. While states retain considerable power, the question of whether they use that power to facilitate the interests of TNCs, to regulate and control them, or to counterpose them, is a political one.

Note

[1] Mohan's use of the terms 'macro', 'meso' and 'micro' is different from that used in the rest of this chapter.

References

Bradshaw, J. (1988) 'Financing private care for the elderly', in S. Baldwin, G. Parker and R. Waller (eds) *Social security and community care*, Aldershot: Avebury.

Cerny, P. (1990) *The changing architecture of politics: Structure, agency and the future of the state*, London: Sage Publications.

Cerny, P. (1996) 'International finance and the erosion of state policy capacity', in P. Gummett (ed) *Globalization and public policy*, Cheltenham: Edward Elgar.

Cm 3968 (1998) *Fairness at work*, London: The Stationery Office.

Cm 4571 (2000) *The National Minimum Wage: The story so far – the second report of the Low Pay Commission*, London: The Stationery Office.

Deacon, B. (1997) *Global social policy: International organisations and the future of welfare*, London: Sage Publications.

Deacon, B. (2000) 'Globalization: a threat to equitable social provision?', *Social Policy Review 12*, pp 250-71.

Deacon, B. (2001) 'International organizations, the EU and global social policy', in R. Sykes, B. Palier and P.M. Prior (eds) *Globalization and European welfare states: Challenges and change*, Basingstoke: Palgrave.

DoH (Department of Health) (2001) *Care homes for older people: National minimum standards*, London: DoH.

Dominelli, L. and Hoogvelt, A. (1996) 'Globalization and the technocratization of social work', *Critical Social Policy*, vol 16, no 2, pp 45-62.

DTI (Department of Trade and Industry) (1998) *Working time regulations*, London: The Stationery Office.

Ebrahim, S., Wallis, C., Brittis, S., Harwood, R. and Graham, N. (1993) 'Purchasing for quality: The providers' view', *Quality in Health Care*, no 2, pp 198-203.

Edmonds, J. (1998) 'A professional approach to supporting care home staff', in Laing & Buisson, *Long-term care of elderly and physically disabled people – Directory of major providers*, London: Laing & Buisson.

Esping-Andersen, G. (1990) *The three worlds of welfare capitalism*, Cambridge: Polity Press.

Esping-Andersen, G. (ed) (1996) *Welfare states in transition: National adaptations in global economies*, London: Sage Publications.

EU (European Union) (1977) *European Acquired Rights Directive 77/187/EEC*.

EU (1992) *Council Directive 92/50/EEC (18.6.92)*.

EU (1993) *Working Time Directive 93/104/EC*.

George, V. (1998) 'Political ideology, globalization and welfare futures in Europe', *Journal of Social Policy*, vol 27, no 1, pp 17-36.

Giddens, A. (1981) *A contemporary critique of historical materialism*, Basingstoke: Macmillan.

Giddens, A. (1984) *The constitution of society*, Cambridge: Polity Press.

Harrington, C. and Pollock, A.M. (1998) 'Decentralisation and privatisation of long-term care in UK and USA', *The Lancet*, vol 351, 13 June, pp 1805-8.

Held, D., McGrew, A., Goldblatt, D. and Perraton, J. (1999) *Global transformations: Politics, economics and culture*, Cambridge: Polity Press.

Hirst, P. and Thompson, G. (1999) *Globalization in question* (2nd edn), Cambridge: Polity Press.

Hoekman, B. and Primo Braga, C.A. (1997) 'Protection and trade in services: a survey', *Open Economies Review*, vol 8, no 3, pp 285-308.

Holden, C. (1999) 'Globalization, social exclusion and Labour's new work ethic', *Critical Social Policy*, vol 19, no 4, pp 529-38.

Holden, C. (2002a: forthcoming) 'British government policy and the concentration of ownership in long term care provision', *Ageing and Society*.

Holden, C. (2002b: forthcoming) 'The internationalisation of long term care provision: Economics and strategy', *Global Social Policy*, vol 2, no 1, pp 47-67.

Jordan, B. (1998) *The new politics of welfare: Social justice in a global context*, London: Sage Publications.

Knapp, M., Hardy, B. and Forder, J. (2001) 'Commissioning for quality: ten years of social care markets in England', *Journal of Social Policy*, vol 30, no 2, pp 283-306.

Laing, W. (1998) *A fair price for care?: Disparities between market rates for nursing/residential care and what state funding agencies will pay*, York: York Publishing Services for Joseph Rowntree Foundation.

Laing & Buisson (1997) *Review of private healthcare*, London: Laing & Buisson.

Laing & Buisson (1999-2000) *Healthcare market review*, London: Laing & Buisson.

Laing & Buisson (2000-01) *Healthcare market review*, London: Laing & Buisson.

Le Grand, J. and Robinson, R. (eds) (1984) *Privatisation and the welfare state*, London: George Allen and Unwin.

Le Grand, J., Propper, C. and Robinson, R. (1992) *The economics of social problems*, Basingstoke: Macmillan.

Mishra, R. (1999) *Globalization and the welfare state*, Cheltenham: Edward Elgar.

Mohan, J. (1996) 'Accounts of the NHS reforms: macro-, meso-, and micro-level perspectives', *Sociology of Health and Illness*, vol 18, no 5, pp 675-98.

Ohmae, K. (1990) *The borderless world*, London: Harper Collins.

Palier, B. and Sykes, R. (2001) 'Challenges and change: issues and perspectives in the analysis of globalization and the European welfare states', in R. Sykes, B. Palier and P.M. Prior (eds) *Globalization and European welfare states: Challenges and change*, Basingstoke: Palgrave.

Perraton, J., Goldblatt, D., Held, D. and McGrew, A. (1997) 'The globalization of economic activity', *New Political Economy*, vol 2, no 2, pp 257-77.

Pierson, P. (1998) 'Irresistible forces, immovable objects: post-industrial welfare states confront permanent austerity', *Journal of European Public Policy*, vol 5, no 4, pp 539-60.

Pollock, A., Shaoul, J., Rowland, D. and Player, S. (2001) *A response to the IPPR's Commission on public private partnerships*, London: Health Policy and Health Services Research Unit, University College London.

PWR (Pay and Workforce Research) (1999) *The impact of the Working Time Directive on the care sector*, Harrogate: PWR.

Reich, R.B. (1991) *The work of nations*, London: Simon and Schuster.

Ruane, S. (2001) 'The general agreement on trade in services, New Labour and the implications for health policy', Paper presented to Social Policy Association Annual Conference, Belfast, July.

Ruigrok, W. and van Tulder, R. (1995) *The logic of international restructuring*, London: Routledge.

Singer, D. (1961) 'The level-of-analysis problem in international relations', in K. Knorr and S. Verba (eds) *The international system*, Princeton, NJ: Princeton University Press.

Sykes, R., Palier, B. and Prior, P.M. (eds) (2001) *Globalization and European welfare states: Challenges and change*, Basingstoke: Palgrave.

Taylor-Gooby, P. (1997) 'In defence of second-best theory: state, class and capital in social policy', *Journal of Social Policy*, vol 26, no 2, p 171-92.

TUPE (1981) *Transfer of undertakings (protection of employment) regulations*, SI 1981 No 1794.

Weiss, L. (1997) 'Globalization and the myth of the powerless state', *New Left Review*, no 225, p 3-27.

Weiss, L. (1998) *The myth of the powerless state: Governing the economy in a global era*, Cambridge: Polity Press.

Wistow, G., Knapp, M., Hardy, B., Forder, J., Kendall, J. and Manning, R. (1996) *Social care markets: Progress and prospects*, Buckingham: Open University Press.

WTO (World Trade Organisation) (1998) 'Health and social services', Background Paper by the WTO Council for Trade in Services Secretariat, S/C/W/50, 18 September.

SEVEN

The 'anti-globalisation' movement and its implications for social policy

Nicola Yeates[1]

Introduction

'Globalisation' is increasingly taking hold as an integrating force for contemporary social movements. With the processes and effects of globalisation spreading throughout the world, a range of groups and organisations – trades unions, women's groups, environmental groups, tribal and indigenous groups, consumer groups, religious groups, human rights groups, civil liberties groups, and anti-nuclear groups – have organised to oppose globalisation at local, national and international levels and on a transnational scale. These groups are increasingly taking their complaints directly to institutions, particularly those of the multilateral economic kind, pursuing a 'free trade' agenda. Through a series of campaigns during the latter part of the 1990s, most notable of which were the anti-MAI (Multilateral Agreement on Investment) campaign (1998) and the 'Battle of Seattle' (1999), they have challenged the infringement of democratic and human rights, drawn attention to the neglect of social and economic justice issues and presented broad alternatives to the neo-liberal approach to globalisation (O'Brien et al, 2000; Ayres, 2001;). Although the focus of these campaigns has been on international institutions, they have also organised against some of the most basic elements of the international economic order.

Through an examination of these protests and the responses to them, this chapter considers the implications of globalisation for social policy. The chapter begins by reviewing recent 'anti-globalisation'[2] campaigns (section one) and then proceeds to examine the composition and methodologies of the 'anti-globalisation' movement (section two). The following two sections focus on the impact of the movement on social policy through a consideration of statist responses to the protests. Thus, section three examines repressive and regulatory/cooptive strategies, while section four focuses on the changes in social policy areas. The final section examines what 'anti-globalisation' movement activity implies for social policy analysis, by outlining in broad terms an internationalist intellectual agenda to structure future scholarly attention in this area.

The anti-MAI and anti-WTO campaigns

The anti-MAI and anti-WTO (World Trade Organisation) demonstrations – particularly those that took place in Seattle in 1999 – are said to have marked a watershed in the struggle against globalisation and free trade. Although by no means the first or the largest protests against international institutions (see Box 7.1 for a chronology of 'anti-globalisation' events), these demonstrations, which Cockburn and St Clair (2000) liken to the 1960s US civil rights movement and French students' movement, have been claimed as a victory of the 'anti-globalisation' movement over the 'social movement for global capitalism' and the 'transnational capitalist class' to use Sklair's (1997, 2001) terms.

Box 7.1: 'Anti-globalisation' events (1996-2001)

Date	Location	Institution	Estimated number of protesters	Comments
November 1996	Manila, Philippines	APEC free trade meeting	130,000	
May 1998	Geneva, Switzerland	WTO	10,000	First mass protest at WTO headquarters
May 1998	Hyderabad, India	WTO	200,000	
5 May 1998	Birmingham, UK	G8 summit	2,000	First 'global street party' organised in 30 countries
September 1998	New Delhi, India	WTO	100,000	
18 June 1999 ('J18')	London, UK	G7	5,000	Carnival Against Capital; 50 stock exchanges world wide targeted
November 1999	Seattle, USA	WTO	50-70,000	
November 1999	Manila, Philippines	ASEAN		Thousands broke through security cordon
January 2000	Davos, Switzerland	WEF	Thousands	

16-17 April 2000	Washington, USA	WB/IMF	20-30,000	1,000 arrested
May 2000	Chang Mai, Thailand	ADB		
May 2000	London, UK		10,000	Guerrilla gardening
July 2000	Okinawa, Japan	WB/IMF	5,000	
11 September 2000	Melbourne, Australia	WEF	5,000	
26 September 2000 ('S26')	Prague, Czech Republic	WB/IMF	9-20,000	Meeting ended a day early; 600 blocked at borders
20 October 2000	Seoul, South Korea	ASEAN	20,000	Workers and students
December 2000	Nice, France	EU	90-100,000	Trades unionists march
January 2001	Davos, Switzerland	WEF	Thousands	
20 April 2001	Quebec, Canada	FTAA	50,000 on trades union march	
June 2001	Gothenburg, Sweden	EU	20,000	Three protesters shot by police, 90 injured. Police raid on protest HQ. Of 539 arrested, 61 deported and 20 sentenced to jail
July 2001	Genoa, Italy	G8	200,000	One death, 240 injured. Genoa Social Forum raided. 200 arrests; allegations of police torture. 2,000 refused entry to city
30 September 2001 ('S30')	Washington, USA	WB/IMF	–	Cancelled due to 11 September attacks
9 November 2001 ('N9')	Doha, Qatar	WTO	100 NGO delegates demon-strated	Agreement in advance not to make any arrests. US delegation shrunk from 300 to 50
10 November 2001	New Delhi, India	WTO	25,000	
16-17 November 2001 ('N16' and 'N17')	Ottawa, Canada	IMF/WB/ G20	2,000 at War Memorial	Attacks on demonstrators
13-15 December 2001 ('D13', 'D14' and 'D15')	Brussels, Belgium	EU	80-100,000 on 'D13' trades union march; 25,000 on 'D14' march, 4,000 on 'D15' march	Legal team members and 150 demonstrators arrested; demonstrators attacked by police using water cannons, tear gas and plastic bullets. 3,000 police on German-Belgian border

Note: ADB = Asian Development Bank; APEC = Asia-Pacific Economic Co-operation (Forum); ASEAN = Association of South-East Asian Nations; EU = European Union; FTAA = Free Trade Association of the Americas; IMF = International Monetary Fund; WB = World Bank; WEF = World Economic Forum; WTO = World Trade Organisation.

Sources: derived from various 'anti-globalisation' and independent media websites and webcast news reports (for example, www.indymedia.org; www.protest.net; www.flora.org).

The anti-MAI campaigns in 1998 set the stage for a battle that saw "for the first time active public participation in the shaping of international relations" (Grimshaw, 1997, p 38). Conceived of in 1995, the MAI was negotiated by the Organisation for Economic Co-operation and Development (OECD) against the background of growing multilateralism as regards international investment issues. Investment issues were included in the GATT's (General Agreement on Trade and Tariffs) Uruguay Round (1987-93) and the NAFTA (North American Free Trade Agreement) (1992) (Dunkley, 2000).

The MAI was designed to provide a single, comprehensive, multilateral framework for the regulation of international investments (Kodama, 1998). Covering all areas and sectors of the economy except national security and defence, the maintenance of public order, and monetary and exchange rate policies (Sanger, 1998), the intention was to outlaw a range of public policy measures available to governments that could interfere with international investment. These measures include performance requirements, which entail the attachment of conditions to the receipt of public money, restrictions on investors' access to national markets on the basis of their unethical operations elsewhere in the world, and social and environmental laws that come into conflict with MAI principles. The MAI included provision for potential investors to challenge domestic laws and policies which they consider breach MAI provisions and are likely to cause them loss or damage. For example, governments accused of interfering 'unreasonably' with the use of private property of an individual or business would be required to pay compensation. Such cases could arise if commercial providers of health or social services claim that their business is, or is likely to be, adversely affected by government plans to expand state services (Sanger, 1998). As the United Nations Research Institute on Social Development (UNRISD) recognised (from a position of opposition), the MAI:

> ... would have allowed foreign private providers to challenge national government prerogatives to provide free services or to subsidize national non-profit providers. The scheme would have embraced the full range of health and social services, including childcare centres, hospitals and community clinics, as well as private labs and independent physicians. (UNRISD, 2000, p 15)

Not surprisingly, given the potentially far-reaching effects of the MAI on domestic social and economic policies, the negotiations were not concluded by the original deadline of May 1997. They were opposed by a broad coalition of citizens' groups, such as consumer, farmer, labour, church, women's, environmental and development groups. At first, critics of the MAI came principally from non-governmental organisations (NGOs) and governments in developing countries, but opposition spread within Europe, Australia, the US and Canada (where the implementation of NAFTA was already generating fierce criticism). Many governments were reluctant to concede control over key areas of their economies, as can be judged by over 1,000 pages of country-specific objections that were lodged, while the French government withdrew from negotiations in 1998. Concessions subsequently made in a revised MAI negotiating text (OECD, 1998, pp 54-5), notably the inclusion of an acknowledgement of core labour standards and a non-binding provision entitled 'Not lowering standards', were intended to allay criticisms of the MAI, but were not enough to put the negotiations back on track (Wilkinson and Hughes, 2000). The negotiations were subsequently moved to the World Trade Organisation (WTO) on the grounds that it is a more global international institution than the OECD, has expertise in negotiating trade and investment agreements, and is already engaging with civic groups (Grimshaw, 1997; Khor, 1998; Wilkinson and Hughes, 2000).

The global citizens' campaign that had disrupted the MAI undertook a massive mobilisation against a WTO ministerial meeting in Seattle in 1999. The purpose of this meeting was to agree a negotiating agenda for the millennium round of trade negotiations. This agenda included agriculture and trade in health, social and education services. The 5,000 delegates to the WTO from 150 countries were met by a programme of seminars, rallies, walkouts and civil disobedience simultaneously in Seattle (US) and in other countries. The 'N30' (November, 30) events succeeded in disrupting the talks, and by the end of the week governments left without an agreement.

Although the anti-MAI and Seattle campaigns claimed victory in disrupting the progress of 'free' trade and investment talks, the variety of causes of the failure of the Seattle talks needs to be stressed, as must their political nature. The most obvious cause was the failure of the national delegations to even agree on the need for a new round. To this can be added the continuing articulation of concern over trade-related intellectual property rights (TRIPs) and trade-related investment measures (TRIMs) by many national social movements since the Uruguay Round (1987-93), and disquiet over the 'cultural imperialism' and disguised protectionism some claimed to see in the demand for labour and environmental clauses (Shiva, 1997). Peripheral nations attending were dissatisfied with the meagre benefits they had gained from previous trade rounds and with their marginalisation from the negotiations. The forthcoming US elections, along with a resurgent labour movement which Gore and Clinton needed to keep on side, determined the strong American line on labour clauses which alienated the peripheral nations even further. The regional fractions within global capitalism were also apparent. The French Education Minister accused the US government of using the trade negotiations to brainwash the world by trying to open its universities around the globe, and the European Union (EU) delegation was split over the proposed liberalisation of agriculture. National delegations were under strong pressure from their own social movements, trades unions, environmental groups and development lobbies (Bayne, 2000). These causes of failure, combined with the well-organised blocking of the opening day and the demonstration of mass opposition (involving an estimated 30,000 people), showed that the push to open markets is not inevitably successful, contrary to the claims of globalisation enthusiasts and defeatists (Yeates, 2001).

Transnational collective action

The 'anti-globalisation' protests have aimed at blocking meetings and suspending negotiations, and have involved tens of thousands of participants (see Box 7.1 previously). The organisational and tactical innovations involved in the international organising of these protests have been the subject of some interest (see for example, Levi and Olson, 2000; *Millennium*, 2000; Smith, 2001). Along with traditional forms of protest, such as education, symbolic mobilisations, demonstrations and disruption, innovations in protest forms were also evident, such as the production of NGO newspapers at global conferences, the borrowing of official templates (for example, Global People's Assembly, People's Tribunal against corporate crimes and participation in government delegations) and electronic activism (Smith, 2001, p 11). The Internet was first successfully used to coordinate the protests that scuttled the MAI in 1998 and the Seattle meeting in 1999. The People's Global Action Against Free Trade, for example, was launched to coordinate resistance globally, making use of the Internet in between major gatherings. The development of alternative media on the Internet, both general sites such as www.indymedia.org and more specific sites such as www.j18.org, are seen as challenging corporate-owned and dominated information channels and media. To say that the Internet brought down the MAI may be an exaggeration, but electronic activism certainly facilitated the campaign. Indeed, the Internet has been cited as central to a number of key social and economic campaigns and to collective action more broadly (Rosenau, 1990; Hoechsmann, 1996;

Cleaver, 1999; Keck and Sikkink, 1999; Warkentin and Mingst, 2000). Thus, the technology that enables economic globalisation is also used to oppose it. One reason for this is that information can be disseminated quickly and relatively cheaply through the Internet, allowing activists to communicate with each other and with the broader public (Warkentin and Mingst, 2000). Others cite the importance of the Internet as a tool which "[privileges] grassroots organisational structures" (Hoechsmann, 1996, p 33); indeed, the revival of direct democracy in the 'anti-globalisation' movement, a movement "with no name, no leaders and no manifesto", was noted by the *New Internationalist* (September 2001, p 13).

The movement in the core countries drew on various innovative political struggles from the previous decades, taking tactics from everywhere: the direct action of Earth First! and others in the US; the heritage of the free party and anti-roads movement in England channelled through Reclaim the Streets; and the Italian white overalls groups ('Tutti Bianchi'). These came together with transnationally operating solidarity groups, organisations of small farmers from France and India and some labour groups and unions[3]. A report by the Canadian Security Intelligence Service (CSIS) provides a succinct account of the 'anti-globalisation' movement's methodology:

> The new protest phenomenon has been characterised by the broad range of interests which have come together to conduct the demonstrations with minimal dissension. 'Reclaim the Streets', a UK-based initiative that originated with street parties or raves in the mid-1990s, is a tactical concept that protesters have adopted to promote their causes en masse, and which gave rise to the massive gatherings at Seattle and Washington. The methodology has been remarkable in terms of organisation, especially because a central 'director' is not evident and, in part, the resulting lack of infighting has been the secret of success. Like the Internet itself, the anti-globalist movement is a body that manages to survive and even thrive without a head.... One of the more impressive innovations has been the method of organising, arranging and directing the operational and administrative activities associated with the demonstrations, accomplished effectively without the obvious influence of central authority, command, or control. In many ways, the system is very similar to that advocated by anarchists of the libertarian socialist philosophy. (CSIS, 2000, p 8)

The composition of the coalition has also been the subject of interest. It should be noted that the mobilisations are often national political demonstrations. The Genoa mobilisation, for example, was a national political demonstration as well as an international one; the vast majority of the 200,000 protestors were Italian. Furthermore, divisions within the movement are apparent. Civic activists at the meetings have been disproportionately drawn from propertied, urban, professional, computer-literate, English-speaking, Western classes. A key division concerns the reproduction of the 'core/periphery' dichotomy. Although Seattle is conventionally regarded as the beginning of the 'anti-globalisation' movement, this ignores decades of anti-World Bank and anti-International Monetary Fund (IMF) campaigns waged in peripheral countries. Similarly, the description of the shooting of protester Carlo Giulani in Genoa in 2001 as the first death of the 'anti-globalisation' campaign ignores the very many deaths outside the core countries over the previous decades. A more accurate history would recognise that Seattle was where a political struggle that had been waged in the periphery finally surfaced in the core.

Seattle was rather prematurely seen as the final emergence of the fabled red-green coalition, encapsulated in the mantra 'teamsters and turtles, together at last' (teamsters representing the trades union movement and turtles representing the environmental movement). The divide between the two movements remains in the core countries, although in the periphery trades unions are strongly involved. According to Cockburn and St Clair "the crucial division was always between the kids et al seizing the streets and the big institutions (notably labor) marching safely: illegal and legal, mutually sympathetic (broadly speaking) but mostly separate and certainly unequal, certainly suspicious of each other" (2000, p 77). What Seattle did see, however, was the coming together of the direct action arm of American environmentalism, an invigorated anarchist movement, and a large variety of more mainstream groups and solidarity campaigns (for a full list of the Seattle coalition, see Box 7.2).

A further compositional division in the 'anti-globalisation' movement concerns tactics, namely reform versus revolution – a division reported in the English media as one between 'fluffy' and 'spiky' protesters. This division between those who wish to reform the WTO and those who oppose its existence has tended to express itself through a tactical disagreement over violence to property. This contradiction was exemplified by the incident reported from Seattle where concerned non-violent protesters defended Niketown from a section of the Black Bloc (Cockburn and St Clair, 2000).

The coalition involved in 'anti-globalisation' mobilisations has been denounced by both Left and Right as incoherent and contradictory.

Box 7.2: Seattle coalition

(as circulated by a subsidiary of PR firm Burston Marstellar)

Abya Yala Fund; A Seed; AFL-CIO; Alliance for Sustainable Jobs and the Environment; Amazon Watch; Anarchist Action Collective; Black Army Faction; Black Clad Messengers; Chinese activist groups; Christian Aid; Committee in Solidarity with the People of El Salvador (CISPES); Citizens' Trade Campaign; Consumer International; Direct Action Network; Earth Justice Legal Defence Fund; 50 Years is Enough; Focus on the Global South; French Peasants Confederation; Friends of the Earth; Global Exchange; Greenpeace; Humane Society; Indigenous Environmental Network; Indigenous Peoples' Network for Political Research and Education; Institute for Local Self-Reliance; International Association of Machinists and Aerospace Workers; International Brotherhood of Teamsters; ICFTU; International Forum on Globalization; No2WTO; National Labour Committee; National Lawyers Guild; Oxfam International; People for Free Trade; People's Decade for Human Rights Education; Peoples' Global Action; Project Underground; Public Citizen's Global Trade Watch; Rainforest Action Network; Ruckus Society; Sheet Metal Workers Union; Sierra Club; Sierra Club's Responsible Trade Programme; Southwest Network for Environmental and Economic Justice; Third World Network; Union of Needle Traders, Industrial and Textile Employees (UNITE); United Auto Workers; United Farmworkers of America; United Steelworkers of America; United Students Against Sweatshops.

Certainly, the issues of concern to the coalition are wide ranging. At the Genoa Public Forum held during the week prior to the official talks in July 2001, an intensive programme of some 200 talks, debates, meetings and caucuses in workshops, plenaries and thematic sessions took place in which some former government ministers, current members of the European Parliament, various citizens' groups, networks and organisations and individual activists took part. A wide range of issues were addressed: the global causes of poverty and inequality; work and employment; global democracy; trade liberalisation; militarisation and war; human rights; debt; World Bank reform; food security; the control of finance; health; genetic manipulation; privatisation; children; immigration; and alternatives to globalisation. These seemingly disparate issues testify to the broad-based nature of the coalition, and to their view of the interconnectedness of the issues themselves. Work is underway to construct more clearly what the campaigners stand *for* rather than against, but it is doubtful that a single 'manifesto' of the 'anti-globalisation' movement will emerge given the diversity of groups, perspectives and interests involved. Indeed, any attempt to create such a manifesto would bring to the fore internal differences on aims, tactics and solutions, possibly dividing the movement.

It is necessary to place the 'anti-globalisation' mobilisations in context. The recent protests may constitute an important episode in transnational mobilisation and collective action (Smith, 2001), but transnational activism long predates the 'anti-globalisation' campaigns (for example, the anti-slavery movement). Moreover, the publicity given to the recent confrontations with global economic institutions ignores the 'global social dialogues' that have been going on for many years in peripheral countries between social movements and international governmental organisations (IGOs) and 'in the shadow' congresses that regularly accompany their meetings. Various such dialogues have also taken place for many decades between campaigners and local branches of transnational corporations (TNCs). A major aspect of this work consists of targeting market processes (boycotts, consumer campaigns, and so on) and influential political associations affiliated with trade, culture, religion, science and production. The public demonstrations at Seattle and since are, in fact, only one of a much wider range of 'anti-globalisation' campaigns waged mostly out of the public gaze: lobbying legislators; letter writing campaigns; exposing illegal activities; class action suits through the courts; strikes and riots; consumer boycotts; and physical attacks on products, centres of consumption and infrastructure.

More generally, the growth of opposition groups to globalisation should be seen against the background of increasing magnitude, simultaneity and coordination in contentious collective action by European social movements since the early 1960s (Walton, 1987; Tarrow, 1995). In the face of the declining power of organised labour and revolutionary groups, alternative strategies of social struggle have been devised to assert local control over the seemingly remote forces of globalisation (Mittelman, 1996). The number, size and professionalism of 'transnational advocacy networks' have grown dramatically in the last three decades, along with the density and complexity of their international linkages with intergovernmental organisations and other NGOs (Keck and Sikkink, 1999, p 92). These new social movements are increasingly cooperating and coordinating on the global level, in addition to the national level, most often in the sharing of information and debate, but increasingly also in their actions.

The transnational organisation and activities of the 'anti-globalisation' movement must also be set in the context of the intensification of transnational policy cooperation, which has altered the way territories and populations are governed, a tendency most clearly seen in regional formations and in relations between developed and developing countries (Pérez Baltodano, 1999). Transnational policy cooperation has also thrown up opportunities and targets for political mobilisation and collective action (Smith, 2001). Governments, TNCs, NGOs, trades unions and professional and trade associations are increasingly directing political action towards global arenas as well as national arenas and IGOs have offered general encouragement to communities of interest to consider themselves part of the international political and policy community. Although some groups are opposed to working with these institutions, others have opted to participate in IGOs' policy processes to try to influence the reform agenda at national and international levels (Weiss and Gordenker, 1996; O'Brien et al, 2000).

State responses: repression, regulation and cooptation

The 'anti-globalisation' protests have made an impact on the ways in which IGOs do business and the state has responded by resorting to increased repression and the denial of civil freedoms and democratic rights. This has involved transnational coordination by police forces whose operations include denying protesters' physical entry to the site or city or even the country in which the negotiations are held, pre-emptive arrests, infiltration and provocation, allegedly. Huge resources have been invested in ensuring security at the meetings, and fortifying the talks, exemplified by locating the WTO talks in Doha, Qatar[4]. Increasingly, free movement, heralded as one of the glories of globalisation and the cornerstone of EU citizenship, is being curtailed as European police apply tactics previously used for football crowd control.

Following Seattle, the free traders have concluded that ignoring civil society was not the most sensible move on their part. Realising that the protests were impeding progress on the deregulation of trade and investment, increasing the economic and political costs of international governance, and that opponents could not be ignored or be seen to be denied their democratic and civil rights for too long, Mike Moore (2001) publicly acknowledged, indeed appeared to welcome, the intense scrutiny that the protests have placed the WTO under. There is likely to be a strong attempt made by IGOs to coopt the 'anti-globalisation' movement. However, cooption is unlikely to succeed given the basic nature of some of the issues involved. While some opposition groups believe the possibility of a dialogue exists, others believe it would be a dialogue of the deaf, given the free traders' position that what is needed is to use the power of argument to convince citizens' groups and other sceptics of the benefits of free trade. A particular problem that those wishing to coopt the movement face was described by *The Economist*, which reported the difficulty Vaclav Havel faced in trying to open negotiations with the protestors at Prague: "Who should represent a disparate collection of websites, all of which take pride in their lack of leaders?" (21 September 2000, p 98).

Given that the movement itself is unavailable for cooption, IGOs and governments are busy coopting the NGO sector, the more formalised section of the opposition. Mike Moore (2001) stated he looked forward to constructive engagement with NGOs who had a genuine interest in helping the WTO do its work, though in reality the WTO has been making efforts to coopt NGOs since 1995 when these groups became more publicly vocal in their opposition to the new multilateral trade regime[5]. These moves to coopt NGOs have occurred alongside attempts to divide the movement into 'non-violent' and 'violent'. The latter segment was dismissed by Moore (2001) as "mindless, undemocratic enemies of open society" and he proposed a set of rules to govern future dialogue between the 'non-violent' NGOs and the WTO. These rules essentially entail greater regulation of NGOs in return for formal channels of access to the WTO. His suggested code of conduct included the rejection of violence and a commitment by NGOs to transparency vis-à-vis their membership, finances and rules of decision making (Moore, 2001). Proposals quickly emerged to regulate the NGO sector: the Foreign Policy Centre, a think-tank sponsored by the British government, proposed a code of conduct for NGOs that includes certification by a regulator. This attempt to enhance the participation of moderate NGOs in the WTO mirrors efforts by other IGOs to court elements of civil society. Both the IMF and WB have made provision for greater NGO involvement in policy making and implementation over the last decade, and the UN is particularly keen to represent itself as an honest broker between the interests of firms, governments and civil society (Deacon, 1999; Weiss and Gordenker, 1996).

Critics argue that these efforts only humanise globalisation and that privileging the relations between civil society and IGOs is a poor substitute for empowering states because it obscures the dominance of powerful states in global institutions, while sustaining the legitimacy of IGOs dedicated to pursuing globalisation (Phillips and Higgott, 1999, p 15). Indeed, enhancing NGO participation in IGO policy making will most probably favour the status quo rather than challenge it. Thus, the business lobby, including bankers, was already the largest sector of civil society present at the mobilisations; a lobby that has already shaped global economic governance far more than reformers and radicals (Scholte, 2000). As Scholte (2000, p 119) argues, "global civic activism can reproduce the exclusions of neoliberal globalisation, even in campaigns that mean to oppose those inequities". Furthermore, most social development NGOs are oriented towards local poverty relief work rather than policy advocacy work at national and transnational levels. They have been encouraged to fill the gaps in existing provision (Owoh, 1996, p 216), challenge state-dominated development policy (Riker, 1995), voice criticisms of existing welfare arrangements and generate demands for policy and institutional reform, often in opposition to corporate, trades union and producer interests nationally (Deacon et al, 1997). Indeed, the greater involvement of the NGO sector may be used to give new strength to a residualist social welfare strategy dressed up in the language of social development, participation, empowerment and civil society, leaving a substantial role for private health and welfare provision for the non-poor population (Vivian, 1995; Deacon et al, 1997; Deacon, 2000).

Of course, it is not only the NGOs that IGOs face difficulties in coopting; IGOs also have to contend with governments. The General Agreement on Tariffs and Trade (GATT) originated in 1947 as a free trade political club of the rich countries, and although the number of governments has since expanded to 117 (China was admitted in December 2001) it has been difficult to shake off this image. Indeed, one of the reasons for the Seattle talks' collapse was that developing countries were dissatisfied with the meagre benefits they had gained from previous trade rounds and with their marginalisation within the negotiations. Developing countries were again excluded from the drafting of a preparatory text for Doha. Desperate for progress to be made on trade talks[6], the US and EU reportedly bent over backwards to (or at least be seen to) address the concerns of the developing nations at Doha in November 2001. India, the largest developing nation at the talks, almost capsized a deal, but its government was eventually bought off by an agreement to delay anti-trust and foreign investment discussions by two years (to start in 2007 rather than in 2005). Developed countries also proved to be no pushover. The French government, in anticipation of the forthcoming elections in 2002, managed to thwart the elimination of all export subsidies to its farmers (Cooper and Winestock, 2001).

State responses: policy change

IGOs have been forced to address at least some of the movement's criticisms of the social, health and environmental consequences of their actions and respond to movement demands placed on them. The protests, combined with the economic effects of the Asian financial crisis in 1997/98, which cost an estimated $2 trillion and which made its effects felt in the West, finally forced transnational political and bureaucratic elites to accept that "an efficient system of global public policy is a necessary ingredient of an efficient global economy" (Kaul et al, 1999, p 451) and that institutions of global governance need to embody socio-political rules, norms and ethics that reflect the common interest of the variety of political actors needed to underpin further globalisation (Evans, 1998; Phillips and Higgott, 1999).

On substantive policy issues, there appears to have been some change in rhetoric. Following the Seattle protests, the WTO, World Bank, IMF and OECD presented their case for more 'free trade' in terms of the contribution that it would make to tackle poverty globally. The IMF reformulated the conditions it attaches to loans it makes to governments to include explicit attention to social, environmental and governance issues, and, together with the World Bank, developed a programme of debt relief for the poorest countries (O'Brien et al, 2000; see www.imf.org and www.worldbank.org). In a review of health and education policy discourse within the World Bank and IMF during the latter part of the 1990s, Deacon (1999, p 19) argued that the World Bank "is learning some of the positive lessons from countries that have primarily public health services" and that it recognises the role of education in relation to social, political, health and environmental stability as well as in relation to production.

More recently, at Doha the WTO "agreed to try to bring its rules in line with environmental treaties and [indicated that it] may give tariff preferences to environmentally sound products" in order to get members of Europe's Green parties on board (Winestock and Cooper, 2001, p 6). The major breakthrough at Doha, from the opposition's side, was a political declaration on TRIPs and public health (public health is one area in which the deleterious effects of TRIPs and TRIMs are anticipated, for example see Koivusalo, 1999). This declaration reaffirmed the WTO's commitment to TRIPs but, crucially, it included the proviso that "the TRIPs agreement does not and should not prevent members from taking measures to protect public health" (WTO, 2001). Essentially, this is a political declaration; it is not the rewriting of legal text on TRIPs, which developing countries had requested, though it does open the way for developing countries to ignore drug patents and buy cheaper, generic drugs to meet public health needs. This acceptance that public health issues could take precedence over the intellectual property rights of the pharmaceuticals industry (which is mostly located in the north) testifies to the strength of the 'anti-globalisation' movement, which outmanoeuvred the drugs companies on the issue and forced a change in the position of the WTO and governments.

Multinational pharmaceuticals companies, which had claimed TRIPs were essential to provide them with an incentive to invest in drug development and production, wanted the declaration only to encompass health pandemics like AIDS. Earlier in 2001, following protests in recent years by HIV/AIDS advocacy groups, the industry had already been forced to make some concessions with regard to the treatment of AIDS in poor countries following a dispute with Brazil and South Africa over the price of AIDS drugs (see www.oxfam.org and www.globaltreatmentaccess.org for further details). However, the deal reached at Doha allowed poor countries to break patents for a much wider range of illnesses, such as cancer, asthma and diabetes. The US government, in the grip of anthrax attacks, had already stated its intention to ignore TRIPs and to manufacture CIPRO, the anti-anthrax drug that was manufactured by a German company, in the interests of the public health of US citizens.

The political declaration on TRIPs showed that concessions are made on core issues when the socially inequitable effects of WTO rules are either politically unjustifiable or when they are no longer deemed to be in the interests of core countries. Although these concessions represent piecemeal advances against fractions of capital (in this case, the pharmaceuticals industry), on balance the gains are relatively minor compared with those achieved by the "transnational capitalist class" (Sklair, 1997, 2001). As Scholte (2000, p 117) argues, "advocates of change have succeeded in placing neoliberal approaches to globalisation under more critical public scrutiny, but the supertanker is slow to turn". Indeed, the WTO is continuing to press ahead with plans to further extend trade and investment deregulation, including trade in services such as in education, health, welfare and financial services provision, and the movement of natural persons (that is, the entry and temporary stay of persons for the purpose of providing a service) (WTO, 1998a, 1998b, 1998c, 1998d). Although the WTO is hopeful as regards the progress it can make, it remains to be seen how far governments will accept multilateral rules on these public services, given their staunch opposition to them previously. Notwithstanding, the WTO's intention to press ahead with the issues potentially opens the way for restrictions on public provision and the extension of private provision of health and welfare services (Deacon, 2000).

In fact, it is questionable how much progress there has been on social policy at all. As regards social protection, the World Bank continues to emphasise the role of sub-national government in promoting economic development and ensuring adequate social safety nets (World Bank, 2000, p 49), particularly through public works schemes with below-market wages (World Bank, 2000, pp 150-1). The IMF also retains a strong aversion to universal social protection, and the UN still talks about social safety nets and risk management, rather than universal social services and redistribution (Deacon, 1999, p 25). Furthermore, the International Labour Organisation (ILO) has partially accepted the World Bank's criticisms of its tripartite system of pensions and it now recommends for developed countries a four pillar model consisting of: a bottom means-tested tier, financed from general revenue; a pay as you go, defined-benefit pension worth 40-50% of lifetime average earnings; a compulsory, capitalised, defined-contribution pension; and an upper tier of voluntary retirement savings and non-pension sources of income. For developing countries, the ILO recommends giving priority to expanding coverage to workers in the informal sector, or a national programme that excludes higher income workers who would be required to participate in a 'more expensive' (probably private) programme. The basic state programme would be limited to disability and survivors' benefits or provide retirement benefits that start at a relatively high age, such as 65 or 70 (Gillion, 2000, p 20; Gillion et al, 2000). The retreat of the ILO from advocacy of universal provision, its acceptance of a larger role for private pension provision, and its adoption of a 'risk management' approach is a particularly significant shift given its previously oppositional stance to much of the Washington Consensus (Deacon, 2000, pp 11-12).

As this discussion has shown, the interventions of the 'anti-globalisation' movement in the global political process have succeeded in demonstrating the mass public support for its criticisms of the institutions and policies of global governance, and bringing to wider public attention issues previously confined to political, diplomatic, bureaucratic, economic and civic elites. The 'anti-globalisation' protests have affirmed the importance of the political domain in the globalisation process; in particular they have shown that a concerted opposition to 'free' trade can be mounted and sustained and that the leverage of governments and political groupings in these fora can be used to advance public interests. Although the achievements of the movement as measured by concrete policy change have so far been limited, to reduce its achievements only to the number of immediate concessions that have been won would be to underplay the importance of this kind of activism in altering the political dynamics and the economics of trade negotiations and enhancing the probability of future concessions. In addition, it may emphasise the policy aims at the expense of the policy outcomes: the degree to which the policy is implemented can still be contested in the domestic political arena by those charged with its implementation, such as civil and public servants and NGOs, which may hold significant bureaucratic and political power nationally, while the effects of popular opposition in shaping how far reforms are implemented cannot be discounted. In fact, implementation is a weak point for any international institution because it does not have a local presence and because implementation has to be enforced by sovereign governments working in the context of the balance of political power nationally.

Towards an internationalist social policy

Whatever one's position on globalisation, there is no doubt that the process has opened up the possibilities of social policy becoming more internationalist than previously. An internationalist approach to social policy essentially means that it has to be studied from both a national and a transnational perspective (see also Townsend, 1993, 1995; Deacon et al, 1997; Stryker, 1998; Morales-Gómez, 1999; Clarke, 2000). The remainder of this chapter sketches what, in broad terms, this entails.

To start with, it entails foregrounding international institutions, both governmental and non-governmental, as social policy 'actors' and the direct or indirect effects of their discourses, policies and actions on national welfare institutions and on individuals', households' and communities' welfare. As Deacon argued in the mid-1990s, there needs to be greater attention to the ways these institutions engage in "transnational redistribution, supranational regulation and supranational and global provision" (Deacon et al, 1997, p 22). In addition to this, analytical frameworks need to be recast to capture the interaction of the national and transnational levels, namely how transnational institutions and practices shape the parameters of domestic economic and social policy, albeit to different degrees across countries and regions, and how the discourses and policies of transnational institutions and actors are in turn shaped by national interests and policies. As the author has argued elsewhere (Yeates, 1999, 2001), the relationship between globalisation and social policy is a 'dialectical' one in the sense that just as the global economy and transnational political processes bear on states, so states pursue a variety of strategies to steer globalisation and advance their national interests. In sum, there needs to be greater recognition of the 'multi-actored', 'multi-tiered', 'multi-sphered' global governance context in which social policy and human welfare are embroiled (Yeates, 2001).

In terms of the scope of focus, an internationalist orientation would include 'traditional' issues of health, social protection, employment and education, but it also has to consider, as 'anti-globalisation' activists have, the impact of national and international monetary, trade, investment and environmental policies and practices on social, health and economic welfare. An internationalist approach would also necessarily be more comparatively focused in order to discern how the ways in which states promote, 'receive' and react to globalisation differ according to their economic and military position, or rank, within the global political economy, their institutional, cultural and historical traditions and arrangements, and the national balance of forces between the state, labour, capital and civil society. To date, comparative social policy has tended to focus on social policies in the advanced industrialised (OECD) countries and to a lesser extent in the newly industrialising countries to the neglect of the much wider variety of arrangements, formal and informal, in place around the world for securing human health and welfare (MacPherson and Midgley, 1987).

MacPherson and Midgley attribute this neglect of developing countries by social policy researchers based in advanced industrialised countries to their parochialism, having "often regarded their own societies as a macrocosm for social policy analysis" (1987, p 5). However, social policy analysis as developed in the north is ill suited in many ways to immediate application to developing countries. Focusing on traditional Western social programmes will miss land policies, micro-credit schemes, agricultural and consumption subsidies and food security programmes, all of which significantly impact on the level and distribution of welfare (Gough, 2000). More generally, concepts such as class, community, identity, territory, justice, rights and citizenship, which have been developed in a national context, may have to be rethought (Deacon et al, 1997; Clarke, 2000). The international social policy agenda is a broad-ranging one, but it is politically and intellectually imperative that the social policy community engage with these issues.

Notes

[1] The author wishes to acknowledge the helpful comments of the Social Policy Review editorial team and Denis O'Hearn on an earlier draft of this chapter.

[2] Quotation marks are used around 'anti-globalisation' to denote the contested nature of this term. Although the media have applied this term to the activists, movement activists themselves often insist that they are not against globalisation per se but against the current form of globalisation.

[3] This global movement varies nationally. In France, for example, the 'anti-globalisation' movement is structured and has strong trades union involvement, which is more characteristic of the periphery, as well as the involvement of the farmers' organisation, Confédération Paysanne. The main group, Association for the Taxation of Financial Transactions for the Aid of Citizens (ATTAC), claims it has over 30,000 supporters and over 200 committees spread throughout France alone (*Red Pepper*, July 2001, pp 26-7).

[4] Six hundred and forty seven NGOs were deemed eligible to attend the Doha Ministerial in November 2001, but due to limited hotel space, fewer than 200 representatives of labour, environmental and other groups opposed to free trade were granted visas by the Qatari government (Blunstein, 2001).

[5] In 1996 the WTO adopted guidelines recognising "the role NGOs can play to increase the awareness of the public in respect of WTO activities" (WTO, 1996). NGOs can apply to the WTO for special status to attend Plenary Sessions. Over 100 NGOs attended the Singapore Ministerial (1996), and over 120 attended the Geneva and Doha Ministerials in 2001. At Prague (2000), a programme of meetings was held by the WTO for non-governmental, non-corporate groups. As part of the WTO's attempts to 'educate' these groups about its good work, it has begun to host symposia on 'issues' confronting the work of the WTO – trade and the environment, trade and development and trade facilitation – at which NGOs, governments, the media and academics are invited to participate.

[6] The attacks on the World Trade Centre and the Pentagon in September 2001 were used by pro-globalisation politicians not only to stress the necessity of a new trade round but also to warn potential protesters of the 'dangers' of demonstrating against the talks. As Bello (2001) reports:

> The smoke had not yet cleared from the ruins of the World Trade Center in New York before US Trade Representative Robert Zoellick ... [asserted] that free trade was one of the best ways of countering terrorism. Others have been more brazen: at a recent conference in Budapest, David Hartridge, an influential senior officer at the WTO Secretariat, openly declared that the 11 September terrorists and activists against corporate-driven globalisation showed a propensity for 'violent behaviour' and warned people from going to Geneva for demonstrations against the WTO in mid-November because 'there will be violence.

References

Ayres, J. (2001) 'Transnational political processes and contention against the global economy', *Mobilization*, vol 6, no 1, pp 55-68.

Bayne, N. (2000) 'Why did Seattle fail? Globalization and the politics of trade', *Government and Opposition*, vol 35, no 2, pp 131-51.

Bello, W. (2001) 'Trade superpowers turn on heat as WTO ministerial opens', *Focus on Trade*, vol 69, no 1 (www.focusweb.org/publications).

Blunstein, P. (2001) 'Protest group softens tone at WTO talks', *Focus on Trade*, vol 71, no 3 (www.focusweb.org/publications).

Clarke, J. (2000) 'A world of difference? Globalization and the study of social policy', in G. Lewis, S. Gewirtz and J. Clarke (eds) *Rethinking social policy*, London: Sage Publications/Open University, pp 201-16.

Cleaver, H. (1999) *Computer-linked social movements and the global threat to capitalism* (www.eco.utexas.edu/Homepages/Faculty/Cleaver).

Cockburn, A. and St Clair, J. (2000) *5 days that shook the world: Seattle and beyond*, London: Verso.

Cooper, H. and Winestock, G. (2001) 'WTO reaches agreement on new round of talks', *Wall Street Journal Europe*, 15 November, vol 11, p 1.

CSIS (Canadian Security Intelligence Service) (2000) 'Anti-globalization: a spreading phenomenon', Report no 8 (www.csis-scrs.gc.ca/eng/menu/menu_e.html).

Deacon, B. (1999) *Towards a socially responsible globalization: International actors and discourses*, Globalism and Social Policy Programme occasional papers, no 1, Helsinki: STAKES.

Deacon, B. (2000) *Globalization and social policy: The threat to equitable welfare*, Occasional Paper 5, Geneva: UNRISD.

Deacon, B. with Hulse, M. and Stubbs, P. (1997) *Global social policy: International organisations and the future of welfare*, London: Sage Publications.

Dunkley, G. (2000) *The free trade adventure*, London: Zed Books.

Economist, The (2000) 'Angry and effective', 21 September, London.

Evans, J. (1998) 'Economic globalization: the need for a social dimension', in D. Foden and P. Morris (eds) *The search for equity: Welfare and security in the global economy*, London: Lawrence and Wishart, pp 11-23.

Gillion, C. (2000) *The development and reform of social security pensions: The approach of the International Labour Office*, Geneva: International Labour Office (www.ilo.org/public/english/protection/socsec).

Gillion, C., Turner, J., Bailey, J. and Latulippe, D. (eds) (2000) *Social security pensions: Development and reform*, Geneva: International Labour Office.

Gough, I. (2000) *Welfare regimes: On adapting the framework to developing countries*, Bath: Global Social Policy Programme, Institute for International Policy Analysis, University of Bath.

Grimshaw, C. (1997) 'The emperor's new clothes. The Multilateral Agreement on Investment', *Corporate Watch*, nos 5/6, pp 36-8.

Hoechsmann, M. (1996) 'Revolution goes global: Zapatistas on the net', *Convergence: Journal of Research into New Media Technologies*, vol 2, no 1, pp 30-5.

Kaul, I., Grunberg, I. and Stern, A. (1999) 'Global public goods: concepts, policies and strategies', in I. Kaul, I. Grunberg and M. Stern (eds) *Global Public Goods: International cooperation in the 21st century*, Oxford: Oxford University Press, pp 450-507.

Keck, M.E. and Sikkink, K. (1999) 'Transnational advocacy networks in international and regional politics', *International Journal of Social Science*, no 159, pp 89-101.

Khor, M. (1998) 'NGOs in OECD countries protest against MAI', *Third World Resurgence*, nos 90/91, pp 25-6.

Kodama, Y. (1998) 'The Multilateral Agreement on Investment and its legal implications for newly industrialising economies', *Journal of World Trade*, vol 32, no 4, pp 21-40.

Koivusalo, M. (1999) *World Trade Organisation and trade-creep in health and social policies*, Globalism and Social Policy Programme Occasional Papers no 4, Helsinki: STAKES.

Levi, M. and Olson, D. (2000) 'The Battle of Seattle', *Politics and Society*, vol 28, pp 309-29.

MacPherson, S. and Midgley, J. (1987) *Comparative social policy and the third world*, Brighton: Wheatsheaf Books.

Millennium (2000) *Millennium: Journal of International Studies*, vol 29, no 1.

Mittelman, J.H. (1996) 'How does globalization really work?', in J.H. Mittelman (ed) *Globalization: critical reflections*, London: Lynne Rienner, pp 229-42.

Moore, M. (2001) 'Open societies, freedom, development and trade', Plenary Opening WTO Symposium on Issues Confronting the World Trading System, 6 July, Geneva (www.wto.org/english/news_e/spmm_e/spmm67_e.htm).

Morales-Gómez, D. (ed) (1999) *Transnational social policies: The new development challenges of globalization*, London: Earthscan.

New Internationalist (2001) 'Global resistance: we are everywhere', issue 38, September, p 13.

O'Brien, R., Goetz, A.M., Scholte, J. and Williams, M. (2000) *Contesting global governance: Multilateral economic institutions and global social movements*, Cambridge: Cambridge University Press.

OECD (Organisation for Economic Co-operation and Development) (1998) *The MAI negotiating text*, Paris: OECD.

Owoh, K. (1996) 'Fragmenting health care: the World Bank prescription for Africa', *Alternatives*, no 21, pp 211-35.

Pérez-Baltodano, A. (1999) 'Social policy and social order in transnational societies', in D. Morales-Gómez (ed) *Transnational social policies: The new development challenges of globalization*, London: Earthscan, pp 19-41.

Phillips, N. and Higgott, R. (1999) *Global governance and the public domain: Collective goods in a 'post-Washington consensus' era*, Warwick: Centre for the Study of Globalization and Regionalisation Working Paper, no 47/99, University of Warwick.

Riker, J.V. (1995) 'From cooptation to cooperation and collaboration in government-NGO relations: toward an enabling policy environment for people-centred development in Asia', in N. Heyzer, J.V. Riker and A.B. Quizon (eds) *Government-NGO relations in Asia: Prospects and challenges for people-centred development*, Basingstoke: Macmillan, pp 91-130.

Rosenau, J. (1990) *Turbulence in world politics*, London: Harvester.

Sanger, M. (1998) 'MAI: multilateral investment and social rights', Paper to International Trade and Investment Agreements, Globalism and Social Policy seminar, University of Sheffield, December.

Scholte, J. (2000) 'Cautionary reflections on Seattle', *Millennium*, vol 29, no 1, pp 115-21.

Shiva,V. (1997) 'How free is free India?', *Resurgence*, no 183, pp 12-17.

Sklair, L. (1997) 'Social movements for global capitalism: the transnational capitalist class in action', *Review of International Political Economy*, vol 4, no 3, pp 514-38.

Sklair, L. (2001) *The transnational capitalist class*, Oxford: Blackwell.

Smith,J. (2001) 'Globalizing resistance: the Battle of Seattle and the future of social movements', *Mobilization*, vol 6, no 1, pp 1-19.

Stryker, R. (1998) 'Globalization and the welfare state', *International Journal of Sociology and Social Policy*, vol 18, nos 2/3/4, pp 1-49.

Tarrow, S. (1995) 'The Europeanization of conflict: reflections from a social movement perspective', *West European Politics*, vol 18, no 2, pp 223-51.

Townsend, P. (1993) *The international analysis of social policy*, Hemel Hempstead: Harvester Wheatsheaf.

Townsend, P. (1995) *The rise of international social policy*, Bristol: The Policy Press.

UNRISD (United Nations Research Institute on Social Development) (2000) *Visible hands: Taking responsibility for social development*, Geneva: UNRISD.

Vivian, J. (1995) 'How safe are social safety nets? Adjustment and social sector restructuring in developing countries', *The European Journal of Development Research*, no 7, pp 1-25.

Walton, J. (1987) 'Urban protest and the global political economy: the IMF riots', in M.P. Smith and J.R. Fagin (eds) *The capitalist city*, Oxford: Blackwell, pp 364-86.

Warkentin, C. and Mingst, K. (2000) 'International institutions, the state, and global civil society in the age of the world wide web', *Global Governance*, vol 6, pp 237-57.

Weiss, T.G. and Gordenker, L. (eds) (1996) *NGOS, the UN, and global governance*, London: Lynne Rienner.

Wilkinson, R. and Hughes, S. (2000) 'Labor standards and global governance: examining the dimensions of institutional engagement', *Global Governance*, vol 6, no 2, pp 259-77.

Winestock, G. and Cooper, H. (2001) 'How activists outmanoeuvred drug makers in WTO Deal', *Wall Street Journal Europe*, 15 November, p 6.

World Bank (2000) *World Development Report 1999/2000: Entering the 21st century*, Oxford: World Bank/Oxford University Press.

WTO (World Trade Organisation) (1996) 'Guidelines for arrangements on relations with non-governmental organisations', WT/L/162, 23 July, Geneva.

WTO (1998a) *Education services. Background note by the Secretariat, Council for Trade in Services*, S/C/W/49.

WTO (1998b) *Financial services. Background note by the Secretariat, Council for Trade in Services*, S/C/W/72.

WTO (1998c) *Health and social services. Background note by the Secretariat, Council for Trade in Services*, S/C/W/50.

WTO (1998d) *Presence of natural persons. Background note by the Secretariat, Council for Trade in Services*, S/C/W/75.

WTO (2001) Ministerial declaration, Doha WTO Ministerial, WT/MIN (01)/Dec/01 (www.wto.org).

Yeates, N. (1999) 'Social politics and policy in an era of globalization: critical reflections', *Social Policy and Administration*, vol 33, no 4, pp 372-93.

Yeates, N. (2001) *Globalization and social policy*, London: Sage Publications.

EIGHT

Migration policy in Europe: contradictions and continuities

Rosemary Sales

Introduction

The announcement in October 2001 by Home Secretary David Blunkett of a new 'green card' system for labour migrants into the UK exposed some of the contradictions that have been at the heart of migration policy in Europe for three decades. With the ending of mass labour migration during the 1970s, many European states declared that they were not countries of immigration. But while they imposed increasingly stringent restrictions on entry and promoted greater selectivity in the skills and geographical origin of potential immigrants, migration continued in a number of forms, both legal (labour migrants, family reunion and asylum) and 'illegal'. During this period, the states of the southern European periphery, traditionally countries of emigration, became countries of 'new immigration'.

The increase in refugee flows in the late 1980s, coinciding with the development of the European Union (EU), brought concerted European Union policies to control the entry of third country (non-EU) nationals. A key element of current policy in relation to asylum, and of the popular discourse surrounding it, has been the distinction between 'genuine refugees' and so-called 'bogus' asylum seekers. The latter, deemed to be 'economic migrants' have been vilified as undeserving of social support, while their dependent status is underlined by their exclusion from formal employment in many states. As demand for migrant labour has increased across a range of sectors, this exclusion comes increasingly into question, not merely from human rights campaigners but also from employers[1]. In practice, the distinction between 'refugee' and 'economic migrant' is blurred: as economic breakdown and social conflict makes basic survival impossible, many people, including those not directly engaged in political activities or individually at risk of persecution, have been forced to migrate in search of work. The use of the expression 'economic migrant' as a term of abuse, even in a period of growing demand for migrant labour, reflects continuing popular hostility to migration.

Recent developments in migration policy in Europe have led to a growing disparity between the rights of migrants with different legal statuses. While legal migrants with settled status have generally secured access to a wider set of rights within the country of migration, others – particularly asylum seekers – have suffered increasing social exclusion. In Britain, for example, restrictions on welfare rights have been a key element in policies aimed at deterring asylum seekers. In France, local prefectures (police) have deployed delaying tactics in the asylum registration process, leaving new asylum seekers completely destitute. The increase during 2001 of asylum seekers attempting to enter Britain from France is partly attributable to these tactics.

This chapter draws on a research project on migration and citizenship rights in Europe[2]. This project examined the processes of exclusion facing two migrant groups: those from Turkey (including Kurds) and those from ex-Yugoslavia. These groups encompass people with diverse migratory histories (including long-term labour migrants and recently arrived refugees), and a range of immigration statuses (from EU citizen to undocumented). The comparative research focused on London, Paris and Rome. As a country of recent immigration, Italy provides a strong contrast with Britain and France with their longer histories of migration, often based on colonial ties, and of ethnic diversity. These states also have different welfare regimes, which have been extensively restructured. The British welfare state's transition from 'universalism' to social exclusion (MacGregor, 1999) has brought increased emphasis on market criteria in service provision. The French model is heavily dependent on work-related benefits (Esping-Andersen, 1990) and support for working mothers (Kofman and Sales, 1996). The Italian model, while developing towards a more comprehensive welfare state, is geographically uneven and, particularly in the south, heavily reliant on the voluntary sector, including religious bodies. The research was based primarily on qualitative methods: it used both life histories of individual migrants and the experience of those working with and for these communities, to provide insight into the complexity of the links between formal and informal processes of exclusion (Kofman et al, 2002). Our research found considerable similarities in London and Paris in terms of the structures of the communities, the patterns of exclusion and the role of community organisations in facilitating access to rights. The situation in Rome was markedly different from both, and therefore the following discussion will focus primarily on London and Rome.

Contemporary immigration flows in Europe: the age of migration?

In 1993, in what has become a major text for students of migration, *The age of migration*, Castles and Miller highlighted four key features of contemporary migration: acceleration, globalisation, diversification and feminisation. Global economic restructuring through the activities of transnational corporations had expanded the scale (acceleration) of migrant flows and their extent, both geographically (globalisation) and in the range of people involved (diversification). The feminisation of migration also reflects changing economic structures in the major countries of immigration (Phizacklea, 1998). The expansion of high level employment associated with leading global companies (Sassen, 1991) feeds demand not only for skilled and elite workers, but also for low status, casualised labour in predominantly female services, such as cleaning, catering and domestic labour. Growing inequalities in wealth between regions and between people has marked these processes. Structural changes in both countries of immigration and emigration have thus brought increased diversification, not merely of migratory streams but of the terms on which migrants are able to settle in Europe.

By 1998, with the second edition of their book, Castles and Miller (1998, p 9) had added a fifth characteristic: *politicisation*. Immigration, particularly asylum, has been constructed as a major political issue in Europe and other main areas of immigration. This reflects an increase in asylum seeking, particularly following the breakdown of state structures in Eastern Europe, but is also an effect of legislation that has made these groups more visible as 'different'.

These migratory movements have altered the relationship between citizenship and the nation state, challenging the notion of national homogeneity (Castles and Davidson, 2000, p 12) and raising questions about how ethnic minorities are incorporated. The increasing divorce between citizenship status and residence also raises issues about the access of non-citizens to the rights – civic, political and social – traditionally associated with citizenship (Marshall, 1950). Some theorists have argued that the existence of stable migrant populations in Europe has diminished the importance of formal citizenship. With settled residence, it is suggested, non-citizens gain significant social rights in the country of migration, producing a new form of 'post-national citizenship' with quasi-citizenship rights and status (Soysal, 1994; Sassen, 1996). Soysal further claims that these rights are guaranteed by an international regime of rights embodied in a series of treaties and other international agreements. This optimistic scenario has some relevance for more secure residents, but recent trends are producing an increasing number of precarious migrants with limited rights. The acquisition of these rights, moreover, owes more to political and economic developments in countries of migration than to international human rights instruments, many of which remain unratified by crucial states (Castles and Davidson, 2000). Formal political rights remain largely confined to nationals, and in some states the issue of granting political rights to non-nationals remains highly contested. The development of 'supranational' EU citizenship has remained limited, and tied to the movement of labour (Ackers, 1998). But this development has, ironically, increased the importance of national belonging, since membership derives from citizenship of a particular national state. Among those without this status, there is an increasing civic stratification, with different sets of rights according to different statuses (Morris, 1997). Immigration policy is still largely the domain of individual states, and the acquisition of national citizenship in particular is jealously guarded at national level. Striking differences remain around the principles by which citizenship is acquired[3] and the ease with which non-nationals can gain citizenship.

European Union policy on migration has produced two interlinked trends. Firstly, European integration and the development of the Single European Market in which capital, commodities and people are able to move freely requires the abolition of internal borders. This development has brought increased efforts to control the EU's external border and concern to distinguish those who are 'in' from those who are 'out' (Leibfried, 1993). The term 'fortress Europe' has frequently been used to describe the controls that have been placed around these borders. This 'fortress' is not, however, impregnable. Policy makers have become increasingly selective about who is allowed to enter (Geddes, 2000) and in the face of growing labour shortages, particularly skilled labour, has opened up considerably towards labour migration since 2000. EU policy depends for its implementation on individual states. A particular concern at EU level has been countries of late immigration such as Italy, which are seen as the 'weak link' in terms of controlling entry; their insecure borders allowing migrants to enter EU territory and then move to northern Europe. Much of this policy development has taken place in intergovernmental bodies, such as the Schengen Agreement outside the

sphere of democratic scrutiny (Geddes, 2000) and then ratified by EU
bodies and individual governments. These measures have focused
particularly on asylum, and include the 'carriers' liability' (fines on airlines
and other carriers who bring in migrants without the correct documents),
a list of 'safe countries' from which asylum applications are automatically
deemed unfounded, and the 'one chance rule' (which allows only one
application for asylum), under which many people have been sent back
to the 'first safe country' in which they landed.

EU states have implemented these policies through national legislation
and administrative procedures. Secondly, there has been the extension of
border controls beyond national boundaries and on to non-state bodies.
Controls on entry at the EU's frontiers are reinforced through a 'buffer
zone' of transit countries (including Turkey and the Balkans), which have
been induced to take on responsibility for securing the European Union's
border, establishing transit checks and controls on illegal immigration
(Geddes, 2000, pp 104-7). Pre-entry checks on immigration status (for
example, by British immigration officers on Roma from the Czech
Republic) have prevented whole groups from travelling to the EU.
Carriers' liability effectively privatises the function of immigration control,
shifting responsibility onto transport operators[4].

These policies have had the effect of making *legal* entry to Europe
almost impossible for asylum seekers. They have not stopped entry,
however, and the past decade has seen a sharp rise in the smuggling of
people to Europe. The activities range from helping friends and comrades
to escape persecution, through to organised criminal gangs. All the refugees
from Turkey interviewed for our study had relied on smugglers.

Refugees recognised by the government of the country of asylum under
the terms of the Geneva Convention[5] ('Convention refugees') are entitled
to the same social rights as citizens. As the rate of recognition fell during
the early 1990s (Duke et al, 1999, p 106), a range of statuses was developed
offering differing social rights and security of residence. These include
temporary protection for groups, such as that offered to Bosnians and
Kosovan Albanians, and individual humanitarian status (for example,
'exceptional leave to remain' – ELR in Britain). Humanitarian status is a
weaker protection since it is granted at the discretion of individual states
and involves no "claim rights against the state" (Schuster and Solomos,
1999, p 61). A major difference is that it offers no right to family reunion,
an exclusion that seriously limits the ability of this group to rebuild their
lives in the country of settlement. Humanitarian status has usually been
renewable, while temporary protection measures have become increasingly
time limited. The trend across Europe has been to reduce the rights of

asylum seekers (those making individual claims for refugee status), in relation to welfare and to security of residence, and to increase detention and deportation.

Immigration legislation has also led to a growing disparity between the rights of labour migrants with settled status and those with temporary or insecure status. New forms of labour migration allow the state to retain "the economic benefits of migration labour while divesting itself of its social cost" (Fekete, 1997, p 1). A common feature has been the casualisation of labour contracts with the removal of permanent rights of residence, and the reduction in social rights. Changes have also occurred in the conditions of family reunion. Those entering under this status (primarily women) are barred from 'recourse to public funds' (welfare benefits), while in many states they are prevented from taking up employment. These conditions impose severe dependency, preventing independent access to income, and force many into informal employment (Kofman et al, 2000). The pattern of change in relation to family reunion has been uneven, for example, Germany has reduced the period during which family members' residence status is dependent on the applicant, but overall more demanding conditions have been imposed.

The changes summarised above have intensified differences between different groups of migrants, creating a widening gap between the rights of the most precarious migrants and those of long-term secure residents. Access to rights is, however, dependent not merely on formal status but also on social divisions based on gender, class, ethnicity, and so on. Restrictive policies on entry at European and national level have had differential impacts on different groups and in different states. The two states discussed in more detail later have introduced policies that have both ratified EU policy, and in many cases gone beyond it.

Migration policy in Britain: from colonial migration to control

Britain's immigration policy has been traditionally preoccupied with control of entry. In the aftermath of the Second World War, mass labour immigration, predominantly from the Commonwealth as part of the decolonisation process, led to significant settlement of ethnic communities, with full citizenship rights. The early politicisation of migration, however, led to a series of measures beginning with the 1962 Commonwealth Immigrants Act, which restricted entry, particularly from the 'old' Commonwealth (Shutter, 1997). With Britain's entry into the Common Market (later the EU), there were attempts to switch labour recruitment towards Europe. Work permits became more difficult for Commonwealth citizens to obtain (Fekete, 1997, p 3) and the conditions attached to them more stringent. Rights to benefits, including Child Benefit, were removed from work permit holders in 1996, and the 1999 Immigration and Asylum Act removed the right to all non-contributory benefits from 'persons subject to immigration control'[6]. In spite of these restrictions, there remains a heavy reliance on immigration from outside the EU in key sectors such as healthcare professions. The announcement of an expansion of work permits in 2001 marked a belated recognition of this dependence, but with the focus of the debate on immigration policy on asylum seekers, this announcement went largely unremarked, and with business supporting increasing openness to labour migration, this was not opposed by the Conservatives in parliament.

Immigration policy since the early 1990s has been dominated by asylum. Until then, Britain had no specific asylum legislation. The Geneva Convention was ratified in 1954, but no legislation was passed to anchor it in domestic law (Schuster and Solomos, 1999, p 57). The first act dealing specifically with this issue was, like other immigration legislation, concerned primarily with controlling entry. The 1993 Immigration and Asylum Appeals Act and the 1996 Immigration and Asylum Act, also restricted social rights of asylum seekers. Labour's 1999 Immigration and Asylum Act, which came into effect in April 2000, extended powers to search and arrest, and to detain asylum seekers. The most controversial clauses concerned the arrangements for social support. The government expressed its determination to reduce the incentive to economic migrants to use the asylum route to enter Britain (Finch, 2001, p 17) and it replaced cash benefits for all asylum seekers with 'vouchers', which asylum seekers must use to make purchases in designated supermarkets. This measure, combined with compulsory dispersal to locations outside London and the South East – often to areas without existing communities of fellow nationals, or even significant migrant or minority ethnic communities – has separated asylum seekers from mainstream society, making them more visible as a group. It also underlined their dependence on welfare benefits, fuelling public perceptions of them as a 'burden'. This created a new social category of 'asylum seeker' increasingly separated in terms of formal rights and official discourse from 'genuine' (that is, recognised) refugees (Sales, 2002).

Welfare provision has thus shifted to the centre of current debate around asylum. Restrictions on social support for asylum seekers coincided with a restructuring of welfare which has made it easier to exclude those deemed 'undeserving'. Service providers have been drawn into scrutinising immigration status (Owers, 1994), a scrutiny that often goes beyond legal requirements. The British Medical Association's ethics committee commented in 1997 "all asylum seekers have the right to be registered with an NHS doctor and therefore there is no obligation or expectation for doctors to check the immigration status of people registering to join their lists" (cited in Coker, 2001, p 38).

These measures provoked strong opposition from a range of organisations, including trades unions, and statutory and voluntary service providers. In response, Home Secretary David Blunkett announced in October 2001 a "fundamental reform of our asylum and immigration policy"[7]. The new proposals include a phasing out of the voucher scheme and its replacement with 'reception centres', which would provide board and lodging. The Refugee Council, while welcoming the commitment to end the voucher scheme, criticised the emphasis on streamlining support structures and on the 'control and tracking' of asylum seekers while their claims are processed (Refugee Council, 2001, p 1). The development of reception centres is, however, likely to represent a further step towards the separation of asylum seekers from mainstream society.

Italy: from emigration to immigration

Although Italy has the fourth highest population of non-EU citizens in Europe, the public perception of immigration to Italy, both abroad and in Italy itself, is of illegality and marginalisation. During the 1970s, Italy started the transition from emigration to immigration, and in the 1990s and 2000s is in the process of a second transformation, from a country of transit towards northern Europe, a 'trampoline' (Petrillo, 1999), to a country of settled immigration. The 2001 edition of the *Immigrazione: Dossier statistico*, the authoritative analysis of immigration trends by Caritas di Rome, reflects this in its subtitle 'the age of integration' (Caritas, 2001).

The Italian model of immigration in the 1970s shared many characteristics with other Mediterranean states (Pugliese, 2000, p 797). There was a heavy preponderance of irregularity, and most migrants who entered in this period have experienced some form of irregularity or precarious status. This was accompanied by official 'toleration' of undocumented migration, which was treated not as a crime but as an 'administrative irregularity'. Entry was facilitated by the long seacoast, which made the border difficult to police. Without a comprehensive immigration policy, new legislation was enacted in response to emergencies during the 1980s and early 1990s and involved regularisation (*sanitoria*) of resident irregular migrants and control of entry, which created a variety of statuses (Morris, 2001). A high degree of sectoral concentration developed in the migrant labour force: men are concentrated in agriculture and petty manufacturing, and women in services, particularly domestic services. Immigrant women are over represented in prostitution, much of it involving coercion and trafficking (Carchedi et al, 2000). Immigrants had severely restricted access to state welfare, with heavy reliance on the voluntary sector (both religious and secular), while the precarious legal and social status of the majority limited political and civil rights.

This model began to change during the 1980s, as settled migrant communities developed. Nearly a quarter of registered immigrants have been resident for over ten years (Caritas, 2000, p 169). With Italy's birth rate among the lowest in Europe and social changes creating gaps in the labour market (Pugliese, 2000), Italy has recognised the need for continuing labour migration. As migration has become a structural, rather than a temporary, feature of Italian society, this has raised the question of the terms on which these communities will be integrated into Italian society, and the deficit in the rights of foreign residents. At the same time, with the increase in asylum seeking during the 1980s, there has been pressure to seal its border, since Italy is seen as the 'weak link' in the EU's defences; the gateway to northern Europe.

A new law, the *Legge Turco Napolitano, 1998* passed under the centre left government that preceded Berlusconi's election in 2001, was an attempt to respond to this situation through a comprehensive policy. It had three main aims (Bonetti, 1998):

- the control of irregular migration through increased detention and expulsion;
- a planned programme of labour immigration;
- the integration of legal migrants through new local and national institutions; increased social rights (particularly in health where all migrants regardless of status are now entitled to basic care); anti-discrimination legislation; and increased security of residence for legal migrants.

The law thus widened the gap between the rights of different categories of migrant, with legal migrants gaining access to the same rights as Italians in some areas, while 'clandestine' migrants are subject to increased controls. Implementation has, however, focused largely on the repressive aspects; integration policies have been left largely to local initiatives and activity has been uneven (Caritas, 2000), while the implementation of the provisions concerning residence rights has been slow. The legislation excluded reference to citizenship, which remains based largely on *ius sanguinis* (Zincone, 2000). In 1992 the minimum residence qualification was increased from five to ten years.

Asylum was also excluded and legislation on this issue, approved by the senate in 1998, is still held up in parliament. The constitution guarantees the right to asylum for those unable to exercise their democratic rights in their own country. A series of Temporary Protection measures were instituted for groups in need of humanitarian protection, for example Bosnians, Kosovans and Kurds (Hein, 2000). These allowed people to work, and generally to convert their status to labour migrant. These temporary protection measures have now ended, and refugees from Kosovo and Turkey must now make individual claims for asylum to the National Commission on Asylum. Asylum seekers are entitled to a small monthly allowance and to a place in a reception centre for 45 days. Since cases generally take up to a year to be decided, many people are largely dependent on the voluntary sector for support. In 2001, in anticipation of the proposed legislation, a National Programme for Asylum was established for the reception, integration and voluntary repatriation of asylum seekers, involving a network of reception centres run by voluntary sector and local state bodies and financed partly through the EU. This programme, however, is limited, both in the number of places available and the period people can remain in the centres.

In spite of Italy's undoubted transformation to a country of settled immigration, and the new comprehensive legislation, many features of the 1970s model remain. In particular there is continuing 'tolerance' of undocumented migrants who gain de facto rights, especially through employment, while many with the right to stay (for example, asylum seekers) have minimal access to social rights (Ruspini, 2001) and are excluded from the formal labour market. There remains a heavy reliance on the voluntary sector for welfare, particularly in relation to health (Geraci et al, 2000).

Civic stratification and exclusion

Our research in London and Rome, which focused on the communities from Turkey and the former Yugoslavia, highlighted the variety of processes of exclusion faced by migrants, and the range of strategies that they employ to overcome them. The structure of the groups in the two cities was very different, particularly those from Turkey. In London, the group included long-established labour migrants, those entering through family reunion, as well as refugees and asylum seekers. There is a well-established network of community organisations and community businesses. However, migrants from Turkey in Rome are almost exclusively Kurdish refugees, predominantly single men. The population is much smaller than in London and extremely mobile, since people usually move north after their case has been decided. Though legally present in Italy, their social conditions are extremely precarious and there is no significant established community in Rome to support them. The communities from former Yugoslavia in both cities are generally less visible and the community organisations weaker. There has been some labour migration, but the majority are spontaneous or programme refugees. In Rome, there is a large population of *Roma* who are seen as largely distinct from migrants or refugees in institutional and policy terms. The majority live in squalid camps (ERRC, 2000) and perceive themselves as the most discriminated against group in Italian society.

The diverse nature of the communities meant that migratory experiences and motives for migration were also diverse, including political and economic motives and family reasons. A striking feature was the dynamic nature of migratory strategies, and the blurring of the boundaries between political and economic motives for migration. The diversity of statuses of our interviewees gave them different sets of rights, but their ability to access these was also influenced by their own personal histories, class position, and so on. Those with greater 'cultural capital' – education, employment experience and language ability – were better able to build a new life, even if along very different lines from the one they had left. But personal circumstances were also important: one Bosnian woman graduate had been able to retrain and take up professional employment in Rome, while her sister, another graduate who arrived at the same time, was confined to menial jobs.

In spite of the diversity of the communities, some common themes emerged in relation to the problems they faced. We can distinguish between immediate problems faced on arrival, short-term and longer-term needs. In very general terms, new arrivals are preoccupied with basic needs for shelter, subsistence and safety. Our work suggested that health problems for example, particularly mental health, often do not appear in this first phase. Similarly acquiring language may not be a priority, beyond a basic level, until some security, legal and social, has been established. Once some form of settlement has begun, language becomes crucial as a means to employment, while health problems often emerge. One interviewee in London had suffered and been successfully treated for depression after he had achieved refugee status and was no longer preoccupied with the day-to-day struggle for survival. This distinction applies particularly to refugees for whom migration was involuntary, generally with little planning or knowledge of their destination. In the longer run, as people start to build a new life in the country of migration, a new set of issues is raised. Employment becomes about more than survival, it may mean rebuilding a career or developing a new one; and language needs are deeper, determining the ability to participate in society. Some with children born or brought up in exile spoke of the children as the future that they themselves had lost, but for these children the future was seen as being in London or Rome. This raises the question of citizenship, not just in the legal sense, but the wider set of social, political and civic rights associated with citizenship, and the sense of belonging to the society.

The main problems noted in all three cities were similar, although due to the precarious nature of the groups, these tended to be more acute in Rome. They concerned language and employment (discussed in more detail later), legal status, welfare benefits, housing and health. For the most recent arrivals legal status was precarious, and several Kurdish and Kosovan asylum seekers were awaiting a result on their asylum claim or appealing a refusal. This caused high levels of anxiety. Many *Roma* people in Rome, even after many years in Italy had uncertain legal status. Those who arrived during the Bosnian crisis, for example, often did not have humanitarian status like other Bosnians: in some cases this was a result of discrimination by the authorities, while others had preferred not to participate in the process and had joined family already living in camps in Italy. Because of legal and informal exclusion from employment, many asylum seekers and other migrants were dependent on benefits or illegal work. Access to benefits has become more strictly conditional on legal status, while lack of language and familiarity with the system was also a barrier to access. Many lived in substandard private housing, especially in the early years. In London asylum legislation in 1996 prevented asylum seekers from being housed in permanent local authority accommodation. In Rome, the limit on the period that asylum seekers can remain in reception centres forces many onto the streets or into dependence on the poorly developed community networks. Barred from public housing, many other migrants were living in overcrowded conditions. Mental health problems were prevalent, particularly among refugees and asylum seekers in London. This was related to trauma and sometimes feelings of guilt following experiences in the homeland, but also to insecurity and isolation in Europe.

Language

Language emerged as a key issue for all our participants. In general the language skills of people from the former Yugoslavia (except Kosovans, the most recent migrants) were greater than those of the Turkish and Kurdish speaking populations, especially in Rome. In London, competence among the Turkish and Kurdish participants ranged from complete fluency to virtually no ability to speak English, even for some who had lived there for many years. Complex attitudes were expressed about the motives for learning the local language. For some it marked an acknowledgement that they were staying, at least for the foreseeable future and therefore represented some kind of defeat. Nevertheless, all our interviewees acknowledged the importance of acquiring the local language. As one Kurd in Italy said, "without the language you are nothing".

The ability to learn to speak a language is affected by gender, class, age, educational level, and so on. Many immigrants from both communities had suffered significant downward mobility in terms of income and status, but those with previous education and experience of study were able to acquire the new language more easily and build a new life. Those with low educational attainment were unused to independent study. This was particularly a problem for Kurdish and Kosovan refugees, many of whom had suffered interrupted education in their home country. Some had attended language classes but given up since they complained that they were too infrequent and they were unable to progress during the intervals between classes. Women, often more isolated and with less contact outside the home, found language acquisition more difficult, while children and young adults learnt more quickly than older people. In both cities asylum seekers were entitled to language classes, although the provision was uneven and inadequate. For many, however, their precarious legal status was a barrier to learning. They did not feel settled and felt it was not worth learning if their stay was going to be short. For some of our interviewees, the experience of torture or imprisonment, or feelings of guilt and anxiety about family left behind meant that they felt unable to concentrate on study. For others, the need to earn income – often through informal work – left little time for study.

Language ability is central to the enjoyment of other rights and the possibilities for integration – for employment, social life, access to services and to a sense of belonging. Many were unaware of their rights in relation to services, and had problems in communicating with service providers. Some people used their children as interpreters, but this could cause problems as parents' dependence placed a heavy responsibility on the children. Inability to speak the local language also reinforces isolation and undermines confidence. In London one refugee said, "I felt like a newborn baby". Many live their lives largely within their community, establishing long-term dependence on other members who are able to act as interpreters and mediators.

The issue of language achieved a high political profile in Britain during 2001, with the announcement that the government is considering proposals to make language classes compulsory for asylum seekers and other migrants. Our research suggests that this would be counterproductive. It would not address the problems that prevent people learning, but on the contrary, compulsion would tend to reinforce them. Compulsion is also unnecessary, since people are keen to learn, provided that tuition is accessible and at appropriate levels. The real problem is not lack of demand for language classes, but lack of resources.

Employment

Employment is often the key to income and other social rights, but also to regaining status and self-esteem and a sense of belonging in the country of immigration. Some of our interviewees had achieved a status commensurate with the one they had left, often through retraining, but most people, particularly in Rome, had experienced periods of unemployment and undocumented work. High levels of unemployment and underemployment were experienced in both cities in both communities, especially among women and older people.

Obstacles to employment take many forms, both formal and informal, and are closely tied to legal status. At one end of the spectrum is complete exclusion from the labour market. This applies to all asylum seekers in Italy, while in the UK they can apply for permission to work after six months. Dependants entering through family migration are also forbidden to work in Italy in the first year of residence. In Italy, public sector employment is restricted to citizens (nationals and EU). This is particularly problematic in Rome where the public sector is the largest employer in the formal sector; one trades union official interviewed described it as "the most serious discrimination against immigrants". This discrimination would be outlawed under a proposed EU directive on the rights of long-term resident third country nationals that is currently awaiting approval from EU states. A third barrier is non-recognition of overseas professional qualifications and experience. Many of our interviewees were forced to study for long periods to regain their professional status, while others abandoned their former discipline and retrained. At the other end of the scale are more informal barriers, including discrimination and stereotyping by employers.

The impact of these obstacles was de-skilling and unemployment, temporary or longer term. Many professional people had retrained into new areas. In many cases this involved work with the community groups as advice workers, mediators and interpreters. A key area of concern was the *ghettoisation* of immigrants into 'community' jobs. Many others worked illegally, often in extremely insecure and underpaid jobs. One interviewee in London reported that his wages doubled when he gained refugee status, while in Rome, interviewees talked of the 'immigrant wage', half of the standard rate. In Rome, the majority of *Roma* people, unable to seek formal work, survive through begging, busking on the metro and other marginal activities. In London, many from Turkey work in community-related businesses, thus increasing dependence on the community and impeding language skills.

A large number of our interviewees took part in voluntary activities within the community or with broader groups of migrants. These activities included teaching and organising language classes, providing advice on migrant rights, counselling survivors of trauma, and organising cultural events. This activity often acted as a bridge between their own community and the wider society, and allowed them to develop skills and experience that were, in several cases, later used in paid employment, both within the community and outside. Our interviews suggested that individual and collective agency could make a real difference to the acquisition of rights.

Conclusion

Current developments in migration policy are producing a growing gap between long-term residents, those with various kinds of temporary residence or protection, asylum seekers and the undocumented. In Britain and Italy, the avowed purposes of recent legislation has been to reduce the numbers of undocumented migrants and asylum seekers and thus to reduce the pool of insecure migrants. In Italy, there has been an attempt to replace clandestine flows with managed migration, but bureaucratic procedures have created a proliferation of legal statuses (Morris, 2001), while the projected numbers of labour migrants have been too low to tackle the problem of illegal entrants. Britain has belatedly recognised its dependence on immigrant labour and extended the issuing of visas, while implementing restrictive policies towards asylum seekers. These have not, however, reduced the flows of asylum seekers, which have continued to follow political and economic crises in the country of origin and to be absorbed into informal labour markets. The impact of these policies, therefore, has been to increase the number of insecure residents. Current policies represent an assertion of state sovereignty in the management of migration, and the selection of those who may enter the national territory. Asylum seekers and the undocumented who evade these selection processes are treated increasingly harshly, while they are prevented from joining the formal labour market even while labour shortages create demands for new migration. With social inclusion associated in policy terms with labour market participation, this group is placed outside the bounds of the 'includable'.

Long-term third country residents may eventually acquire rights almost on a par with European citizens. The restrictions on access to benefits, however, which increasingly apply to labour and family migrants, underlines the continuing importance of formal citizenship status in securing these rights. At the other end of the scale, the growth in undocumented migration is creating a population that is tolerated but barred from participating fully in society. The restrictive legislation in Britain in relation to access to employment and welfare for the undocumented and asylum seekers has forced them to rely increasingly on their own communities and charities. In Italy, the 1998 legislation gave some new minimum rights to all migrants, especially in relation to health, but the limited nature of social support for asylum seekers and other insecure migrants has forced many into extreme destitution and dependence on charity. In both cities, the majority of these groups are likely to remain resident for the foreseeable future. The processes of social exclusion that they experience will have long-term implications for them, their families and for the society in which they now live.

Notes

[1] A conference in October 2001 on *The business case for immigration* organised by the United Kingdom Race Equality Network attracted business leaders as well as researchers and campaigners. The British magazine *Personnel Management* launched a campaign in 2001 to ease the restrictions on asylum seekers.

[2] This project, *Civic stratification, exclusion and migrant trajectories in three European states* was funded by the Economic and Social Research Council through its *One Europe or Several* programme. The principal researchers were Eleonore Kofman (Nottingham Trent University), Cathie Lloyd (Oxford University) and Rosemary Sales (Middlesex University) with Giuliana Candia (Parsec, Rome).

[3] Citizenship is traditionally acquired through *ius soli*, that is, through birth on the national territory, or *ius sanguinis*, that is, birth to a national (that is existing members of the national group). The most common way for non-nationals to acquire citizenship is through marriage.

[4] The imposition of fines by the UK government on drivers and transport companies for bringing asylum seekers into the UK has now been deemed contrary to the EU's human rights legislation.

[5] The Geneva Convention defines refugees as persons who are outside their country because of a well-founded fear of persecution for reasons of race, religion, nationality, membership of a particular social group or political opinion.

[6] This includes non-European Economic Area nationals whose leave to remain is conditional.

[7] Statement to the House of Commons, 29 October 2001.

References

Ackers, L. (1998) *Shifting spaces: Women, citizenship and migration within the European Union*, Bristol: The Policy Press.

Bonetti, P. (1998) 'La nouvelle loi italienne sur l'immigration', *Migrations Societe*, vol 10/57.

Carchedi, F., Picciolini, A., Mottura, G. and Campani, G. (eds) (2000) *I colori della notte*, Milan: Franco Angeli.

Caritas di Roma (2000) *Immigrazione: Dossier statistico 2000*, Rome: Anterem.

Caritas di Roma (2001) *Immigrazione: Dossier statistico 2001*, Rome: Anterem.

Castles, S. and Davidson, A. (2000) *Citizenship and migration: Globalization and the politics of belonging*, Basingstoke: Macmillan.

Castles, S. and Miller, M. (1993) *The age of migration*, Basingstoke: Macmillan.

Castles, S. and Miller, M. (1998) *The age of migration* (2nd edn), Basingstoke: Macmillan.

Coker, J. (2001) 'Access to health, employment and education', in Immigration Law Practitioners' Association *Asylum seekers: a guide to recent legislation*, London: ILPA/Resource Information Service, pp 38-43.

Duke, K., Sales, R. and Gregory, J. (1999) 'Refugee resettlement in Europe', in A. Bloch and C. Levy (eds) *Refugees, citizenship and social policy in Britain and Europe*, Basingstoke: Macmillan, pp 105-31.

ERRC (European Roma Rights Center) (2000) *Campland: Racial segregation of Roma in Italy*, Country Report series, No 9, Budapest: ERRC.

Esping-Andersen, G. (1990) *The three worlds of welfare capitalism*, Cambridge: Polity Press.

Fekete, L. (1997) 'Blackening the economy: the path to convergence', *Race and Class*, vol 39, no 1, pp 1-17.

Finch, N. (2001) 'The support and dispersal of asylum seekers', in Immigration Law Practitioners' Association *Asylum seekers: a guide to recent legislation*, London: ILPA/Resource Information Service, pp 17-25.

Geddes, A. (2000) *Immigration and European integration: Towards fortress Europe?*, Manchester: Manchester University Press.

Geraci, S., Marceca, M. and Mazzetti, M. (2000) 'Migrazioni e salute in Italia', in Agenzia Roma per la preparazione del Giubileo *Migrazioni. Scenari per il XXI secolo*, Convengno internazionale 12-14 luglio, Dossier di ricerca, vol II, pp 1298-355.

Hein, C. (2000) 'Italy: Gateway to Europe, but not the gatekeeper?', in J. Van Selm (ed) *Kosovo's refugees in the European Union*, London and New York: Pinter, pp 139-61.

HMSO (1999) *Immigration and Asylum Act, 1999*, London: The Stationery Office.

Kofman, E. and Sales, R. (1996) 'The geography of gender and welfare in the new Europe', in M.D. Garcia Ramon and J. Monk (eds) *South and North: Women's work and daily lives in the European Community*, London: Routledge, pp 31-60.

Kofman, E., Phizacklea, A., Raghuram, P. and Sales, R. (2000) *Gender, migration and welfare in Europe*, London: Routledge.

Kofman, E., Lloyd, C. and Sales, R. (2002: forthcoming) *Civic stratification and migrant trajectories in three European cities*, End of award report, ESRC award no L213252016, London: ESRC.

Leibfried, S. (1993) 'Conceptualising European social policy: the EC as social actor', in L.L. Hantrais and S. Mangen (eds) *The policy making process and the social actors*, Cross National Research Papers, third series, Loughborough: European Research: University of Loughborough, vol 3, no 1, pp 5-14.

MacGregor, S. (1999) 'Welfare, neo-liberalism and new paternalism: three ways for social policy in late capitalist societies', *Capital and Class*, vol 67, Spring, pp 91-118.

Marshall, T.H. (1950) *Citizenship and social class*, Cambridge: Cambridge University Press.

Morris, L. (1997) 'A cluster of contradictions: the politics of migration in the European Union', *New Community*, vol 19, no 3, pp 459-84.

Morris, L. (2001) 'The ambiguous terrain of rights: civic stratification in Italy's emergent immigration regime', *International Journal of Urban and Regional Research*, vol 25, pp 497-516.

Owers, A. (1994) 'The age of internal controls?', in S. Spencer (ed) *Strangers and citizens: A positive approach to migrants and refugees*, London: Rivers Oram Press, pp 264-81.

Petrillo, A. (1999) 'Italy: Farewell to the 'Bel Paese'?', in R. Dale and M. Cole (eds) *European Union and migration labour*, Oxford: Berg, pp 231-62.

Phizacklea, A. (1998) 'Migration and globalization: a feminist perspective', in K. Koser and H. Lutz *The new migration in Europe*, Basingstoke: Macmillan, pp 21-38.

Pugliese, E. (2000) 'L'Italia tra migrazioni internazionali e migrazione interne', in Agenzia Roma per la preparazione del Giubileo *Migrazioni. Scenari per il XXI secolo* Convengno internazionale 12-14 luglio, Dossier di ricerca, pp 751-81.

Refugee Council (2001) *The Home Secretary's asylum proposals, October 2001*, Refugee Council Briefing, London: Refugee Council.

Ruspini, P. (2001) 'Irregolari: alla ricerca del capro espiatorio', *IMSU informa*, vol 27, no 26, Milan: Fondazione Cariplo, pp 10-11.

Sales, R. (2002: forthcoming) 'The deserving and the undeserving? Refugees, asylum seekers and welfare in Britain', *Critical Social Policy*, vol 22, no 1 (in press).

Sassen, S. (1991) *The global city: New York, London, Tokyo*, Princeton, NJ: Princeton University Press.

Sassen, S. (1996) 'New employment regimes in cities: the impact on migrant workers', *New Community*, vol 22, no 4, pp 579-94.

Schuster, L. and Solomos, J. (1999) 'The politics of refugee and asylum policies in Britain: historical patterns and contemporary realities', in A. Bloch and C. Levy (eds) *Refugees, citizenship and social policy in Europe*, Basingstoke: Macmillan, pp 51-75.

Shutter, S. (1997) *Immigration, nationality and refugee law handbook: A user's guide*, London: Joint Council for the Welfare of Immigrants.

Soysal, Y. (1994) *Limits of citizenship: Migrants and postnational membership in Europe*, Chicago, IL: University of Chicago Press.

Zincone, G. (2000) 'Immigrati: quali politiche per l'integrazione?', *Il Mulino* 387, January-February, pp 80-91.

NINE

The European Union's social policy focus: from labour to welfare and constitutionalised rights?

Monica Threlfall

One of the perennial frustrations for social policy specialists interested in Europe used to be sauntering through the maze of EU institutions, laws and policies only to miraculously arrive at the exit without ever passing anything that looked recognisably like social policy, and to be left wondering how they missed it. Much had been written about the possible Europeanisation of the welfare state, so why did it prove elusive to pin down in hard, let alone legal, copy? All this began to change with the treaty amendments of the 1990s, but even then the casual browser through the myriad Europa.eu.int websites would have found most documents with any legal validity (such as treaty titles or directives and recommendations) on education, health or social protection to be high sounding, yet flimsy on policy-prescriptive substance. The reason is that social policy in the context of European integration has had the meaning of labour policy more than broader social welfare policy. EU social policy developments have consequently focused in the past on the needs of workers – both female and male – and on employment-related problems.

There is a growing awareness that the labour focus of social policy has changed to become more inclusive. Indeed social protection is now a subtitle of the Commission's Employment and Social Affairs 'major concerns' list. But it is not easy to assess how far the EU has really shifted attention towards the social welfare of citizens in general. Does the fact that the Nice Presidency summit of heads of state in December 2000 adopted a social agenda that vows to prevent and eradicate poverty and modernise and improve social protection, mean citizens are going to see action that directly affects them? Did the endorsement of a Charter of Fundamental Rights represent a definitive coming of age of social policy in Europe? Is there now a strong legal base to matters traditionally associated with welfare states and falling within the purview of the discipline of social policy, as opposed to labour rights and the working environment? Or are those Charter chapters engagingly entitled 'Equality' and 'Solidarity' still only vague intentions with little chance of development? Is EU social policy moving from its 'labourist' origins to a more 'welfarist' character?

Before discussing the very recent developments and assessing the current situation, this chapter will review the historic milestones in collective decisions made by the member states that have cumulatively developed the social *acquis communautaire* – the body of laws that all applicant states must adopt to become full members. Such decisions form the precedents that gradually provide 'European' legitimacy to major social issues. These then gain a place in the Community's current social agenda, in a consolidated treaty, in a Charter and eventually in a future Constitution for Europe. Our approach aims to bridge the gap between the labourist and the welfarist understandings of social policy, while emphasising developments in the latter, for reasons of space.

Developments at treaty level: the 'green lights' for action

Despite the original aim of building an economic community, Part 1 of the 1957 Treaty of Rome entitled 'Principles' manifested the nascent Community's commitments to maintaining a high level of social protection for workers, to increasing standards of living and the quality of life, as well as to improving living conditions. Such expressions of concern are usually found in labour-related contexts rather than constituting stand alone objectives in themselves, especially in the early decades of European integration. In line with this, the Treaty of Rome's specific facilitating articles in 'Part 3, Title III on Social Policy' did not in fact provide a clear legal basis for any initiatives connected with welfare matters. The Title was short and Article 118 restricted the fields in which the Commission was to act, merely to promote *cooperation* between member states, all of which refer to the world of employment rather than the broader social policies.

Article 118 establishing the European Communities (Treaty of Rome):

> ... the Commission shall have as its task the promotion of close co-operation between member-states in the social field, particularly in matters relating to: -employment; -labour law and working conditions; -basic and advanced vocational training; -social security; -prevention

of occupational accidents and diseases; -occupational hygiene; -the right of association, and collective bargaining between employers and workers[1].

Even cooperation over social security was only to refer to Community migrant workers. Nevertheless the historic Article 119 (now 141) on equal pay was to prove that the European legal order could be ahead of its time, and was to provide the green light for the Commission's subsequent equality actions – although only once it had had its consciousness raised by feminist advocates (Hoskyns, 1996). For the Council of Ministers of the European Economic Community, as it was then called, adopted virtually no 'legal instruments' (legally valid, though not necessarily binding policies or decisions) to develop the potential role of the Commission in any of the above-mentioned areas for well over a decade until the mid-1970s, with the exception of measures to facilitate the free movement of workers. The first directives concerned the procedures to be followed in the case of companies wishing to make collective redundancies; the protection of workers' acquired rights where their employers transfer the undertaking to another owner; and the three historic sex equality directives on equal pay, equal treatment and social security (for a full list, see Appendix to this chapter).

Not until the launch in the mid-1980s of Commission President Jacques Delors' new vision of a greater social dimension to the integration project and the ensuing initiative to bestow some guiding social principles on the EEC does one detect an interest in the kind of social policies that affect the well being of people in general, in the form of the Community Charter of Fundamental Rights. Examples of such groups are the elderly, the young, the excluded, in addition to rights for workers already firmly in the labour market, whether male or female. Women's rights as a gender and not just as workers, had not yet been recognised, let alone adopted as policy, despite the European Parliament women's committee's pioneering reports on a variety of aspects of 'the feminine condition', as it was still called.

The 1989 Community Charter of Fundamental Rights of Workers (see Gold, 1993, pp 221-7 for full text) can be said to be the EEC's first move towards the public adoption of a set of social welfare policies insofar as it gave rights to social protection to "persons who have no means of subsistence" and "any person who has reached retirement age" and "all disabled persons", while endorsing the "protection of children and adolescents". Had it been incorporated into the treaty, it would have moved the EEC markedly away from an economic community towards one manifesting concerns typical of a welfare state, or at least a state with social-democratic leanings. However, it was not to be, due largely to British objections. Even though this Charter remained non-binding, the Commission continued to request that each member state report periodically on progress towards the goals set out therein (for example, European Commission, 1996). Furthermore, the principles embedded in it, if not the rights, have arguably been developed in a piecemeal fashion by directives and by later treaty amendments, as well as by a growing social philosophy which the Commission has generated through policy documents, comparative social research and the growth of a community of advocates and non-governmental organisations (NGOs) promoting social policy, such as the European Social Forum (1999).

The Maastricht summit of December 1991 marked a new departure and therefore a milestone in the growing status of social policies. Despite the UK's struggle to slow down or even prevent the development of social policy-making initiatives, the new Treaty on European Union (TEU) adopted at Maastricht nevertheless contained new Titles which suggested the 'Europeanisation' of areas such as education and youth policy (in its Title VIII, Chapter 3: Education, Vocational Training and Youth) and public health (Title X Public Health), though the wording of these specified that no harmonisation measures bringing member state laws into harmony were to be initiated. Thus the Commission's role in education was circumscribed to the added-value aspect of the 'European dimension' of education and did not (and still does not) impinge on curricular issues, educational philosophies or education systems. Its role in public health similarly excluded individual healthcare and healthcare systems, limiting itself to major public health questions, such as the frontierless health scourges of smoking and drugs[2]. The UK approved the TEU, so refraining from blocking the expansion of EU competencies where these were limited in their scope, but it did block the adoption of a redrafted and reinforced Title on social policy that was to have reflected the aims of the Community Charter of Fundamental Rights more closely.

The rejected draft title ended up as an appendix to the treaty, known as the Agreement on Social Policy. It was approved by the remaining 11 member states who were willing to see the expansion of Commission and Council prerogatives in the social field, to the point of taking on board a further, hitherto marginal, area of concern, namely poverty ('social exclusion'). They also made it easier for decisions to be taken in the Council of Ministers by qualified majority voting (QMV) for equality between men and women (with regard to employment matters), and on the integration of persons excluded from the labour market, in addition to the existing mainstream policies on working conditions and health and safety.

Paradoxically, the renamed European Union's (EU) next formal steps into the field of welfare and integration of the excluded – a Council Recommendation that specifically committed member states to certain welfare policies – were approved by John Major's government with Norman Lamont as chief signatory, and with the UK occupying the Presidency of the EU at the time. In the *Council Recommendation on common criteria concerning sufficient resources and social assistance in social protection systems*, member states agreed to ensure that all legal residents are to have access to healthcare, access to vocational training of some kind and are given sufficient resources 'in keeping with human dignity' (Council of Ministers, 1992a).

A further point of significance for social policy regarding the Maastricht Treaty agreements was that they consolidated European citizenship rights, confirming in particular the expansion of free movement rights beyond 'workers' and their 'dependants' to virtually all categories of persons, including students, pensioners and jobseekers (for details, see Appendix). While such rights did not directly involve rights to welfare in other countries or any EU social protection harmonisation, they were, in time, to lead the EU to take up numerous further social policy questions such as:

- the rights of free movers (also called intra-community migrants) to social security benefits and to housing support schemes in other member states;
- the exportability of pensions and access to benefits in kind for older people (such as meals on wheels, reduced entry to museums, cheaper travel, and so on);
- students' expanded choices of universities to study at, and their rights regarding fees, grants and scholarships;
- the recognition of all kinds of higher education qualifications generally;
- free movers' access to healthcare while temporarily or permanently settled in another member state.

Most of these issues were dealt with as questions of equal rights between different EU nationals; in other words, as issues of equal treatment and non-discrimination rather than of improving living conditions for all, as the original Community principles had stated in the Treaty of Rome. This raft of new social policy decisions taken by the Council and the European Court of Justice (ECJ) were thus *not* fundamentally about member states losing their prerogatives in any field by transferring responsibility up to the supranational level. They did not involve the actual 'Europeanisation' of social policies, only their wider application to include more varieties of movers from other parts of the EU.

The Treaty of Amsterdam, adopted by the heads of state and government in 1997[3], marked another milestone in the status of social policies in general. It also introduced a new form of member state coordination over employment policy. The main new elements in the area of civil and social rights were as follows. The status of gender equality was raised to become a main goal of the EU (articulated in Article 2), and positive action to advance sex equality was allowed (Article 141). A new article (6A, consolidated as Article 13) widely banned discrimination on the grounds of sex, racial or ethnic origin, religion or belief, disability, age or sexual orientation, and allows the Community to take action to combat it, although only via unanimity in the Council of Ministers. The declaration on the death penalty, while not being prescriptive, states that it is rejected by all member states. Finally, the wording on European citizenship rights was strengthened, confirming more clearly that all have the right to reside in any member state, not just workers.

Title XI 'Social Policy, Education, Vocational Training and Youth' became the new 'social chapter', confirming the Union's commitment to promoting employment and improved living and working conditions (Article 136). Combating exclusion was now recognised as legitimate Community activity. In addition, the Commission was to encourage cooperation between member states and facilitate coordination of their action in all social fields, reporting annually on their progress in achieving the goals of Article 136 – an indication that the EU has moved beyond good intentions to exerting gentle pressure on member states. In addition, the Commission's role in pan-European labour relations facilitation agreements between the major actors (employers and trades union organisations), which had been launched by the Single European Act of 1986, is reiterated in a stronger form. However, the Amsterdam agreements hardly strengthened the Commission's competence in the fields of education, healthcare or social protection established in Maastricht. However, the Consumer Protection title (XI – now XIV) was boosted with the addition of a Community commitment 'to promote the interests' and to 'protecting the health, safety and economic interests' of consumers in a way that allows the Commission a freer hand (Article 129A, now 153).

A marked innovation at Amsterdam, which launched the member states into extensively coordinated activities, was the new Title VIII on

'Employment' dealing mainly with job creation and 'active' labour market policies. As a result, member states, the Council of Ministers and the Commission are now to develop a coordinated strategy (known as the open method of coordination) with a view to contribute to a 'high level of employment'. This is a policy-prescriptive method of operation in which the European Council (the summit of heads of state and government) approves the broad strategy and more specific Guidelines drawn up by the Commission. Member states respond with their own National Action Plans and then report on their progress in implementing the Guidelines to the Commission. Mutual scrutiny takes place in the Council. Member states may even be given recommendations (one could almost say ticked off) for not responding adequately.

Labour and social rights legislation introduced so far

All in all, it could be said that ordinary citizens reading the Consolidated Treaty for the first time would undoubtedly come to the conclusion that the Union clearly did have a set of social policies. Yet if they were looking to see what specific benefits they were entitled to, they would find it difficult to pin down a treaty wording on which to base a strong claim. Nonetheless, many treaty provisions have led to the development of secondary legislation, and this is what we turn to now. For clarity's sake, and because the only user-friendly official printed lists of social laws are mostly out of date or out of stock, a new list has been compiled (Appendix) covering the main binding directives that have been transposed into member state legislation, and have either confirmed existing laws or forced some national legislatures to pass new texts in order to implement the directives.

A search of EU legislation in force (see www.europa.eu.int/eur-lex/en/lif/index.html) shows that the largest number of directives adopted by the Council of Ministers, and, since co-decision, by the Parliament and Council together, were aimed at ensuring the health and safety of workers through the maintenance of a safe working environment, which prevents employees from getting ill or injured at work. In the wake of the 1989 broad 'framework' directive setting out the parameters of industrial health and safety, a series of specific aspects of workplace safety have been regulated and the list of directives continues to grow. Therefore, a broadly harmonised, healthier working environment could be said to be the EU's major contribution towards the well being of the workforce. The degree of improvement depends on whether these directives force member states to improve their own standards, as in Spain (Threlfall, 1997), or whether standards were already well protected. Despite the UK's 1974 Health and Safety at Work Act, which also created the Heath and Safety Executive (HSE) to implement it, James (1993, p 147) considers that the directives imposed more detailed obligations on employers and therefore led to major changes to UK law.

Another numerous set of directives was designed to help workers and their dependants move to and work in another country under the exact same conditions as that country's nationals, whether those conditions were better or worse than in the mover's home state, under the 'equal treatment' principle (for details see www.europa.eu.int/eur-lex/legislationinforce/freemovement). They ensure that the EU migrant workers receive the same treatment as others for social security arrangements, and have traditionally covered contributory benefits and those provided by national social insurance schemes.

A glance at the accumulated *acquis* of directives shows that the equal treatment principle quite clearly also applies to gender, ensuring that women enjoy the same entitlements, social security and equal pay for work of equal value to their male counterparts. In particular the EU has managed to make dismissal on grounds of pregnancy and maternity extremely difficult. And when women are sacked or discriminated against, the Burden of Proof directive seeks to make it easier for the employee to prove their case by shifting a certain onus of disclosure of evidence onto the employers, who may be obliged to show that they have not discriminated. Mothers have also benefited from the introduction of a minimum 14-week period of paid maternity leave with a minimum level of pay. Parents of both sexes have been given rights to a cumulative minimum of three months of leave from work to attend to their pre-school children and for family emergencies. The equal treatment principle has also been applied successfully to benefit part-time workers by giving them entitlements on a pro-rata basis.

Furthermore, equal treatment was even more widely applied with the adoption in 2000 of two significant directives to combat discrimination. The first addresses racism and provides an entitlement to equal treatment in the context of employment irrespective of race (equal treatment between persons irrespective of racial or ethnic origin [2000/43/EC]). The second wraps up the remaining well-known claims of discrimination on the grounds of a person's religion or belief, disability, age or sexual orientation in employment (2000/78/EC). It should be noted that all the equal treatment provisions in theory only incur costs to employers who were practising discrimination in their workplaces. They do not introduce a new right to benefits in cash or kind, although as social policies, if the sex equality directives are anything to go by, they will foreseeably have a long 'tail' of effects. All in all, it can be said that the coverage of the 'negative' right to freedom from discrimination is wide and substantially established in the EU.

As to working conditions other than health and safety, a glance at our list shows that EU coverage is still patchy. True, EU law stipulates that employees must have a written statement of their terms of employment, that their working hours are subject to a limit of an average of no more than 48 hours a week and that they are entitled to a minimum of one rest day a week and to paid holidays. However, if their employer wanted to sack them, they could do so within the terms of a member state's own law. In terms of job protection, the EU has only succeeded in introducing mandatory consultation of workers' representatives in cases of collective redundancy, and in protecting employees' acquired rights in cases of a transfer of the company to another owner or of employer insolvency, nothing more. Even in the area of the 'social dialogue', which has long been close to the Commission's heart, the most that is regulated at European level is that employees in large companies with branches in at least two member states must be informed and consulted by the management on a series of issues through a joint committee known as a European Works Council. Only at the end of 2001 has this right been extended to smaller companies without a 'European' presence, although the final text is not yet in force.

EU welfare-oriented policies in practice

Apart from the legal *acquis* listed previously, ordinary EU citizens seeking to know their pan-European entitlements would have to rely on their country of residence's statutory provision. Nonetheless, it would be wrong to assume that the EU is not concerned with fields that do not appear on our list of the binding legal *acquis*. Let us briefly consider fields in which policy initiatives have been taken, such as in social protection and social exclusion and in public health, that develop an EU competence in practice, going beyond the letter of the law.

Poverty and social exclusion is a field that, despite lacking a legal base for regulation, has been of concern to European institutions ever since the 1969 Paris summit, and has grown over time to acquire a budget line, with Council of Ministers approving the Commission's Action Programmes. Known as Poverty I, Poverty II and Poverty III, they supported innovative schemes to combat social exclusion, with the intention that these should play a role as examples of good practice in other member states (see Commission of the EC, 1989; Room, 1993). By 1992 consensus had reached the point where member states agreed a Council Recommendation stating that they would each ensure a guaranteed minimum income for all legal residents in keeping with human dignity. This was not to be a universal entitlement to a social income, but state-funded programmes for 'insertion' into the labour market in exchange for certain commitments on the part of the recipient. Though sometimes derided for being only the subject of a non-binding agreement, the issue has nevertheless crept up the agenda and it should be noted that minimum income schemes have since been introduced in Spain, Italy and Portugal.

In 1999 the Commission, invited by the European Parliament, published a concerted strategy for modernising social protection, asking the Council to approve four major objectives for the member states' systems that would also bring them closer together through political debate and the exchange of experiences. These were (European Commission, 1999):

- make work pay and provide a secure income;
- make pensions safe and pension systems sustainable;
- promote social integration;
- ensure high quality and sustainability of healthcare.

The strategy was approved by the Council, and a high level committee of experts named the European Social Protection Committee was set up in 2000 (Council of Ministers, 2000b). It must be underlined that these are not initiatives aimed at introducing new rights or entitlements or at harmonising the types of benefit available across Europe, but rather at modernising member state systems along lines that, in a nutshell, could be termed 'New Labour', given their emphasis on accessing employment and reducing any disincentives to work, accompanied by state aids and safety nets (see European Commission's Scadplus site for more details: http//europa.eu.int/scadplus)[4]. At the Lisbon European Council of 2000 it was decided that the member states would take steps towards the eradication of poverty by setting targets. At Nice they agreed to use the Open Method of Coordination (OMC), similar to that used for the employment strategy. Member states were to submit two-year national action plans to promote social inclusion (abbreviated as NAPIncl) in June 2001. The Commission drafted an initial Joint Report on Social Inclusion that pulled them all together, which was submitted to the Council of Ministers of Employment and Social Affairs on 3 December 2001. The Belgian Presidency organised a European Meeting of People

Living in Poverty (1-2 December 2001) in order to give the excluded a voice and a chance to exchange ideas.

As to practical outcomes, so far the EU's main efforts have centred on finding or constructing robust statistical indicators that would be valid across member states. A list of commonly agreed EU indicators for social inclusion was agreed at the end of 2001 (Belgian Presidency, 2001b).

The last few years have seen a rather different set of developments in the field of healthcare available to EU citizens, which do not directly come from intergovernmental arrangements or the Open Method of Coordination on Social inclusion. For the right of access of patients to healthcare was unexpectedly extended in 1997 and 1998 in landmark decisions that attracted little attention at the time but have rather suddenly had an impact on the UK and in effect heralded the arrival of 'patient mobility' (Wavell, 1998). A Council Regulation issued in 1997 stated that citizens have the possibility to travel to another member state with the sole intention of receiving treatment, the cost of which will be reimbursed by their own health insurance institution, though only with prior authorisation. Such authorisation cannot be refused, even if the type of treatment needed is provided by the country in which the person is insured, if it is not available within a time limit compatible with their state of health (European Commission DGV, 1999, p 2). The following year, in the cases of Kohll and of Decker[5], the ECJ ruled that citizens purchasing treatments (in this case spectacles) in another member state did *not* have to seek *prior* authorisation from their insurance fund in order to get their medical expenses reimbursed on returning home.

This prompted the Commission to talk of a "Europe of patients" (European Commission DGV, 1999, p 1), a good example being the case of the UK citizen, Chris Davies, who had a heart bypass and a kidney transplant in Brussels, after a 15-year wait on dialysis due to the shortage of organ donors in Britain. He later obtained authorisation from the NHS (that is, they would reimburse him) to return to Belgium for a hip replacement operation after one year's wait and several cancellations. Another example was Crawley Primary Health Care Group, which negotiated to send 50 patients to a hospital in Germany, paying their full costs. A further six British health regions had talks about similar packages in 2001 (Marsh, 2001, p 6). By the end of August 2001, the British government had accepted the feasibility of making use of spare operating theatre capacity in other parts of Europe in a move that was hailed as 'a historic shift in NHS policy'. Frank Field believed that teams of French, German, Italian or Spanish specialists might also operate in NHS hospitals at weekends (Carvel, 2001).

The ECJ rulings did, however, recognise that a barrier to implementing the principles of the internal market (for example, preventing citizens moving to obtain treatment elsewhere in the EU) *could* be justified "where the financial balance of the social security system might be seriously undermined" (European Commission DGV, 1999, p 1). In other words, it envisaged a situation where an excess of claims for payment of health services received in another country might be a serious burden for the home health system. But it is foreseeable that the rulings will put pressure on governments, the British government in this case, to reduce hospital waiting times for urgent cases, so as to avoid the adverse publicity that would doubtless arise from any refusal to authorise a patient who requested it to travel to another EU hospital. Consequently, some experts believe it necessary "to undertake a revision of the whole legal framework regulating access to health care across the EU" (Mossialos et al, 2001, p 4), which would obviously lead to many further developments. The Commission has taken up the banner of pan-European access to healthcare by announcing the replacement of the E111 card with a European Health Card.

The implications of the Charter of Fundamental Rights for social policies

Even as the ink on the Amsterdam Treaty was drying, the EU was already engaged in a new debate that encompassed social policy and rights. An Expert Group on Fundamental Rights was set up to decide how the Community could bring together both its own established principles and rights as well as those normally associated with a liberal democratic state, such as those enshrined in the member states' own Constitutions and legislation (Expert Group on Fundamental Rights, 1999). This process culminated in the Charter of Fundamental Rights, which was adopted by the member states at Nice in December 2000, but not incorporated into a new treaty or given legally enforceable status. To this day, the Charter's rights cannot be judicially invoked. Discussions at the Laeken summit of heads of state and government in December 2001 did not advance its status either, as they merely concluded that "thought would have to be given to whether the Charter [...] should be included in the basic treaty", in the context of a possible "simplification and reorganisation" of the European treaties that might "lead in the long run to the adoption of a constitutional text" whose "basic features" might include the "fundamental rights and obligations of citizens" (Belgian Presidency, 2001c, p 7). The wording does not raise hopes that the Charter will soon become justiciable.

But what really matters for social policy analysts is how far the Charter would serve to establish social policy principles that would have a ratchet effect on lagging member states, particularly those with rudimentary or incipient welfare states. Might it serve to create a minimum floor of rights beneath which social protection could not fall in times of crisis or as the result of a lurch towards extreme forms of economic liberalism? Two chapters of the Charter stand out in this respect, Chapter III on 'Equality' and Chapter IV on 'Solidarity'. The former contains a series of principled affirmations of mainly formal equality of the usual categories of social groups, men, women, children, older people and persons with disabilities, as well as a wide ban on discrimination covering a newly extended set of grounds and circumstances.

Charter of Fundamental Rights

Article 21
Non-discrimination
1. Any discrimination based on any ground such as sex, race, colour, ethnic or social origin, genetic features, language, religion or belief, political or any other opinion, membership of a national minority, property, birth, disability, age or sexual orientation shall be prohibited.

Several, but not all, of these grounds are included in the discrimination Directive (Council of Ministers, 2000c) for which the deadline for transposition into domestic legislation has not yet been reached. Given that the member states are currently faced with combating discrimination on the grounds of religion, belief, disability, age and sexual orientation as regards employment and occupation, it can be safely surmised that the even wider grounds of discrimination provided for in Article 21 would *not* be one of their priorities for development. As regards sex equality, Article 23 repeats the formulation, but with the wording, "Equality between men and women must be ensured in all areas, including employment, work and pay". Two aspects open the way for the development of measures for *substantive* equality. Firstly, the words 'all areas' could possibly be interpreted as including freedom from violence or the right to bodily integrity, opening the way for measures regarding domestic violence, rape, birth control, abortion, trafficking and sexual exploitation, on the grounds that in practise women often cannot enjoy their freedom nor assert practical equality in such areas – a point made by the European Women's Lobby (2001) when it pressed the Expert Group with its own submission at the time of drafting. In fact, the Commission has already proposed to harmonise national penalties and to agree a minimum six-year prison sentence for trafficking[6]. Secondly, the separation of 'employment' and 'work' may be taken to refer to unpaid work, which would open up the issue of how carers can earn a living outside the labour market. In addition, Article 23 of the Charter also permits "the maintenance or adoption of measures providing specific advantages in favour of the under-represented sex", which again reinforces the already established public policy concept that it is necessary to go beyond formal equality to achieve gender equity – a concept that the current treaty supports through its acceptance of positive action.

On the rights of the child, the Charter introduces a novel (in the EU context) paragraph on a child's "right to maintain on a regular basis a personal relationship and direct contact with both his or her parents". If enforced, this would have considerable implications for member states' divorce laws and for the practices of family courts and of social services, and would foreseeably lead to EU-wide harmonisation measures in order to maintain the principle of free movement and equal treatment of member state nationals (see Threlfall, 2001). There is already a Council of Ministers regulation on the EU-wide recognition and enforcement of judgements in matrimonial matters and in matters of parental responsibility for children (Council of Ministers, 2000d), showing that the EU has not shied away from regulating such areas via judicial cooperation.

On the rights of older people, Article 25's single sentence wording lays out the issue primarily in terms of substantive equality: "The Union recognises and respects the rights of the elderly to lead a life of dignity and independence and to participate in cultural and social life". It avoids – unlike with men and women – any implied equality or comparison with the young. As with the rights of the child, it is a policy-prescriptive formulation of possibly wide but unpredictable consequences, because the current state of play of EU law regarding older people seeks to prevent discrimination in employment on the grounds of age – a much more circumscribed area than the Charter's.

By contrast, the article on persons with disabilities is much more weakly formulated. It offers only a right "to benefit from measures designed to ensure..." (independence, integration and participation) without further specification. As formulated this is likely to have little direct impact, because at present most member states already have measures designed for persons with disabilities (Hantrais, 2000, pp 153-6). These not surprisingly fall short of the demands of disability lobbies such as the

European Disability Forum and given that the Commission has a history of actions to support disabled people, such as the HELIOS programme (see Hantrais, 2000, pp 140-7, 160-4).

Nonetheless the significance of the Equality chapter is, arguably, that it confirms the status of groups that are not part of the labour market in a much more explicit way than before, and thereby shifts the EU's view of its own 'constituents' (at least in theory if not in law) towards the whole range of citizens rather than just the business and labour communities it has traditionally addressed. It also suggests that social protection issues could rise to become a formal part of EU concerns. The Commission has long had an interest in social protection (see its extensive comparative data gathering on this topic) and the Council of Ministers did entrust it with a coordinating role in a 1992 Recommendation in which member states envisaged the convergence of their social protection aims and outcomes (Council of Ministers, 1992a, 92/441/EEC).

These aspects of the Equality chapter should be read in conjunction with sections of Chapter IV on Solidarity, which also has some striking elements. Article 34 is entitled *Social security and social assistance*, which seems rather bold considering the weakness of any EU social security competency other than for free movers. It introduces a new recognition, not present in the treaties, of "the entitlement to social security benefits and social services providing protection *in cases such as* maternity, illness, industrial accidents, dependency or old age and in the case of loss of employment..." (emphasis added: note it does not say 'in cases of...'). However, it is qualified by the next clause: "in accordance with the rules laid down by Community law and national law and practices", which implies that any innovations would be of limited impact. Yet Article 34 also states that the Union '*respects*' the citizen's entitlement, suggesting a simultaneous wish to curb any retrenchment of existing benefit provision. Furthermore, in paragraph 3 of Article 34, the Union "recognises and respects the right to social and housing assistance so as to ensure a decent existence to those who lack sufficient resources". So far the EU has been concerned with the economic aspects of housing, such as mortgage markets and competition in the construction industry (Kleinman, 2002b, p 350). There are no legal instruments on housing so far and the Commission spending programmes, such as URBAN, have been concerned with physical regeneration rather than citizens' access to housing. So perhaps Article 34 represents a step forward which enlarges the parameters of the EU's commitment to social welfare: social assistance with housing is declared to be a right. Does it follow that there is to be a policy convergence around those member states that follow such policy? It all depends on the status the Charter eventually acquires. All in all, Article 34 may turn out to constitute a useful lever for those concerned to increase the Europeanisation of social protection. This is not to forget that the Charter is a mere declaration, but also to remember that declarations of principle set precedents which allow the Commission to claim there is a green light for it to take new initiatives – one only has to look at the list of 'Whereas...' clauses, which list all the preceding policy steps introducing all new proposals, to see how the legitimacy of a new initiative is built out of small scale precedents. A compelling example is the far-reaching Social Action Programme that followed hard on the heels of the declarative, non-binding Community Charter of Fundamental Rights of Workers in 1989, although it took over a decade to implement, being dependent on political will in the last instance.

Another significant innovation is contained in Article 35 on healthcare. As explained previously, the Treaty on European Union agreed at Maastricht, introduced a circumscribed Commission competency in public health (Title X Article 129, later consolidated as Title XIII Article 152). It starts by stating that "a high level of *human health protection* shall be ensured in the definition and implementation of Community policies and activities" (§ 1), but ends with a reminder that the member states have responsibilities "for the organisation and delivery of health services and medical care", which Community action had to fully respect (§ 5). The Nice Charter on the other hand, moves into the realm of individual health by stating that: "Everyone has the right of access to preventative health care and the right to benefit from medical treatment under the conditions established by national laws and practices". What it does is to raise to the status of a universal right a concept already embodied in a 'soft' policy instrument, namely the Council Recommendation on sufficient resources and social protection systems (Council of Ministers, 1992a), in which member states had agreed that all legal residents should have access to a healthcare system. In the Charter the wording is stronger and can be interpreted as an attempt to convert an intergovernmental agreement, in which beneficiaries are dependent on their own state's policies and laws, into a generalised right. Developments towards pan-European consumption and provision of healthcare services, discussed above, should also be borne in mind.

Finally, Articles 27 to 32 in the Solidarity chapter focus on employment and mainly reiterate concepts that are already covered in the treaties and by a series of directives. The reiterative, confirmatory articles are: (Article 27) workers' rights to information and consultation; (Article 31) working conditions which respect health and safety and include rest periods and annual leave; and (Article 32) the protection of young people at work; and (Article 33) the reconciliation of family and professional life. Nonetheless, path-breaking articles are also to be found, such as Article 30:

Article 30
Protection in the event of unjustified dismissal
Every worker has the right to protection against unjustified dismissal, in accordance with Community law and national laws and practices.

Up to now, EU job protection regulation has been scant. Amsterdam used a wording on protecting workers "where their employment contract is terminated" (Article 137) that had not been acted on. So the Charter proposes what is in effect a new pan-European right to protection against unjustified dismissal. In Article 28 the right to strike, long excluded from any Community action in all treaties up till now, is proposed: "Workers and employers, or their respective organisations, have, in accordance with Community law and national laws and practices, the right to [...] take collective action to defend their interests, including strike action". This could therefore be considered a particularly challenging, even audacious article. It is probably significant that there is no mention in the Charter of the right to join a trades union – trades union law being another area deliberately not covered by the Treaty of Rome. Given their phrasing, neither Article 30 nor Article 28 herald the introduction of harmonisation of member state laws on dismissal or the right to strike, since they expressly recognise them. But were the Charter justiciable, there is mileage to be found in these articles, first and foremost in a protective sense, to defend against encroachment of such rights by governments. And even if it is not justiciable, it remains to be seen whether the ECJ will take it into account when making a ruling – it has, after all, been adopted by the member states. It is not difficult to imagine a challenging test case being taken by a trades union, which could lead to the strengthening of protective legislation, at least at member state level. Lastly, the Commission itself is entitled to take the new Charter and see what proposals for directives it can devise on its basis. Whether it wishes to do this and whether the member states' governments are persuadable, is a political matter.

Summary

At first sight therefore, the new Charter of Fundamental Rights appears to be a hybrid creation. On the one hand, it is selective of the social rights that it chooses to cover and does not emulate the comprehensive nature of some national constitutions' social provisions (for example Spain's). It is also selective in the citizen's political rights and rights to justice that it introduces, in keeping with what the EU, as a supranational body, is able to offer. On the other, it incorporates well-established Community rules such as free movement and residence, workers' rights to information and consultation together with extensive applications of the equal treatment principle that are not typical of European constitutions. In other words, it both falls short of and spills over the boundaries of what the average member state citizen, informed by a national perspective on her/his rights, might expect. This makes it an exciting initiative bound to have an extensive impact if it becomes justiciable. However, perhaps for this very reason – if it is a view shared by member states – the likelihood of it becoming so may recede.

Conclusion

The theme explored in this chapter has been the long-term shift in the European Community's social concerns, from the time when it was still called an economic community through to the period after it saw itself as a political Union. The question asked at the beginning was has its social policy evolved from a labourist to a welfarist focus? The conclusion is that, undeniably, its evolution has been more complex and multi-layered, even at the formal levels of treaties and laws reviewed here. While the general pace of development is clearly incremental, the accretion has taken place within quite strict boundaries, moving along the vectors of free movement and equal treatment – deeply embedded Community principles – and of workplace health and safety, the most consensual field of regulation. At the same time, and paradoxically, the EU has become increasingly active in the wider social policy fields of social security, healthcare and social exclusion, while regulating less and less of them, as our 'bottom line' list of directives shows.

The fact remains, as analysts have pointed out, that the major elements of social policy at national level have only a limited involvement at European level, and direct provision of services remains non-existent (most recently, Kleinman, 2002a, p 221). Nor are the benefits that the member states are supposed to provide even benchmarked, small exceptions being maternity pay (which should be no less than statutory sickness benefit) and social assistance (an unspecified minimum 'in keeping with human dignity'). The latter is not even enforceable. So one is bound to conclude that the EU has become a supranational welfare state. But the focus of policy is now undoubtedly more oriented towards the general welfare of the citizenry, and the member states' new Open Coordination Method on social inclusion that is being launched with the aim of eradicating unacceptable levels of poverty will involve governments in closer discussion of the causes and consequences of exclusion as well as committing them to poverty reduction measures. This constitutes an expansion of welfarist concerns at the intergovernmental level, suggesting that the EU has moved from a focus on the workplace to one on social protection generally. At the same time, the adoption of a new Charter signals a return to an interest in regulation, at least at the level of declarations of principles and of constitution building. Taking the 1989 Community Charter of Fundamental Rights of Workers as a precedent, a steady trickle of regulation can be predicted to occur, even if the new Charter does not become enforceable. Furthermore, the Convention on the Future of Europe headed by Giscard d'Estaing is supposed to give thought to whether it should be included in the basic treaty (Belgian Presidency, 2001c, p 7) giving it a constitutional basis. Yet, as always, the future of EU social policy remains unpredictable.

Notes

[1] Reproduced from HMSO (1988) in Gold (1993).

[2] Not to be confused with health product standards, the testing of medicines and the operation of pharmaceutical markets in which the EC has long played a role under its market regulation and competition powers.

[3] The Treaty of Amsterdam came fully into force in 1999. The final text, called *Consolidated version of the Treaty establishing the European Community*, is the one in force until the Nice consolidated version is ratified. Accessing the correct text can be confusing as one of the Europa websites currently publishes both the [Maastricht] Treaty on European Union (with a confusing publication date of 1997, even though the signatories and date at the end of the text are from 1992), as well as the *Consolidated version of the treaty establishing the European Community* (also dated 1997), which contains the current key social provisions. The Nice Treaty amendments and the Charter of Fundamental Rights have not been consolidated or approved for incorporation into a new text.

[4] On 13 January 2002, http//europa.eu.int/scadplus/leg/en/cha/c10101.htm featured a text entitled *The legal framework following the Treaty of Amsterdam* with the sentence: "As for pay, the right of association, the right to strike and the right to impose lockouts, they are still excluded from the Community competence".

[5] Kohll case C–120/95 and Decker case C–158/96, of 28 May 1998 (not to be confused with the well-known Dekker case).

[6] Trafficking, as opposed to smuggling of immigrants, is defined by the EP Citizens' Rights Committee as, "using force, violence, deceit or threats", according to this source, that is associated with the abuse of women.

References

Belgian Presidency (2001a) *EU cooperation in the field of social inclusion*, Information Paper of 3 December 2001 (http://vandenbroucke.fgov.be/Eframe.htm).

Belgian Presidency (2001b) Report of the conference on 'Indicators for social inclusion: making common EU objectives work', Antwerp 14–15 September, forthcoming (2002) in T. Atkinson (ed) *Social indicators: The EU and social inclusion*.

Belgian Presidency (2001c) 'Laeken declaration on the future of Europe', Annexes to the Presidency Conclusions, Annex 1, SN 300/01 ADD1.

Carvel, J. (2001) 'NHS to fund operations in Europe: change in NHS rules to allow more operations in EU', *The Guardian*, 27 August (www.guardian.co.uk/Archive/Article/0,4273,4245986,00.html).

Commission of the EC (1989) 'Medium-term community action programme to foster the economic and social integration of the least privileged groups', *Bulletin of the EC*, Supplement 4/89, p 33.

Council of Ministers (1992a) *Council Recommendation of 24 June 1992 on common criteria concerning sufficient resources and social assistance in social protection systems* (92/441/EEC).

Council of Ministers (1992b) *Council Recommendation on the convergence of social protection objectives and policies of 27 July 1992* (92/442/EEC).

Council of Ministers (2000a) *Conclusions of 17 December 1999 on the strengthening of cooperation for modernising and improving social protection* (OJ C8, 12 January).

Council of Ministers (2000b) *Council Decision of 29 June 2000 setting up a Social Protection Committee* (COM 2000) 134 final, Official Journal L172, 12 July).

Council of Ministers (2000c) 'Council Directive 2000/78/EC of 27 November 2000 establishing a general framework for equal treatment in employment and occupation', *Official Journal of the European Communities*, L303/16, 2 December.

Council of Ministers (2000d) *Regulation on the recognition and enforcement of judgments in matrimonial matters and in matters of parental responsibility for children*, (EC) No 1347/2000 of 29 May 2000, Official Journal L160, 30 June, pp 19-29.

Euroconfidential (1999) *The Rome, Maastricht & Amsterdam Treaties: comparative texts*, Brussels: Euroconfidential.

European Commission (undated) *Social policy and social protection, a concerted strategy for modernising social protection* (http://europa.eu.int/scadplus/leg/en/cha/c10618.htm, last visited 13.01.01).

European Commission (1996) *4th Report on the application of the Community charter on the fundamental rights of workers*, Luxembourg: Office of Official Publications of the European Community.

European Commission (1999) *Communication of 14 July 1999: A concerted strategy for modernising social protection*, COM (99) 347 final (not in OJ).

European Commission DGV (1999) *Free movement and social security, citizens' rights when moving within the EU*, Bulletin No 2.

European Social Forum (1999) *Summary report of the European social policy forum 98*, Brussels, 24-6 June, Mark Carley (ed), Luxembourg: Office of Official Publications of the European Community.

EU (European Union) (2000) 'Charter of fundamental rights', *Official Journal of the European Communities*, C 364 18 December.

European Women's Lobby (2001) Policy documents (www.womenlobby.org).

Expert Group on Fundamental Rights (1999) *Affirming fundamental rights in the EU*, report, Luxembourg: Office of Official Publications of the European Community.

Geyer, R. (2000) *Exploring European social policy*, Cambridge: Polity Press.

Gold, M. (ed) (1993) *The social dimension: Employment policy in the European Community*, Basingstoke: Macmillan.

Hantrais, L. (2000) *Social policy in the European Union* (2nd edn), Basingstoke: Macmillan.

Hoskyns, C. (1996) *Integrating gender: Women, law and politics in the European Union*, London/New York, NY: Verso.

James, P. (1993) 'Occupational health and safety', in M. Gold (ed) *The social dimension: Employment policy in the European Community*, Basingstoke: Macmillan, pp 135-52.

Kleinman, M. (2002a) *A European welfare state?*, Basingstoke: Palgrave.

Kleinman, M. (2002b) 'The future of European Union social policy and its implications for housing', *Urban Studies*, vol 39, no 2, pp 341-52.

Marsh, B. (2001) 'Hip replacement patients may be sent to Europe', *The Daily Mail*, 30 July, p 6.

Mossialos, E., McKee, M., Palm, W., Karl, B. and Marhold, F. (2001) *The influence of EU law on the social character of health care systems in the European Union*, Executive Summary, Report submitted to the Belgian Presidency of the EU (final version), Brussels 19 November, p 7.

Nice Treaty (2000) *Consolidated text of the future Treaty of the EU including Nice amendments* (http://euobserver.com/onm/media_upload/TreatieothEconsolidated.pdf).

Room, G. (1993) *Anti-poverty action research in Europe*, Bristol: SAUS Publications.

Threlfall, M. (1997) 'Spain in social Europe: a compliant or a laggard state?', *Southern European Society and Politics*, vol 2, no 2, Autumn, pp 1-33.

Threlfall, M. (2002) 'Social integration in the European Union: towards a single social area?', in M. Farrell, S. Fella and M. Newman (eds) *European unity in diversity – Challenges for the twenty-first century*, London: Sage Publications, pp 135-57.

Treaty of Rome (1957, 1988 edn) Treaties establishing the European Communities as Amended by Subsequent Treaties, Cmnd 455, London: HMSO.

Wavell, S. (1998) 'Your very good health – in a foreign body', *The Sunday Times*, 31 May, p 11.

Appendix
The *acquis communautaire* – main Directives in the social field*

- Equal Pay for women and men (75/117/EEC)
- Collective Redundancies (mandatory consultation of employee representatives) (75/129/EEC)
- Equal Treatment of women and men in access to employment, vocational training and promotion (76/207/EEC)
- Transfer of Undertakings (protection of acquired rights of employees) (77/187/EEC)
- Statutory Social Security schemes (equal treatment of women and men) (79/7/EEC)
- Insolvency of Employers (protection of employees) (80/987/EEC)
- Protection from Hazards (health and safety of employees) (80/1107/EEC)
- Occupational Social Security schemes (equal treatment of women and men) (86/378/EEC)
- Equal Treatment for the Self-employed (86/613/EEC)
- Health and Safety at work (consolidated Framework Directive 89/391/EEC) and many other derived Directives on specific aspects of health and safety, totalling over thirty
- Residence rights for persons of independent means in other member states (90/364/EEC)
- Residence rights for pensioners, providing substantial new mobility rights (90/365/EEC)
- Residence rights for students engaged in vocational training (90/366/EEC, replaced by 93/96/EEC)
- Health and Safety Protection for Temporary Workers (91/383/EEC)
- Proof of the Employment Relationship (contract of employment) (91/533/EEC)

Since the 1992 Maastricht Treaty on European Union:

- Health and Safety Protection of Pregnant Workers and workers who have recently given birth (92/85/EEC)
- Working Time (organisation of rest periods and holidays) (93/104/EEC)
- Young People at Work (protection against abuses) (94/33/EC)
- Posted Workers (local conditions of work should apply) (96/71/EC)

- European Works Councils for the purpose of informing and consulting employees (94/45/EC). *Adopted under the Social Agreement (excluding UK)*
- Parental Leave (96/34/EC). *Adopted under the Social Agreement (excluding UK) and via the Social Partners procedure*
- Part-Time Workers (97/81/EC). *Adopted via the Social Partners procedure*

Since the 1997 Treaty of Amsterdam:

- Reversal of the Burden of Proof (employers to prove non-discrimination) (97/80/EC)
- Collective Redundancies (approximation of the laws) (98/59/EC)
- Equal Treatment between persons irrespective of racial or ethnic origin (2000/43/EC)
- Equal Treatment in employment and occupation; combating discrimination on the grounds of religion or belief, disability, age or sexual orientation as regards employment and occupation (2000/78/EC)
- Safeguarding of employees' rights in the event of transfers of undertakings, businesses or parts thereof (2001/23/EC)
- Information and involvement of employees (supplementing the Statute for a European company) (2001/86/EC)
- Working Time in mobile road-transport activities [Common Position reached June 2001]
- Equal Treatment for women and men as regards access to employment, vocational training and promotion, and working conditions (strengthens Directive 76/207/EEC and includes sexual harassment at work) [about to be adopted]
- Information and consultation rights of employees (general framework for improving these) [common position reached October 2001]

Note: Directives only. Official titles have been abbreviated for easier recognition. The list excludes free movement of workers, recognition of qualifications, consumer affairs and the full list of over 30 health and safety at work directives.

Part Three:
Conceptual developments

Each of the chapters that make up this section concentrate on one key theme: the making and remaking of policy-relevant theory. In an era of rapid social, political and economic change, it is important that we (re)examine theory 'reflexively' for at least three reasons. First, there is a need continually to assess the capacity of accepted theoretical perspectives to provide insights into, and explanations of, changing policy arenas – literally to maintain, and where necessary to readjust, their explanatory power. Second, it is important that new theories are 'tested' against social and political actuality in an effort both to judge their policy relevance and to gauge their influence on policy making. Third, and conversely, it is equally important that new departures in policy making are used to inform theoretical debate in ways that stimulate new thinking about, and new interpretations of, the policy process.

The section begins with Chris Crowther's piece, which revisits "recent analyses of the policing of the underclass by considering old and newly emergent theorisations of developments in police policy and practice in relation to social exclusion". The theoretical approaches under review are neo-Marxist and Foucauldian, and the chapter assesses the capacity of these perspectives to 'explain' or conceptualise the policing of the 'underclass'. Crowther notes that, while neo-Marxist analyses favours 'macro', or structural, social, political and economic changes as factors capable of explaining how populations, surplus to production requirements, are excluded and criminalised, Foucauldian thinking privileges the 'micro' influences of "discursive practices and political rationalities". Both perspectives need refining, however, if they are to take proper conceptual account of what Crowther refers to as the new "police-policing continuum", a concept that focuses theoretical attention on the ways in which the role of the police is being increasingly supplanted, as well as complemented, by the policing and control activities of non-police agents and agencies. The linkages between macro- and micro-level changes have to be re-examined in this evolving context, Crowther argues, because forms of exclusion and criminalisation are continually being made and remade in this new and highly complex, multi-agency policy environment. In addition, if these processes are to be fully understood, greater attention needs to be paid not only to new agencies of social control but, in an increasingly fluid policy context, also to the role of agency itself.

For Caron Caldwell, the problem is not so much the explanatory failings of a particular theory – in this case ecological theory – but the difficulties associated with its dissemination and acceptance by policy relevant audiences. As she states at the outset, despite general acknowledgement that it is important to human welfare, "concern for the environment has not yet been translated into comprehensive policy initiatives". Drawing on Dobson's three-stage typology of environmental sustainability, which categorises ecological theories according to the strength of their anthropocentric or ecocentric leanings, Caldwell reports preliminary results of her empirical study of politicians' awareness of the relationship between welfare and environmental issues. Importantly, the study shows that the politicians interviewed do make connections between social policy and the environment – although some struggle to reconcile the apparent contradiction between economic prosperity and a more ecocentric agenda. Indeed it seems that politicians are likely to favour only the most anthropocentric versions of eco-theory and that the current New Labour government is itself only committed to this rather unchallenging approach. In view of these prevailing concerns about the potential impact of Green policies on continued growth, Caldwell suggests that this discourse of "weak ecological modernisation may be a good place for the government to start". However, she remains hopeful that more radical Green discourses may yet come to influence the social policy agenda.

Martin Roche examines the concept of 'social capital'. He argues that there needs to be an effective means of 'measuring' the possession of social capital if the idea is to be effective as a policy tool. Noting that "social capital is a notion still very much in its infancy when it comes to being applied in practice", Roche argues that the innate value of the term itself is in danger of being compromised through ill thought out attempts to operationalise it. He attempts to rescue the situation by constructing a methodology which is, first, robust in terms of its capacity to develop categories – 'trust', 'participation', 'altruism', 'sociability' – that reflect the theoretical underpinnings of social capital as an idea and, second, accessible to empirical measurement. The point, of course, is to make theory 'useful' for (social) policy analysis. In this case, the methodology Roche outlines seeks to bring theory and policy together by acting as a mechanism which allows policy makers "to assess both the value and nature of social capital to deprived communities". The focus on deprivation is important here. Because social capital can be used by dominant interests to exclude others, for example by denying them access to particular resources or forms of expression, Roche argues that we must guard against the assumption that its simple possession somehow acts as a panacea for the alleviation of poverty and social exclusion. It may not, and, just as other chapters in this section suggest, the underlying point is that it is important for academics, service users and policy makers alike to engage consistently in attempts to think (and rethink) the nature of theory and policy practice not so much as an end in itself but in the interests of greater social justice.

Where ideas of participation are concerned, the irony is that theory, such as it is, has become radically divorced from what Peter Beresford refers to as the "technicalities" of participation, as these are "reflected in the production of a large and rapidly growing body of 'how to do it' manuals, courses and consultants". Asking whether this technicist approach can really illuminate understandings of participation, Beresford argues that it cannot because it ignores the inherently ideological and political nature of participatory processes. The chapter investigates the ideological, political and economic relations of participation both conceptually and in practice, from a social policy perspective. Writing from a service user's perspective, Beresford comments that traditional theories within social policy failed to advance understandings of participation. He also notes, that, while 'New Right' and 'Third Way' thinking do indeed stress the importance of participation, they do so only in ways that emphasise a 'consumerist/managerialist' dimension, which can actually work to obstruct involvement. In contrast to this position, the chapter assesses the merits of a democratic model, which encourages an explicitly user-oriented, bottom-up political approach to participation, and which, through its emphasis on the redistribution of power and personal and political empowerment, holds out the prospect of personal and social liberation. As Beresford acknowledges, such a model clearly has implications for social policy: for example, how policy should be produced and who should shape and control welfare policy and welfare institutions.

TEN

The politics and economics of disciplining an inclusive and exclusive society

Chris Crowther

The key area of concern in this chapter is the relationship between crime, the police and social exclusion. It has been argued, for example, that the main function of the modern British police service since its inception in 1829 is to regulate the underclass (Reiner, 2000b). The racialised disorders occurring in the north of England throughout 2001 are recent examples of the police service's role in containing excluded sections of society (Home Office, 2000, 2001a). The connection between police policy and practice, and marginalised, deprived and criminogenic populations has been described by two schools of thought. First, by writers drawing on the sociologists of modernity, in particular Marx, Weber and Durkheim (Choongh, 1997; Crowther, 2000a, 2000b; Reiner, 2000b) and second, by those drawing on post-structuralist commentators indebted to Michel Foucault (Feeley and Simon, 1994; Ericson and Haggerty, 1997; Stenson, 1998, 2000). The former concentrate on the dynamics of the capitalist political economy; a structure that reflects the economic interests of the ruling class and maintains its superiority in relation to the working and underclasses. The police are a component of the 'repressive state apparatus' safeguarding the productive and profit-making activities of the ruling elite by containing the potentially unruly and rebellious behaviour of an economically redundant crime-prone *lumpenproletariat* (Hall et al, 1978; Brake and Hale, 1992; Cook, 1997). The latter approach consists of several strands of thought and a detailed review of this rich literature is beyond the remit of this discussion. However, for heuristic purposes there are two principal schools of thought: (i) the governmentality approach (Foucault, 1991; Feeley and Simon, 1994; Dean, 1999; Rose, 1999); and (ii) the 'dispersal of discipline' and 'carceral society' thesis (Foucault, 1977; Cohen, 1985; Squires, 1990; Hillyard and Watson, 1996). There are crucial differences between these two perspectives, but what they share in common is their suspicion of totalising theoretical claims, such as those made by neo-Marxists about the functions of the capitalist economy. For Foucauldians, power is not concentrated in the hands of a sovereign, in the form of a state elite or ruling class, but is dispersed throughout various networks of agents and agencies and does not systematically represent the unitary interests of dominant groups. Instead of class, risk society is more important. Moreover, Foucauldians are concerned with the local or micro levels, rather than the meso and macro levels of analysis favoured by neo-Marxists.

Critics have attacked the latent or implicit functionalism underlying neo-Marxist explanations and a similar criticism has been extended to Foucault, for example by Poulantzas (1978), but on the whole Foucault's anti-realist and relativist stance allows the deflection of this accusation. However, both perspectives ignore human agency and social action, prompting Crowther (2000b) to attempt an integration of watered-down versions of Marxist and implicitly Foucauldian-type thinking to redress this deficiency by addressing practical matters in social and crime policy.

Much of the work mentioned above was published in the 1980s and 1990s as a reaction to the New Right and neo-liberal led policies implemented in the UK and USA, which reformed at macro and meso levels the social structure of welfare regimes and at a micro level the moral economies of individual citizens (Lister, 1996; Bauman, 1998; Murray, 1999). More recently, different beliefs about the relationship between political economic conditions, social exclusion, social divisions, crime and policing have evolved. Since their election victories in 1997 and 2001, New Labour's policy agenda has been premised on a different set of assumptions to those promoted by the New Right and neo-liberals. This is demonstrated by the decision to treat the behavioural and structural causes of, and solutions to, problems in criminal justice and social policy as if they are intertwined, confirmed by New Labour's 'joined-up' policies: the Crime Reduction Programme; the 1998 Crime and Disorder Act (CDA); and the Social Exclusion Unit (SEU) (Hughes, 2002). Although there remains a residual influence of neo-liberal thinking and practice, New Labour's political philosophy has been described as the 'Third Way', arguably a hybrid of left of centre and centre right social democratic and neo-liberal ideas, which has led to a partial reorientation of crime and public policy (Giddens, 1998). More fundamentally, there are different intellectual, legislative and policy frameworks now informing the policy response to the excluded society at different levels.

Thus, the main intention of this discussion is to revisit recent analyses of the policing of the underclass by considering old and newly emergent theorisations of developments in police policy and practice in relation to social exclusion. In earlier work the author suggested that the distinction between behavioural and structural perspectives on the underclass thesis needs to be made more explicit to account for the processes leading to exclusion, crime and the workings of the 'care-control complex' in crime reduction and community development (Crowther, 2000c). This emphasis was particularly important in the light of the crime and public policy agenda, which four successive Conservative governments (1979-97) handed down to the first New Labour government (1997-2001). However, as noted previously, recent conceptions of, and policy responses to, social exclusion attest to a more complex social reality which is interpreted and acted on through a different set of ideologies, cultural sensibilities and political rationalities (Crowther, 2000c; Garland, 2001; Stenson and Edwards, 2001). It is here that the author intends to reinstate an appreciation of agency into analyses of crime, policing and poverty.

The chapter consists of three main sections. It begins with an outline of the contemporary policy context in the fields of social and crime policy. The second part reviews the main currents in neo-Marxist and Foucauldian theorisations of crime and control. The final section suggests an alternative approach, which attempts to assimilate elements of both these perspectives. Some elaboration of the rationale for dwelling on these thematic threads is necessary.

The first section recounts the shift of emphasis in social and crime policy signalled by the New Labour government's pledge to be "tough on crime and tough on the causes of crime". It considers the main principles underpinning 'joined-up' government at central and local levels in the context of the SEU and the Regional Development Agencies (RDAs). The main provisions of the CDA are then outlined, including the relationship between the central government's, or the Home Office's, Crime Reduction Programme and local Community Safety Partnerships (CSPs) and Crime Reduction Partnerships (CRPs). The government demands that all of these innovations need to be evidence based, satisfy the requirements of the 'what works' agenda (Wiles, 1999; Davies et al, 2000) and fulfil the aims and objectives of the New Public Management (NPM) or the 'three Es' – economy, effectiveness and efficiency (Hood, 1991; Clarke and Newman, 1997). It is too early to anticipate, let alone audit, the actual impact of these anti-social exclusion and anti-crime and disorder strategies, but there are some emergent issues of theoretical interest (Bradshaw, 2000; Percy-Smith, 2000; Reiner, 2000a; Savage and Atkinson, 2001). Among other things, the aforementioned changes have led to a closer relationship, and arguably the blurring of the boundaries, between criminal justice and social policies.

The second section briefly reviews neo-Marxist and Foucauldian interpretations of police and policing policy and practice, including an initial assessment of the feasibility of making connections between them. The integration of these perspectives may be partly achieved with the concept of the 'police–policing continuum', which is applied to refine and re-conceptualise an earlier argument (Crowther, 2000c) that built on neo-Marxist and neo-Weberian sociologies and criminologies to make sense of contemporary changes in relation to crime, exclusion and various types of police activity (Hay, 1999; Jessop, 2000; Reiner, 2000a). While this work offers some useful ideas to understand these developments the writings of a number of scholars drawing on Foucault's work may also be incorporated as a conceptual complement to these commentaries (Feeley and Simon, 1994; Johnston, 1999; Reiner, 2000a; Stenson, 2000). At this stage, because of the radically different epistemologies and ontologies underpinning neo-Marxist and Foucauldian analyses, a meaningful synthesis of these different bodies of work is a long way off, but some tentative suggestions for future work are discussed.

It seems that there is a significant difference between the two perspectives, which ironically may bring the two closer together, hence the police-policing continuum. Neo-Marxists concentrate most on the *police* as a specialist, formal state apparatus, endowed with the legitimate use of force, which is the 'thin blue line' responsible for crime reduction, order maintenance and quasi-social service tasks. Where the police work with other statutory and non-statutory agencies, the latter's work is coopted by the former and is essentially an extension of the police force's influence and control (Gilroy and Sim, 1987). Foucauldians have tended to work more closely with the notions of police and policing in terms of *polizeiwissenschaft* or 'police science', which connotes more general forms of administration and regulation. Rather than the narrow function of crime control, policing focuses on general social order, including the provision of security, welfare in its widest sense, and general social stability and economic prosperity (Pasquino, 1991; Dean, 1999; Rose, 1999). Moreover, such functions are performed by the police as well as other governmental agencies, whose respective activities may interpenetrate one another. The Foucauldian framework is arguably more useful for analysing the current policy agenda in community safety set in train by the Crime Reduction Programme and CDA, where a plethora of agencies beyond the state participate in social control. For instance, the specialised roles of agencies such as the police, local authorities, housing, social security, health, are simultaneously becoming increasingly fragmented and divided.

The third section argues that the paradigms described above do not fully consider the agency or the intellectual and practical activities of policy makers and practitioners. An attempt is made to complement the above analyses by calling for an appreciation of what police officers and other actors carrying out policing activities, for example, actually say and do throughout their involvement at different stages and levels of the policy-making process. The critical insights offered by neo-Marxists and Foucauldians are not rejected outright but require refinement to recognise the situated activities of social actors. This calls for an awareness of the centrality of discourse in the constitution of social life (Foucault, 1967) and language in the social construction of reality (Berger and Luckmann, 1966). Although human beings use language in their day-to-day lives there are structural properties, such as power and ideology, which affect what individuals think, say and do (Gramsci, 1971).

Above all, more attention needs to be given to the complex articulation of social exclusion and crime in the context of the police-policing continuum. This includes consideration of the structural and agentic factors implicated in the policy response of the *police service* and other statutory, private, not-for-profit and voluntary agencies involved in the more general activity of *policing*.

The policy agenda: social exclusion and crime

Social exclusion

Before addressing policing, some attention needs to be paid to the notion of 'social exclusion'. This term is the latest variation on a number of other ideas referring to poverty, such as the 'underclass' and 'social deprivation' (Townsend, 1979; Morris, 1994). Each of these concepts refers to essentially the same social problems: lone-parent households; households dependent on Income Support and the Jobseeker's Allowance; households with no paid workers; local authority and housing association tenants; large families; separated/divorced households; families with a child aged under 11; adults living in one person households, including single pensioners; children; young people; those who left school aged 16 or under and women (Rahman et al, 2000). Missing from Rahman et al's inventory, but variables that are frequently attached to other lists, are crime and disorder (Jones-Finer and Nellis, 1998; Young, 1999). There are many different methods of defining, conceptualising and measuring exclusion. The author has argued elsewhere that there are two distinctive approaches, the structural and behavioural (Crowther, 2000a, 2000b, 2000c), but Levitas' (1998, 2000) typology comprising three perspectives offers a more sophisticated characterisation: the redistributionist discourse (RED); the social integrationist discourse (SID); and the moral underclass discourse (MUD). As Levitas puts it:

> ... a redistributionist discourse (RED) developed in British critical social policy, whose prime concern is poverty; a moral underclass discourse (MUD) which centres on the moral and behavioural delinquency of the excluded themselves; and a social integrationist discourse (SID) whose central focus is on paid work. (1998, p 7)

Each of these models may be influential at different times and in different places, with unique policy implications. Under four successive Conservative regimes (1979-97) MUD was the explanation preferred by ministers and the mass media. New Labour retains a degree of MUD, but following the government's launch of the SEU shortly after the 1997 election victory, the drive has been towards SID which embodies a 'joined-up' understanding of the main causes of poverty and crime. Tony Blair's oft-quoted mantra that government needs to be "tough on crime and tough on the causes of crime" epitomises SID. For example, New Labour's palliative for the excluded society is paid work and inclusion or integration into the labour force. The solutions to social exclusion involve holistic or multidimensional cross-departmental and multi-agency strategies and policies, including initiatives such as the New Deal for Communities, Sure Start and Connexions (Prescott, 2002). At the time of writing there are nine Regional Development Agencies (RDAs) charged with developing strategies of economic and social regeneration (Percy-Smith, 2000).

New Labour's multifaceted response to social exclusion and crime is buttressed by a distinctive moral and political philosophy. A founding principle is that all citizens must exercise personal responsibility in exchange for rights. This relates to the next supposition: the main right is to act responsibly by taking up opportunities at school and in the labour market; state support such as welfare services are made available only to those who are not able to carry out these fundamental responsibilities. These assumptions rest on the premise that money in the form of increased welfare will not solve social exclusion. Finally, New Labour politicians have promoted a view similar to their Conservative predecessors by refusing to accept a strong causal link between exclusion and crime. Wiles and Pease's (2001, p 224) comment about the *imperfect relationship* between crime and deprivation nicely summarises New Labour's policy orientation: "The simple presumption that economic inequality causes crime is seductive but far too simple. Remedying material inequality is not the royal road to crime reduction".

Recent changes in the rates of social exclusion and a decrease in crime and disorder may attest to the accuracy of Wiles and Pease's (2001) more complex appraisal of these problems. Under the first New Labour government, the available evidence indicates that its anti-exclusionary policies have made some headway in improving the lot of some poor people, but that low income and multiple deprivation are potentially persistent and intransigent problems (Bradshaw, 2000; DSS, 2001; Hattersley, 2001; Rahman et al, 2001; Wintour, 2001). Tony Blair also made it clear in an interview shortly before the election in June 2001 that New Labour is not specifically committed to narrowing the gap between the richest and poorest (http://news.bbc.co.uk/hi/english/events/newsnight/newsid_1372000/1372220.stm). However, more recently John Prescott, who heads up the SEU, has made a pledge to set "floor targets" to end "postcode poverty" (Prescott, 2002, p 22). Crime, on the other hand, has for the fifth successive year decreased. The British Crime Survey demonstrates a 33% fall in crime rates between 1995-2000, averaging out at 6% per year. Crimes recorded by the police have also fallen, but at a slightly less dramatic rate (Kershaw et al, 2001). The discussion now turns to contemporary crime policy.

Crime reduction and community safety: the merger of social policy and crime policy

The Morgan Report (Home Office, 1991) first put the idea of community safety onto the agenda of policy makers, but it was not formally recognised until more recently (Crawford, 1997; Hughes, 2002). According to the Home Office, community safety is:

> ... an aspect of quality of life in which people, individually and collectively, are protected as far as possible from hazards or threats that result from the criminal or anti-social behaviour of others, and are equipped or helped to cope with those that they do experience. It would enable them to pursue and obtain the fullest benefits from, their social and economic lives without fear or hindrance from crime and disorder. (Home Office, 1998, p 7)

Community safety encompasses more than crime and unlawful activities but also relates to 'chronic' social conditions brought about by anti-social behaviour, as well as low level disorder and incivilities which cause people to fear for their own safety. Behaviour such as drug misuse and drug dealing, racial harassment and hate crime; and phenomena including tackling social exclusion, consumer protection, household safety, road safety, fire prevention, as well as mental health and public health are all community safety issues. It would be fair to say that the boundaries between crime and social policy, and police and policing activity are less clear-cut, equating in some instances to the displacement of social policy through crime policy (Stenson, 1998) and arguably vice versa. Clearly it is not just the police who deal with these 'joined-up' problems and the roles and responsibilities of different agencies are being contested and negotiated along the police-policing continuum. For example, a diverse array of tactics are used that cut across the different government departments and focus on social exclusion, school performance, drug-related crime, economic regeneration, and the promotion of family life. This is congruent with the view that the causes of crime include poverty, poor housing, poor parenting, associating with delinquent peers, poor school performance, and persistent truanting (Percy-Smith, 2000).

In July 1998 the government introduced its Crime Reduction Programme and passed into law the CDA (1998). The Crime Reduction Programme is coordinated by the Crime Reduction Task Force (CRTF), which includes representatives from police forces and local and central government. The CRTF supports, advises and guides Regional Crime Reduction Directors (RCRDs) by giving them a national focus. For example, guidance may be given in relation to target setting, the best ways of involving different agencies and the development of good practice. These inform what takes place at a local level in the context of CSPs and CRPs. The Crime Reduction Programme is intended to use available resources prudently, initially to slow down, but eventually to curb, the long-term growth rate in crime (Reiner, 2000a). It is concerned with five broad themes, with varying degrees of relevance to social policy and social exclusion: working with families, children and schools to prevent young people from becoming offenders in the future (that is, the Sure Start programme); tackling crime in communities, particularly high volume crime such as domestic burglary; developing products and systems that are more resistant to crime; more effective sentencing practices; and working with offenders to ensure that they do not reoffend (Home Office, 2000, p 59). These initiatives are required to tackle crime and its structural or social and individual or behavioural causes. However, each programme has to satisfy the principles enshrined in the NPM by proving that they are 'cost-effective', provide 'value for money' and evaluated according to its effectiveness, efficiency and economy (Faulkner, 2000). Initiatives presently include burglary reduction, targeted policing, tackling school exclusions, the installation of CCTV systems in high-crime areas, improving the information available to sentencers and tackling domestic violence (Home Office, 2000, p 59).

These centrally determined aims and objectives are translated into practice at a local level: Sections 5-7, 17 and 116 of the CDA provide a statutory framework for police, local authorities and other interested agencies or CSPs and CRPs (Home Office, 1998). As an ideal type there are three elements:

- partnership group: Assistant Chief Constable (police); Chief Probation Officer; Chief Executive of Local Authority; Director of Social Services; Director of Education; voluntary sector; transport; magistrates;
- publicly accountable bodies: police authorities; health authorities; elected members of local authorities; probation committee;
- working groups: street robberies working group; car crime working group; domestic burglary working group; anti-social behaviour working group; racial harassment working group (Home Office, 2000, p 59).

These partnerships conduct audits of local crime and disorder problems, including community consultation, to set out the main priorities, objectives and targets of Community Safety Plans. The rationale of these audits is to produce information about the scale of, the impact on, and the cost of, each crime and disorder related problem for communities. This information enables participating agencies and groups to discover those problems they share in common and the best method of deploying resources to resolve them. These audits are used to formulate effective crime prevention and community safety strategies derived from a basic problem-solving structure. Crime and disorder are not actually defined in the CDA but burglary, racially motivated crime, witness intimidation, fear of crime, domestic violence, and repeat victimisation, are all designated as requiring special attention. Consideration would also be given to multi-agency strategies to tackle youth crime, take action against drugs misuse and create partnerships to crack down on general crime and disorder problems at a local level (Home Office, 1998).

The next section examines the social context in which these policies are embedded and the different modes of police and policing response.

Policing the excluded society

Neo-Marxist accounts

Until relatively recently, the argument that the police orient their resources towards an underclass has been grounded in neo-Marxist and neo-Weberian sociology. Although these sociological perspectives are markedly different, they share an emphasis on the political economy of violent crime and disorder and its structural and behavioural causes (Taylor, 1999).

Historically discussions about the issues of poverty, crime and policing tend to cluster in the aftermath of public disorder, such as the inner- and outer-city riots of 1981/85 and 1991 respectively. The former confirmed for many critical criminologists that the police were there to control the criminal classes in the inner-cities on behalf of an authoritarian state (Hall et al, 1978; Gilroy and Sim, 1987). One influential argument was that the state's economic and political marginalisation of the underclass was compounded by the criminalisation and breakdown of policing by consent following on from the police's coercive strategies (Hall et al, 1978). Lord Scarman's (1981) Inquiry into the Brixton disorders called for a less authoritarian and crime fighting type of response from the police, and instead called for more community-based policing policies including interagency communication. Although these two tendencies are sometimes characterised as hard/soft and malign/benign police forms, both were critiqued extensively for their anti-democratic, non-accountable and unjustifiably aggressive nature and a proclivity for net widening and the dispersal of disciplinary mechanisms and controls (Cohen, 1985; Brake and Hale, 1992). The police and other statutory, private and voluntary agencies with whom they worked, allegedly regulated poor communities through repression, surveillance and control.

Much of this work, therefore, describes the police's usage of force to impose order on disorderly groups and spaces, and while it offers a convincing overview of some aspects of police-community relations, the focus on a relatively narrow range of police activities such as their legitimate use of force, means that other aspects of police work are not duly considered. For example, there is a tendency to overstate the police's reliance on tough and coercive strategies (that is, paramilitarist policies) to manage the underclass (Waddington, 1994). This means two important issues are neglected. First, a wider range of community policing tactics such as police-community consultation and multi-agency partnerships do not rely on force. Second, the influence of neo-liberal and Third Way political rationalities associated with the New Public Management (NPM)

(O'Malley, 1997; Faulkner, 2000; Fionda, 2000; McLaughlin and Murji, 2001), which reduces the resources available to the police to impose control over problem groups.

The relationship between the aforementioned developments in policing and underclass formation may be seen in the context of the incomplete structural repositioning of the Keynesian Welfare National State (KWNS) into the Schumpeterian Workfare Post-National Regime (SWPR) (Jessop, 2000). The 'regulation approach' stands as an explanation of some of these transformations by focusing on changes in the global political economy which are gradually restructuring the process of capital accumulation, producing irregular effects on national, regional and local economies. The consequences of this ideal typical representation of the substitution of one state form by another for the police are as follows.

By the end of the 1980s, but particularly since the early to mid-1990s, the police were no longer given the unconditional support they previously enjoyed (Rose, 1996). New Right and neo-liberal politicians were worried about the failure of the British economy to remain competitive with other national economies in the global order, leading them to accept the inexorable logic of globalisation and the need for reform of the different organisations belonging to the KWNS, including the police (Crowther, 2000c). The objective of remaining economically competitive with other economies across the world was to be achieved by substituting the KWNS's demand side measures with the supply side measures manifest in the emergent SWPR. The welfare state did not disappear and in many instances its size increased, but there was increased rationing, targeting, privatisation, civilianisation and a general lack of investment in the infrastructure, leading to the subordination of social policy to economic policy (Hay, 1999; Jessop, 2000).

The impact of the shift from the KWNS to the SWPR on the police service is not clear-cut, but it has been suggested that it sustains the neo-liberal principles of the NPM, which were introduced to reorganise and restructure the police to ensure more effective, economical and efficient performance and service delivery (Fionda, 2000). As well as being affected by this agenda the police at local levels have also been given more centrally determined responsibilities. For example, under New Labour a Third Way version of the NPM (McLaughlin and Murji, 2001) underlines the Crime Reduction Programme and bears down on police policy at a local level through the CDA's anti-crime and disorder audits, CSPs and CRPs. For the police service this has led to more targeted forms of policing that lack the authoritarian and coercive capacities of strategies mobilised in the 1980s, such as the use of the 'sus laws' and paramilitary-style tactics, which criminalised whole groups such as the inner-city unemployed and racialised subgroups. For example, popular police strategies now include problem-oriented policing (POP), intelligence-led policing and 'crackdowns' like zero-tolerance policing are relatively intensive but short-lived interventions (Jordan, 1998). These policing tactics sometimes allow the police to impose their sovereignty in particular geographical areas. However, in contrast to the 1980s, these approaches to police work have not led to the mass criminalisation and control of entire communities. Currently, in stark contrast, the police are being criticised for abandoning, under-policing or under-protecting minority ethnic groups (Bowling, 1998; MacPherson, 1999; Marlow and Loveday, 2000) and women (Campbell, 1993). Despite these dilemmas, the police continue to aspire to police by consent, be democratically accountable and operate ethically (Neyroud and Beckley, 2001).

In short the dystopian scenarios sketched in the 1980s have not become manifest. It is now important to consider recent changes in crime policy and the contribution of Foucauldian accounts, specifically the significance they attach to political rationalities, especially the risk society thesis (Beck, 1992).

Foucauldian paradigms: the politics and economics of the risk society

The influence of Beck's *Risk society* (1992) on the social sciences cannot be overstated and Foucauldian criminologists have readily absorbed his key observation that risk society has replaced social class. These approaches consider relatively recent changes in crime control and its practical orientation towards the poor through a range of discursive and political rationalities. For example, strategies of risk assessment and risk management embedded in the logic of actuarial justice have been deployed to segregate the hazards presented by an unruly underclass (Feeley and Simon, 1994; Ericson and Haggerty, 1997). Other analysts, referred to later, draw on the governmentality literature (Dean, 1999). Here the focus is on the workings of politically constituted, differentiated and hybridised networks of statutory, voluntary and private agencies. In contrast to neo-Marxists, proponents of the governmentality approach argue that these networks do not reflect the unitary interests of elite-type groups. Having said that, the police sometimes mobilise themselves in order to impose sovereign control over given territories and specific social groups, some of which may be socially excluded (Stenson and Edwards, 2001, p 74).

Feeley and Simon (1994) have focused on the concept of actuarial justice to explain innovations in crime and control in the US. Actuarial justice is contrasted with liberal conceptions of justice belonging to the Enlightenment project of modernity, which are concerned with establishing the guilt, responsibility and obligations of individual suspects and offenders as part of a more general aim to reform and reintegrate them into society. Towards the latter stages of the 20th century the usefulness and viability of this objective was questioned. Actuarial justice is less attentive to either the rehabilitation or punishment of individuals and is preoccupied with devising "techniques for identifying, classifying and managing groups assorted by levels of dangerousness" (Feeley and Simon, 1994, p 173). Justice is no longer individualised but determined by assessing and managing the risks and hazards presented by 'groups' and 'aggregates' such as 'permanent-marginal' underclass-type populations.

Like other Foucauldians the issue of social class is not at the forefront of Feeley and Simon's (1994) analysis, but what it does show is that some groups of offenders, for instance sex offenders, share characteristics equated with a predisposition to specific types of behaviour. With regard to this group of offenders, risk assessment and management have been defined by the Probation Service: the former is "an assessment carried out to establish whether the subject is likely to cause serious physical or psychological harm to others" and the latter an "action taken to monitor a person's behaviour and attitudes, and to intervene in his/her life, in order to prevent them harming others". The "desired outcome" of "risk assessment" and "risk management" is "public protection" and enhanced security (HM Inspectorate of Probation, 1995, cited in Hebenton and Thomas, 1996, p 434).

The production of knowledge about risks and dissemination of this knowledge or 'communication about risk' are prerequisites for 'knowledge-for-security' (Hebenton and Thomas, 1996, pp 428, 431). Furthermore, the reduction of risk and creation of security is reliant on both, hence the term 'security through knowledge'. For example, the police service survey and monitor populations to produce knowledge, which may be applied in the context of risk management strategies to regulate specific categories of suspects or offenders (Hebenton and Thomas, 1996, p 432).

In principle, intelligence systems are in place to store the data used to inform and harmonise the policy responses of the different agencies involved in community safety and crime reduction (Hebenton and Thomas, 1996, pp 435-6). In practice the attainment of security through 'risk management' is far from simple as local intelligence systems are not adequately equipped to actively assess, monitor and keep track of all offending groups. Furthermore, multi-agency networks coexisting along the police-policing continuum (that is, the police, education, probation) are rarely coordinated.

Ericson and Haggerty (1997) develop similar ideas in their characterisation of the police as 'information brokers' who collaborate with other organisations, such as welfare organisations and insurance companies, to identify the crime risks imposed on society in order to control and govern crime. They process and reproduce knowledge for security through systems of information technology, bureaucracy and surveillance. Then they refer to prudential and actuarial models to calculate and measure the risk of particular behaviours and the scale of harm or loss they cause. The application of scientific knowledge enables different expert groups to classify, target and exclude deviant populations.

However, there would appear to be fundamental problems with this type of analysis because risk is not always calculable (that is, the prudential paradigm) and all knowledge of risk is finite and entangled with ignorance and uncertainty (MacVean, 2001). Police officers operate with different risk management strategies not only in relation to traditional and specialised police activities such as investigative techniques or styles of detective work, but also to a wider range of policing activities that they carry out with multi-agency partnerships. Crawford (1997) suggests that actuarial principles are invoked when agencies amass crime data, which is in turn used to inform crime prevention and community safety initiatives in specific geographical territories, such as incapacitation and community-based punishments.

MacVean (2001) rightly disagrees with such representations of risk because they are over coherent and too systematic. According to MacVean (2001), Ericson and Haggerty (1997) have conceptualised an ideal typical model of risk assessment and management, instead of considering how different strategies are combined in many different ways, producing hybrid forms of risk management. In other words, models of risk found in policy documents are not implemented straightforwardly as they come into contact with traditional police practices and procedures, as well as more novel policing techniques and strategies found along the police-policing continuum. The pure conceptions of risk imagined by policy makers are thus hybridised in practice.

Interim summary

As in the 1980s the police currently work with other agencies in crime reduction, providing further evidence of the development of a new policing complex or the police-policing continuum where the role of the police is concurrently being displaced, supplanted, strengthened or complemented by the policing activities of non-police agents and agencies. This is also an example of 'responsiblisation' and 'governance at a distance' (Garland, 2001) whereby non-statutory agencies (that is, Safer Cities, Crime Concern UK and the Jill Dando Institute of Crime Science) and individual citizens (Neighbourhood Watch) are expected to contribute towards the 'war on crime'. Due to finite resources policing activities carried out by non-police agencies are also increasingly short-term and targeted initiatives that displace, and are displaced by, other policies. The 'net widening' scenario outlined in the 1980s by Foucauldians (Cohen, 1985; Squires, 1990) and neo-Marxists (Brake and Hale, 1992) has not come into being. The conflicts between social, political and economic priorities in the prevailing political economic environment, characterised in terms of the shift from the KWNS to the SWPR, rarely result in an overarching strategy of inclusion or exclusion through policies of care or control and discipline, while the rhetoric of 'joined-up' thinking is rarely realised in policy and practice. For instance, the many policies and strategies mentioned previously do not operate in all areas and nowhere in the UK would communities receive all the support and services. Consequently, there is still scope for neglect and abandonment (Crowther, 2000b).

Reinstating agency in the political economy of policing

The critical lesson to be learnt from the above is that neo-Marxist and Foucauldian analyses do not pay enough attention to the situated activities of a range of policy makers and practitioners. In the case of the former there is too much emphasis on state power and the privileging of system needs, and the latter attributes too much significance to the political and discursive rationalities applied in theories of governmentality and the disciplinary society thesis. In short, both analytical frameworks tend to reify political and economic processes and understate the significance of agency and social action in the social construction of reality (Crowther, 2000b).

The claim that the police's resources are dedicated to monitoring the underclass has also been made by researchers focusing on the micro level of analysis who have uncovered the racist and sexist banter sustained by the occupational culture of the rank and file (Holdaway, 1983). What police officers say and do at this level has rightly been treated as a cause for concern but there are problems. For one thing, there is no necessary correspondence between thought, word and deed, but more fundamentally the processes implicated in the police's response to social groups such as the underclass are more complex and multidimensional and not reducible to the utterances and behaviour of just one level of the police policy-making process (Keith, 1993). For example, the organisational structure of the police service consists of three main players: the Home Office; chief constables; and police authorities; and the constitution of the CDA's (1998), CSPs and CRPs show that policing functions are undertaken by many agents and agencies. Their respective ideas and practices do not necessarily have a fit with the vignettes described in neo-Marxist and Foucauldian narratives. Thus there is a need for more research into the complex and diverse processes and structures within which practitioners and policy makers conduct themselves.

Crowther's (2000b) earlier work on the policing of the underclass intended to utilise a Foucauldian version of discourse analysis, drawing on archaeological and genealogical approaches (Foucault, 1967, 1977). After a period of prolonged reflection on this matter it was decided that these approaches are useful for understanding the utterances of police officers and other policy makers involved in the police policy-making process, but that the adoption of a discourse analytical framework would have entailed a close and highly detailed reading of a range of texts, which raised three epistemological and methodological issues. First, the selection of a relatively small number of texts could be criticised for selective or biased reading. Second, an exclusive focus on discourse could be seen as an attempt to reduce reality to a linguistic construction. Third, if it is accepted that reality is contingent on discourse, the potential pitfalls of relativism, solipsism and nihilism are never far away.

However, discourse and text need not be jettisoned. An attentive reading of Berger and Luckmann (1966), for example, reveals some conceptual parallels between their ideas and Foucault's thinking, in particular their mutual recognition of language or discourse. Where they part company, though, is expressed clearly in Luckmann's (1983, p 88) statement that: "language is the main, although not the only, medium for the constitution of social reality. It is also the most important medium for the transmission of social realities". Foucauldians are not likely to refer to reality or realities in this way, however. Jessop (1990) makes a similar point when he identifies the 'empty realist ontology' (1990, p 302) characterising discourse analysis. Like Luckmann, Jessop partly endorses discourse theory by accepting the importance of language and discourse in shaping social reality, but suggests that "analyses of discursive strategies and mechanisms may be one-sided but this makes them incomplete rather than wrong" (Jessop, 1990, p 392).

Studies of the policing of social exclusion therefore may be based on various textual data sources, such as legislation, government documents and policy makers' speeches, but these may be insufficient in themselves. The issue of social exclusion and any policy response to it is not just a linguistic construction but permeates various kinds of social action such as police work and policing, which are both the substance of the police-policing continuum. Luckmann's (1983, p 91) statement that: "as a rhetoric and a reservoir of justificatory devices, language is a partial guarantee of socially constructed normal worlds of entire societies, classes and social groups". The use of the word 'partial' is significant, giving a firm indication that there are other relevant factors apart from discourse. It is always possible to treat ideas and concepts as if they have a predetermined objective reality, thus negating the creative capacity of social agents as they recurrently recreate the social world as an ongoing process. However, there is also the danger of reification, which means that so much power is attributed to human agency that it loses sight of the fact that constructs are continually created and recreated. A possible consequence of this is that causal powers may be attributed to ideas such as social exclusion and models of risk, without due consideration of the fact that it is social agents who first make the ideas meaningful. The concept of social exclusion is therefore persistently made and remade by the social actors and the different organisational groups to which they belong. For example, the government's rhetoric about crime and social exclusion may be more well known in society and effectively cancel out other narratives, but this is not necessarily so. Crowther (2000b) showed that in the mid-1990s chief constables acted in concert to reject the predisposition of their political paymasters to blame the underclass for its behaviour without giving due attention to structural influences on the actions of poor people. Moreover, chief officers' views have a bearing, albeit indirect, on the police policy-making process. In other words there are different ideas about policy problems, which are understood and acted on in different cultural, organisational and structural circumstances.

Berger and Luckmann's (1966) social constructionism – including its implicit relationship with Foucault's work – is of utility for understanding the creativity of the human subject at a micro level, but the ability to change and recreate is constrained by wider macro-structural properties. Social actors' ideas and perceptions are significant, but in the context of this wider social structure some individuals and groups tend to be more persuasive and provide more influential ideas than others. Human creativity and social action is restricted because of the impositions of relatively more powerful and permanent structures in wider society. A major influence, for want of better terms, occurs at an ideological level. To clarify this, Gramsci's (1971) notion of 'common sense' is helpful.

Debates about social exclusion and crime are an element of policy maker's 'common sense' views of the world. Gramsci (1971) defines 'common sense' as the ambiguous, incoherent and, sometimes contradictory, assumptions, attitudes and beliefs that are part of our worldview. There is not one 'common sense', but rather the term comprises a 'multiform' and 'collective noun' (1971, p 325), which does not refer to a single, unitary perspective. For this reason, Gramsci maintains that common sense does not:"constitute an intellectual order, because it cannot be reduced to unity and coherence within an individual consciousness" (p 325). Gramsci expands this point:

> ... where one's conception of the world is not critical and coherent but disjointed and episodic, one belongs simultaneously to a multiplicity of mass human groups. The personality is strangely composite: it contains Stone Age elements and principles of a more advanced science, prejudices from all past phases of history at the level and intuitions of a future philosophy which will be that of a human race united the world over. (1971, p 324)

Gramsci's particular conception of 'common sense' is derived from one of Karl Marx's observations outlined in the *Critique of Hegel's philosophy of right,* namely the necessity of articulating 'popular beliefs' with 'material forces'. In distinguishing these two phenomena, Marx's preoccupation is not with the coherence of attitudes and beliefs but the effects of such ways of thinking on their conduct. Even if perceptions are amorphous and inchoate, they have the potential to be a force at work in the social construction of reality (Marx, cited in Gramsci, 1971).

To relate this to the main concerns of this chapter, there are many different representations of social exclusion and crime, which come into conflict with each other. These diverse ideas focus on various ways of explaining interrelated economic, political and social processes. However, some ideas are more influential because certain powerful agents and institutions are in relatively privileged positions to mobilise ideologies, which in turn shape the policy response to given policy dilemmas. Returning to the author's earlier example, chief constables effectively voiced their collective concerns about particular aspects of government rhetoric, in this instance its willingness to blame and condemn the socially excluded for their predicament. In practice, though, the government has more authority, exercises its power more effectively and almost always wins (Crowther, 2000b).

Conclusion

This chapter has critically reflected on the practical relevance of neo-Marxist and Foucauldian analyses of the local, national and global processes impinging on social and crime policy, particularly developments in police policy and practice. These respective analytical perspectives have identified a complex mix of political and economic interventions, which create uneven patterns of social inclusion and exclusion mediated through the usage of contradictory styles of police and policing as part of a new police–policing continuum. Traditionally neo-Marxists have concentrated on macro changes, such as globalisation and political economic restructuring, resulting in the criminalisation and exclusion of populations surplus to the requirements of the system of production. Foucauldian commentators have instead described the influence of discursive practices and political rationalities, such as risk, which are deployed to assess and manage dangerous populations.

The central argument is that these approaches need to be reworked because they overstate the accomplishments of police and policing agencies. For example, the mutual interaction of changes in the political economy at global and local levels and their impact on the poor and policed is becoming more and more complex. The relationship between the police and the poor was once explained in terms of the police reflecting the interests of an authoritarian and repressive state. Nowadays police activities do not simply mirror the interests of the state and the assumed relationship between social exclusion, crime and policing is less straightforward than sometimes imagined. One reason for this change is that in the context of 'joined-up' policy the linkages between different problems become more complex due to the different discursive and practical agendas of the different organisations involved.

There are other countervailing processes, such as the tension between state set priorities at a macro level and their interpretation, application and reprioritisation at meso and micro levels. In addition there is a diversity of structures in place to deal with crime and social exclusion and many different methods of spreading scarce resources ever more thinly. For example, the police and partners from the private and voluntary sectors involved in policing are required to distribute resources according to 'evidence based' and managerial or performance oriented criteria based on 'what works'; hence targeted community-based policing strategies. Elsewhere the author has argued that the underclass are the beneficiaries of this attention, either through increased control or care (Crowther, 2000c). The author would like to suggest that current police-policing mechanisms and processes no longer lead to the scenarios outlined in the 1980s and 1990s, and that further empirical research is required to assess the extent to which the socially excluded are controlled, cared for or abandoned as a consequence of the effects of the new police-policing continuum. Moreover, future research requires a reorientation to address more fully the complexity of social reality and practical matters in social policy through reinstating an appreciation of human agency and social action.

References

Bauman, Z. (1998) *Work, consumerism and the new poor*, Milton Keynes: Open University Press.

Beck, U. (1992) *The risk society*, London: Sage Publications.

Berger, P. and Luckmann, T. (1966) *The social construction of reality*, London: Allen Lane.

Bowling, B. (1998) *Violent racism*, Oxford: Oxford University Press.

Bradshaw, J. (2000) 'Prospects for poverty in Britain in the first twenty five years of the next century', *Sociology*, vol 34, no 1, pp 53-70.

Brake, M. and Hale, C. (1992) *Public order and private lives: The politics of law and order*, London: Routledge.

Campbell, B. (1993) *Goliath: Britain's dangerous places*, London: Meuthen.

Choongh, S. (1997) *Policing as social discipline*, Oxford: Clarendon Press.

Clarke, J. and Newman, J. (1997) *The managerial state: Power, politics and ideology in the remaking of social welfare*, London: Sage Publications.

Cohen, S. (1985) *Visions of social control*, Cambridge: Polity Press.

Cook, D. (1997) *Poverty, crime and punishment*, London: Child Poverty Action Group.

Crawford, A. (1997) *The local governance of crime*, Oxford: Oxford University Press.

Crowther, C. (2000a) 'Crime, social exclusion and policing in the twenty-first century', *Crime Prevention and Community Safety*, vol 2, no 1, pp 37-49.

Crowther, C. (2000b) *Policing urban poverty*, Basingstoke: Macmillan.

Crowther, C. (2000c) 'Thinking about the "underclass": towards a political economy of policing', *Theoretical Criminology*, vol 4, no 2, pp 149-67.

Davies, H., Nutley, S. and Smith, P. (eds) (2000) *What works?: Evidence-based policy and practice in public services*, Bristol: The Policy Press.

Dean, M. (1999) *Governmentality: Power and rule in modern society*, London: Sage Publications.

Dennis, N. (ed) (1997) *Zero tolerance policing: Policing a free society*, London: Institute of Economic Affairs.

DSS (Department of Social Security) (2001) *Households below average income*, London: The Stationery Office.

Ericson, R. and Haggerty, K. (1997) *Policing the risk society*, Oxford: Oxford University Press.

Faulkner, D. (2000) 'Policy and practice in modern Britain: influences, outcomes and civil society', in P. Green and A. Rutherford (eds) *Criminal policy in transition*, Oxford: Hart, pp 79-89.

Feeley, M. and Simon, J. (1994) 'Actuarial justice: the emerging new criminal law', in D. Nelken (ed) *The futures of criminology*, London: Sage Publications, pp 173-201.

Fionda, J. (2000) 'New managerialism, credibility and the sanitisation of criminal justice', in P. Green and A. Rutherford (eds) *Criminal policy in transition*, Oxford: Hart, pp 109-27.

Foucault, M. (1967) *Madness and civilisation: A history of insanity in the age of reason*, London: Tavistock.

Foucault, M. (1977) *Discipline and punish*, Harmondsworth: Penguin.

Foucault, M. (1991) 'Governmentality', in G. Burchell, C. Gordon and P. Miller (eds) *The Foucault effect: Studies in governmentality*, Brighton: Harvester, pp 87-104.

Garland, D. (2001) *The culture of control: Crime and social order in contemporary society*, Oxford: Oxford University Press.

Giddens, A. (1998) *The third way: The renewal of social democracy*, Cambridge: Polity Press.

Giddens, A. (2002) *Where now for New Labour?*, Cambridge: Polity Press.

Gilroy, P. and Sim, J. (1987) 'Law, order and the state of the left', in P. Scraton (ed) *Law, order and the authoritarian state: Readings in critical criminology*, Milton Keynes: Open University Press, pp 71-106.

Gramsci, A. (1971) *Selections from the prison notebooks*, London: Lawrence and Wishart.

Hall, S., Critcher, C., Jefferson, T., Clarke, J. and Roberts, B. (1978) *Policing the crisis: Mugging, the state and law and order*, Basingstoke: Macmillan.

Hattersley, R. (2001) 'New labour's creeping poverty gap', *The Guardian*, 16 July.

Hay, C. (1999) *The political economy of new labour: Labouring under false pretences?*, Manchester: Manchester University Press.

Hebenton, B. and Thomas, T. (1996) 'Sexual offenders in the community: Reflections on problems of law, community and risk management in the USA, England and Wales', *International Journal of the Sociology of Law*, vol 24, pp 427-43.

Hillyard, P. and Watson, S. (1996) 'Postmodern social policy: a contradiction in terms', *Journal of Social Policy*, vol 25, no 3, pp 321-46.

Holdaway, S. (1983) *Inside the British police: A force at work*, Oxford: Blackwell.

Home Office (1991) *Safer communities: The local delivery of crime prevention through the partnership approach* (Morgan Report), London: Home Office.

Home Office (1998) *The crime and disorder act: Community safety and the reduction and prevention of crime – A conceptual framework for training and the development of a professional discipline*, London: Home Office.

Home Office (1999) *Mission statement*, London: The Stationery Office.

Home Office (2000) *A guide to the criminal justice system in England and Wales*, London: Home Office.

Home Office (2001a) *Building cohesive communities: A Report on the Ministerial Group on Public Order and Community Cohesion*, London: Home Office.

Home Office (2001b) *Community Cohesion: A report of the independent review team chaired by Ted Cantle*, London: Home Office.

Hood, C. (1991) 'A public management for all services', *Public Administration*, vol 69, no 1, pp 3-11.

Hopkins-Burke, R. (ed) (1998) *Zero tolerance policing*, Leicester: Perpetuity Press.

Hughes, G. (2002) 'The shifting sands of crime prevention and community safety', in G. Hughes, E. McLaughlin and J. Muncie (eds) *Crime prevention and community safety: New directions*, London: Sage Publications, pp 1-10.

Jessop, B. (1990) *State theory: Putting capitalist states in their place*, Cambridge: Polity Press.

Jessop, B. (2000) 'From the KWNS to the SWPR', in G. Lewis, S. Gerwitz and J. Clarke (eds) *Rethinking social policy*, London: Sage Publications, pp 171-84.

Johnston, L. (1999) *Policing Britain: Risk, security and governance*, Harlow: Longman.

Jones-Finer, C. and Nellis, M. (eds) (1998) *Crime and social exclusion*, Oxford: Blackwell.

Jordan, P. (1998) 'Effective policing strategies for reducing crime', in P. Goldblatt and C. Lewis (eds) *Reducing offending: An assessment of research evidence on ways of dealing with offending behaviour*, Home Office Research Study 187, London: Home Office, pp 63-81.

Keith, M. (1993) *Race, riots and policing*, London: UCL Press.

Kershaw, C., Chivitie-Mathews, N., Thomas, C. and Aust, R. (2001) *The 2001 British crime survey*, Home Office Statistical Bulletin, 18/01, London: Home Office.

Levitas, R. (1998) *The inclusive society?: Social exclusion and new labour*, Basingstoke: Macmillan.

Levitas, R. (2000) 'What is social exclusion?', in D. Gordon and P. Townsend (eds) *Breadline Europe: The measurement of poverty*, Bristol: The Policy Press, pp 357-83.

Lister, R. (ed) (1996) *Charles Murray and the underclass*, London: IEA.

Luckmann, T. (1983) *The life world and social realities*, London: Heinemann.

MacPherson, Sir W. (1999) *Report of an inquiry into the Stephen Lawrence murder*, London: Home Office.

MacVean, A. (2001) 'Risk, policing and the management of sex offenders', *Crime Prevention and Community Safety: An International Journal*, vol 4, no 2, pp 7-18.

Marlow, A. and Loveday, B. (eds) (2000) *After MacPherson: Policing after the Stephen Lawrence inquiry*, Lyme Regis: Russell House Publishing.

McLaughlin, E. and Murji, K. (2001) 'Lost connections and new directions: neo-liberalism, new public management and the "modernization" of the British police', in K. Stenson and R.A. Sullivan (eds) *Crime, risk and justice: The politics of crime control in liberal democracies*, Cullompton: Willan, pp 104-22.

Marx, K. (1970) *Critique of Hegel's 'Philosophy of Right'*, London: Cambridge University Press.

Morris, L. (1994) *Dangerous classes*, London: Routledge.

Murray, C. (1999) *The underclass revisited*, Washington, DC: American Enterprise Institute for Public Policy Research.

Neyroud, P. and Beckley, A. (2001) *Policing, ethics and human rights*, Cullompton: Willan.

O'Malley, P. (1997) 'Policing, politics and post-modernity', *Social and Legal Studies*, vol 6, no 3, pp 363-81.

O'Malley, P., Weir, D. and Shearing, C. (1997) 'Governing thrift: Insurance, political rationalities and working class security', Unpublished paper, School of Law and Legal Studies, Melbourne: La Trobe University.

Pasquino, P. (1991) 'Theatricum politicum: the genealogy of capital-police and the state of prosperity', in G. Burchell, C. Gordon and P. Miller (eds) *The Foucault effect: Studies in governmentality*, Brighton: Harvester, pp 105-18.

Percy-Smith, J. (ed) (2000) *Policy responses to social exclusion: Towards inclusion?*, Buckingham: Open University Press.

Pitts, J. and Matthews, R. (eds) (2001) *Crime, disorder and community safety*, London: Sage Publications.

Poulantzas, N. (1978) *State, power and socialism*, London: New Left Books.

Prescott, J. (2002) 'The heart and soul of the nation', *The Guardian*, 16 January.

Rahman, M., Palmer, G., Kenway, P. and Howarth, C. (2000) *Monitoring poverty and social exclusion 2000*, York: Joseph Rowntree Foundation.

Rahman, M., Palmer, G. and Kenway, P. (2001) *Monitoring poverty and social exclusion 2001*, York: Joseph Rowntree Foundation.

Reiner, R. (2000a) 'Crime and control in Britain', *Sociology*, vol 34, no 1, pp 71-94.

Reiner, R. (2000b) *The politics of the police* (3rd edn), Oxford: Oxford University Press.

Rose, D. (1996) *In the name of the law*, London: Jonathan Cape.

Rose, N. (1999) *Powers of freedom: Reframing political thought*, Cambridge: Cambridge University Press.

Savage, S. and Atkinson, R. (eds) (2001) *Public policy under Blair*, Basingstoke: Palgrave.

Scarman, Lord L. (1981) *The Brixton disorders 10-12 April, report of an inquiry by the Rt. Honourable Lord Scarman*, Cmnd 8427, London: HMSO.

Squires, P. (1990) *Anti-social policy: Welfare, ideology and the disciplinary state*, London: Harvester Wheatsheaf.

Stenson, K. (1998) 'Displacing social policy through crime control', in S. Hänninen (ed) *Displacement of social policies*, SoPhi: University of Jykväskylä, pp 117-44.

Stenson, K. (2000) 'Crime control, social policy and liberalism', in G. Lewis, S. Gerwitz and J. Clarke (eds) *Rethinking social policy*, London: Sage Publications, p 229-44.

Stenson, K. and Edwards, A. (2001) 'Crime control and liberal government: the "third way" and the return to the local', in K. Stenson and R.A. Sullivan (eds) *Crime, risk and justice: The politics of crime control in liberal democracies*, Cullompton: Willan, pp 117-44.

Taylor, I. (1999) *Crime in context: A critical criminology of market societies*, Cambridge: Polity Press.

Townsend, P. (1979) *Poverty in the United Kingdom*, London: Harmondsworth.

Waddington, P.A.J. (1994) *Liberty and order: Public order policing in the capital*, London: UCL Press.

Walker, A. and Walker, C. (eds) (1997) *Britain divided: The growth of social exclusion in the 1980s and 1990s*, London: Child Poverty Action Group.

Wiles, P. (1999) 'The contribution of research to policy', Speech given at the Centre for Criminal Justice Studies (ISTD), AGM, November.

Wiles, P. and Pease, K. (2001) 'Distributive justice and crime', in J. Pitts and R. Matthews (eds) *Crime, disorder and community safety*, London: Sage Publications, pp 219-40.

Wintour, P. (2001) 'Blair fails to close rich-poor gap', *The Guardian*, 13 July.

Young, J. (1999) *The exclusive society: social exclusion, crime and difference in late modernity*, London: Sage Publications.

ELEVEN

Green social welfare: an investigation into political attitudes towards ecological critiques and prescriptions concerning the welfare state

Caron Caldwell

The environment has now firmly established itself as an issue that society can no longer afford to ignore, and there is currently a general consensus both among political parties and the public that the quality of the environment is important to human welfare (George and Wilding, 1999). However, despite this increased importance, concern for the environment has not yet been translated into comprehensive policy initiatives. There is a growing recognition that such concern needs to be incorporated into all policy areas, including social policy but, both theoretically and practically, Green social policies continue to remain something of an enigma.

Since the 1990s social policy's neglect of environmental issues has been partly addressed by Cahill (1999), Ferris (1991), Fitzpatrick (1998a, 1998b), Huby (1998) and Shaw (1999). Indeed, Fitzpatrick (1998b) argues that if Green critiques are even marginally accurate in terms of the explanations that they offer and the predictions that they make, then the social policy community cannot afford to disregard environmental concerns indefinitely. One reason is that studies have begun to demonstrate that the environment has a direct impact on health. However, more importantly, the contemporary welfare state is dependent on economic growth to provide the financial resources with which to deliver welfare goods and services (Shaw, 1999). The ecological critique challenges this perception; unlimited, indiscriminate economic growth is neither desirable nor possible (Meadows et al, 1972, 1992). Therefore, if economic growth is limited the welfare state as we know it is under threat. But, with economic growth continuing to be the yardstick by which countries measure their success, the idea that such limits to growth exist has yet to find favour either with politicians or the electorate.

This chapter reports preliminary findings from research currently being undertaken by the author, which examines the extent to which politicians and Green activists make an association between welfare reform and environmentalism. It argues that Green social policies and welfare reforms can only be developed if we have a clear idea about how they understand the nature of this relationship. From discursive analysis it has been possible to 'map' a tentative diagram of different environmental discourses that highlight potential areas of rapprochement alongside those of diversity. Such an approach, it is argued, may indicate what alliances are necessary/ possible in order to create a political agenda of social sustainability.

Environmentalism

One problem when discussing environmentalism is that it is an 'umbrella' term used to cover a wide range of differing perspectives. The environmental movement may have at its core a unifying desire to protect the environment, but there is considerable debate within the movement as to how humans relate to nature, what counts as 'value', how the environmental crisis can be known, and what strategies are required to pursue sustainability. This is because the environmental movement itself spans a broad church, from lobbyists and activists on the one hand, to a sort of New Age, counter-cultural force on the other. Therefore, it is first necessary to identify some of the environmental discourses that currently predominate.

Sustainability

Debates around the concept of sustainability have expanded over recent years to embrace a multitude of theoretical perspectives and policy applications. At their core lies the dilemma of how to reconcile human and social activities with the long-term resilience, vulnerability and regenerative capacity of ecological systems (Sneddon, 2000). At present, sustainability remains a contested concept both in terms of definition and how it can be achieved. While this allows room for debate, negotiation and more radical interpretations, it can also mean that the term itself is at risk of being applied too liberally without any clear indication of what it actually means.

Dobson (1998) offers one of the best of the most recent treatments of sustainability. According to Dobson, it is possible to identify three main conceptions of environmental sustainability:

- Conception A: (Dobson, 1998, pp 41-7) is concerned with sustaining critical natural capital. Critical natural capital refers to those aspects of natural capital that are considered essential for the continuation of human life. Within this conception critical natural capital is preserved primarily through processes of renewal and substitution. Therefore, sustainable forests are those that are constantly renewed with trees being replanted as they are used. For capital that cannot be renewed in this way due to its finite resources, for example oil, alternatives or substitutes can be found. According to this conception it is only when critical natural capital cannot be renewed or substituted that it needs to be conserved.
- Conception B: (Dobson, 1998, pp 47-50) acknowledges that there are certain aspects of the natural world whose loss would be irreversible and therefore non-renewable. For example, when a species becomes extinct, it cannot, by definition, be renewed. This conception also acknowledges that substitution has its limits. Again, if a species becomes extinct, it is not possible to replace it with a human-made substitute. Consequently, this conception gives priority to the needs of present generations of non-humans over the needs of future generations of humans, on the grounds that the loss of a non-human species cannot be justified in terms of the potential benefits of that loss to future generations.
- Conception C: (Dobson, 1998, pp 50-4) accepts that nature has its own intrinsic value. Accordingly, neither renewability nor substitution can compensate for this loss. Therefore, in this conception, it is the idea of conservation that is the main instrument to be used to achieve sustainability. This position does not necessarily mean that human needs are not important but it does argue for the needs of non-humans to be granted higher priority in the decision-making process.

These three conceptions can be thought of in terms of the anthropocentric/ecocentric positions that make up two extremes of Green thought. This dichotomy represents one of the central tenets of Green thinking; the status of the non-human world and its treatment by humans. Whereas the former argues that humans stand separate and above nature, the latter argues that all nature has intrinsic value.

Conception A adopts a distinctly anthropocentric approach. Critical natural capital is preserved in order to protect human welfare. Conception

B adopts a midway position between anthropocentrism and ecocentrism. Therefore, while it acknowledges and accepts the importance of human welfare, it also recognises that some elements of non-human nature, even if it does not impact upon human welfare, should be conserved. Conception C, on the other hand, by identifying the intrinsic value of nature adopts a more ecocentric position. Nature should be protected not because of its use value to human welfare, but because it has value in its own right. Nature can be beneficial to human welfare but this should not be the overriding consideration for its protection.

Perhaps more importantly, moving on from the debate about what it is that actually needs to be sustained, it is also necessary to consider whether achieving sustainability would require a move beyond market capitalism. If Dobson's conception A can be identified as 'weak' sustainability, then conception B would be 'middle' and conception C 'strong'. Only the weak version could happily remain within a framework of liberal democratic capitalism, whereas radical versions of moderate and strong sustainability begin to push beyond it. Consequently, it is important to examine how current policy making understands the concept of sustainability. To do this it is necessary to examine the equally contested concept of sustainable development.

Sustainable development

Sustainable development is a term that has been frequently used over recent years as a blueprint for achieving sustainability. It has become common political currency across the political spectrum, from radical bio-regionalists to neo-liberal free marketeers (Huby, 2002: forthcoming). However, its wide range of interpretations and breadth of deployment undermines this consensus. As sustainability is a contested concept, then how it is to be achieved through the process of sustainable development is obviously dependent on which interpretation of the concept you subscribe to.

If Dobson's conception A is favoured then sustainable development will involve the natural world being regarded as there for the benefit of the human world. This pragmatic interpretation would allow for the continuation of current patterns of growth, as long as they were modified to reduce environmental impacts. Conception B would involve preventing the loss of any of the natural world that would be irreversible. However, this criterion could be applied too stringently within the conception because it does not distinguish between those elements of the natural world, such as pathogenic organisms, whose eradication would be desirable for the good of humankind. Sustainable development implies progress, so for example, it would be considered both progressive and desirable to free the world from harmful pathogenic organisms, but this would not sit easily with conception B. Conception C, on the other hand, can be associated with radical Green interpretations of sustainable development. These recognise the intrinsic value of the natural world and challenge the current capitalist economic and political paradigm.

The interpretation of sustainable development that has been adopted in the UK is predicated on the influential Brundtland Report that attempts to reconcile Third World development with environmental protection: "development that meets the needs of present generations without compromising the ability of future generations to meet their own needs" (WCED, 1987).

The notion of social justice is important within the discourse because it recognises the importance of the need to alleviate poverty so that poor people will not abuse their environment in order to survive. Justice within this discourse should also refer to future generations as well as the present, although it remains distinctly anthropocentric in its approach. Therefore, this definition tends, at best, towards Dobson's conception A of sustainability. While there is a recognition that the legitimate developmental aspirations of the world's people cannot be met by all countries following the growth path already taken by the industrialised countries, economic growth continues to be promoted but in ways that are both environmentally benign and socially just.

The Brundtland definition of sustainable development (WCED, 1987), with its emphasis on the mutual reinforcement of economic growth, social development and environmental protection, is the one that was readily adopted by the UK government in the 1990s. It therefore embodies an acceptance that industrial capitalism is not going to be overturned, and that modern science and technology can help to solve environmental problems (Jacobs, 1999, p 7). However, although this interpretation of sustainable development has official government endorsement it has not become part of mainstream political discourse (Jacobs, 1999, p 2).

Jacobs (1999, p 11) argues that sustainable development is not a New Labour discourse because it is still perceived essentially as a Green philosophy. Therefore, according to Jacobs, there needs to be a new environmental discourse that chimes with Labour's core concerns. Consequently, what is required is a discourse that not only focuses on growth as an environmental good but also enables more ambitious, radical Green concepts to be included within the debate. One such discourse is 'ecological modernisation'.

Ecological modernisation

Ecological modernisation has emerged recently and suggests one pathway to sustainable development. It derives from an interpretation of sustainability that has evolved from the Brundtland Report in an attempt to 'put flesh on' the reformist version of sustainable development (Garner, 2000, p 42). This emerging discourse or the so-called 'third wave' of environmentalism has therefore developed from a discourse of radical change into a pragmatic acceptance of the status quo (Van der Heijden, 1999, p 217).

Ecological modernisation was first observed and identified in German environmental policy in the early 1980s (Dryzek, 1997, p 141). It is a discourse that implies a partnership between government, businesses, moderate environmentalists and scientists who would cooperate in the restructuring of the capitalist political economy along more environmentally defensible lines. The importance of this perspective lies in the fact that it is seen as an immanent critique that represents a realistic theory about how to deal with environmental problems (Barry, 1999). What is important is not reducing economic growth, but making sure that growth is sustainable.

Thus sustainability, it is argued, can be achieved through developments in science and technology within existing social practices and administrative structures. Ecological modernisation can be considered as both a set of reforms and a political discourse (Christoff, 1996; Van der Heijden, 1999) whereby environmental goals and traditional objectives are regarded as mutually achievable through the application of greater efficiency in the use of resources and energy. Nature is treated as a source of resources and a recycler of pollutants (Dryzek, 1997, p 144), making ecological modernisation unashamedly anthropocentric in its approach. It is a discourse of progress and reassurance in which not only can environmental protection and economic prosperity proceed hand in hand, but environmental protection can also be re-conceptualised as a potential source of growth rather than an economic burden (Weale, 1992). As Blair (*The Guardian*, 25 October 2000) has stated, "we can be richer by being greener and by being greener we will enrich the quality of our lives".

The essential question is: does ecological modernisation represent little more than a rhetorical tool that enables the government to control the political agenda or does it genuinely provide the opportunity for Green values and principles to be raised politically through the state (Barry, 1999, p 101)? In attempting to answer this question it is important to note that ecological modernisation remains a contested concept. Christoff (1996) has devised a typology that differentiates between 'weak' and 'strong' interpretations of ecological modernisation. Whereas the strong interpretation denotes a democratic, international approach with a strong ecological influence, weak ecological modernisation can be regarded as a narrow, national approach with economic considerations continuing to take precedence over environmental ones. However, it is essential not to consider the weak and strong features of ecological modernisation as mutually exclusive binary opposites but to recognise that aspects of weak ecological modernisation need to be subsumed into and guided by the normative dimensions of the strong interpretation (Christoff, 1996, p 491). Similarly, the latter must be guided by the pragmatism of the former.

Ecological modernisation is not without its critics (for example, Pepper, 1998). It has been understood as a discourse that neglects social justice and also one that underestimates how developing countries are to reach the position where they can afford to practice ecological modernisation. It also allows those who subscribe to the 'limits to growth' argument to challenge the notion that environmentally responsible growth is an adequate substitute for low or zero growth. However, others take a more positive stance and argue that this discourse may offer a viable theoretical framework that can be utilised both as a device to persuade governments to act on Green demands and as a means of judging how 'sustainable' their response is (cf Fitzpatrick with Caldwell, 2001).

Green social policies in the polity

So just how sustainable has New Labour's response been to the heightened awareness of environmental issues? The election of the Labour government in 1997 had the potential to be a significant event in the development of British environmental policy. Not only was the Blair government the first Labour administration to come to power since the environment had become an important issue, but the transformation of the Party over the course of the late 1980s and early 1990s seemed to remove the ideological and organisational obstacles that had previously prevented Labour from wholeheartedly endorsing environmentalism. Now, protecting the environment and promoting sustainable development were not to be add-on extras, but instead "inform the whole of government, from housing and energy policy through to global warming and international agreement" (Labour Party, 1997, p 4).

However, recent research (Ross, 2000) has concluded that there continue to be problems surrounding cross-departmental policies like sustainable development.

This is primarily because government is not a single entity but a complex diversity of interrelated bodies with each department or agency having its own identity, objectives, culture, organisation and priorities. For some departments like the now-defunct Department of the Environment, Transport and the Regions (DETR), sustainable development was a key objective; for others, like the Treasury, it is one of many often conflicting policy objectives; and for others, it is a non-issue. Therefore, it is easy to see how cross-departmental policies like sustainable development can falter due to the diverse ambitions of individual departments.

As for explaining what is meant by the term 'sustainable development' the government published *A better quality of life: A strategy for sustainable development for the UK* (DETR, 1999) on 17 May 1999. This document stated that "ensuring a better quality of life for everyone, now and for future generations to come lies at the heart of the government's sustainable development strategy" (DETR, 1999, p 3). It is therefore possible to identify similarities with the popular Brundtland definition. However, it is also possible to identify a range of issues that are either missing or understated in the document. Poverty, education and health are cases in point but the need to tackle unsustainable consumption is also clearly under-represented. Indeed, the document appears to confuse the distinction between improving the 'quality of life' and achieving higher living standards.

Attaining a higher standard of living has traditionally been concerned with increased income and purchasing power within the marketplace. The 'quality of life' argument promotes the idea that individual and collective welfare is not solely provided by consumption, but must also include such environmental 'goods' as clean air and lack of noise pollution. Recognising and highlighting this difference is considered to be of vital importance to those who are promoting the link between social policy and environmentalism (Huby, 1998; Cahill, 1999). New Labour's working definition of sustainable development has therefore yet to resolve the perception of conflict between the pursuit of economic growth, low levels of taxation and personal prosperity and autonomy on the one hand, and protecting the environment on the other.

Significantly in this regard a recent review of Labour's performance in government argues that growth consistently trumped the environment in all areas of policy (Toynbee and Walker, 2001). Disappointingly, Labour's commitment to the environment continues to be primarily channelled towards the traditional environmental areas and, for example, honouring their manifesto commitment by agreeing to a 20% cut in CO_2 emissions. Where there are links between social policy and environmentalism these are mainly to be found at the local level under the auspices of the Local Agenda 21 programme. However, even under this programme there is little consensus as to what Green social policies might actually look like and how they could be effectively implemented.

Empirical research

Given this lack of consensus it is not surprising that preliminary investigation reveals Green social policies as barely registering on the political and policy-making agenda. Because we are studying the preconditions of what *might* exist rather than what already exists, to get to where we want to be we have to start from where we are now. Subsequently, two research propositions are being explored within the study:

- The future direction of the welfare state is partly dependent on the outcome of the debate between conflicting ideas regarding Green social policy making.
- Green social policies and welfare reforms can only be developed if we have clear ideas about how and why politicians and Green activists formulate the link between environmentalism and welfare systems.

While it is acknowledged that individual perspectives can have only minimal influence on institutional policies, it was considered necessary to canvass individuals for their views in order to explore individual perceptions of some of the environmental concepts described in the first part of this chapter. Only once these perceptions have been analysed and common links identified would it be possible to suggest how environmental policies might be introduced onto the social agenda.

Six in-depth qualitative interviews have so far been carried out; three with national politicians (2 Labour, 1 Conservative), one with a member of the European Parliament (Labour), one with a Green Party political activist and one with a local government officer. Alongside these interviews a questionnaire was devised and distributed to 659 Members of Parliament in an attempt to access the views of as many MPs as possible: 366 were sent through the post and 281 by e-mail containing a website address where the questionnaire could be accessed. The decision to use the two separate methodologies was born partly out of financial considerations and partly due to an attempt to offer MPs the chance to fill in a questionnaire as quickly as possible. However, both methods produced a very low response rate: postal 8.7%, e-mail 5.7%. The survey therefore generated an overall response rate of 7.4%. The e-mail response rate was consistent with other e-mail research (cf Mehta and Sividas, 1995; Tse, 1998). Of course, given the low response rate, the results cannot be considered valid or representative of the views of national politicians in general; however, they do provide an 'audit' of differing perspectives.

Preliminary findings

Overall the questionnaire demonstrated that there was considerable homogeneity within the answers pertaining to both environmental and welfare issues. For example, all but two of the respondents believed global warming to be either very or fairly important and well over three quarters of respondents believed the welfare state to be both popular with the general public and necessary for both society and the economy. Another area around which there appeared to be consensus was the role of the environmental movement to raise both public and politician's awareness of environmental issues. However, cross-tabulation of the survey data along party political lines suggests that there may not be the same degree of ideological homogeneity across all issues, with some Labour MPs adopting a more egalitarian, redistributional and regulated stance to welfare than Conservative respondents. One of the disadvantages of using a questionnaire to gauge politicians' attitudes, values and beliefs is that there is no way of knowing how the respondents interpreted the questions, so qualitative analysis of the interviews was also employed to expand on some of the themes.

Five topics have emerged from the preliminary analysis as being particularly significant:

- economic growth and consumption
- social justice
- local government and Europe
- community
- science and technology.

Economic growth and consumption

The subject of economic growth is central to the debate around ecological concern and social policy. However, it can be argued that since the emergence of the sustainable development and ecological modernisation discourses, economic growth and environmental concern need no longer be viewed as incompatible.

When asked whether economic growth and environmental protection were compatible the three Labour politicians (two national and one European MP) strongly agreed that they were. All three also spoke in the language of ecological modernisation; not only were economic growth and environmental protection compatible but there was also a sense that environmental protection should be viewed as a source of future growth, which could be achieved through initiatives such as prudent use of resources:

> "... opportunities for using the environment for advances as far as economic prosperity is concerned are amazing." (Labour MEP)

Growth therefore does not necessarily have to be reduced but needs to be made sustainable. In this discourse, consumption needs to be addressed, and indeed, analysis of the questionnaire demonstrated that the majority of Labour MPs who responded (17 out of 25) agreed that consumption should be the concern of social policies, but it is indiscriminate consumption, or that which causes resource depletion and pollution, not consumption per se. However, one Labour MP who was interviewed appeared unable to see the distinction between achieving a better quality of life and raising standards of living:

> "How can you possibly advocate to people that they should be more environmentally aware if at the same time you are preventing them enhancing their quality of living or you're condemning them to poor housing or you're saying you are not having job opportunities in this area. It's completely nuts." (Labour MP)

With regard to taxation, which is one way of regulating consumption (and also the ultimate resource for social policy), findings from the survey indicated that one third of the Labour MPs who responded agreed with the need for higher income tax.

The one Conservative MP who has so far been interviewed, did not share the belief that environmental protection can be viewed as a source of future growth. Instead he saw environmental protection as a necessary cost of continued growth:

> "... environmental protection is a necessary cost, not a source of growth. Ultimately growth creates resources which can be used to help protect the environment." (Conservative MP)

This belief is consistent with what Dryzek (1997) calls the 'Promethean' discourse. Within this discourse is the belief in the infinite capacity of the earth to cope with human exploitation and the ingenuity of humans to solve problems that arise. Therefore, within this discourse, continued growth and consumption are not only desirable but also essential in order to protect the environment. These sentiments are echoed in the responses from those Conservative MPs who answered the questionnaire. When asked whether the issue of consumption should be the concern of social policies none of the 12 who replied agreed that it should be and in fact, over half of them (seven out of 12) thought that it should not be. Unsurprisingly, not one of the Conservative MPs who answered the questionnaire thought that there was a need for higher income tax either.

The Green Party politician and the Local Agenda 21 officer talked less about growth per se, but instead about how to link social and economic factors with economic development. This stance is more compatible with the discourse of sustainable development and demonstrates a recognition that achieving individual and collective welfare is not purely about materialistic consumption and indiscriminate growth. Instead, the sustainable development discourse can encompass some Green policy solutions that prescribe restraining one's own consumption, not only to improve your own well being, but also for the benefit of others in the recognition that consumption, and the materialist values underlying it, can cause resource depletion and pollution (Martell, 1994). This discourse therefore has at its core the notion of social and environmental justice.

Social justice

There was an acknowledgement of the importance of social justice to the environmental debate by all those politicians who took part in the interviews, but it was only the Green politician who made this link explicit in the debate around economic growth. One potential explanation for this is that the other politicians were still focusing on traditional environmental areas rather than making links between environmentalism and social issues. The Conservative MP, while also acknowledging that the poor suffered environmental impact harder than most, when asked if the term 'environmental justice' meant anything to him stated:

> "No. I remember Hayek saying when you put an adjective in front of the word justice you normally reverse its sense." (Conservative MP)

The Green politician however argued that sustainability and social justice "could and should not be separated" and indeed, there is a growing consensus on this relationship between these two concepts (Hayward, 1998). If this is the case then environmental policies should also address those issues surrounding poverty and redistribution.

The relevance of poverty and income maintenance to the environmental debate has been well illustrated by Huby (1998), who highlights how the activities of poorer people in more affluent countries have negative effects on the environment. She argues that the demand for cheap food creates pressure for agricultural intensification and on the provision of frozen and pre-packaged foods, which are wasteful in terms of energy and packaging. People on low incomes are less likely to live in well-insulated homes and more likely to use resources inefficiently since they cannot afford to buy energy and water efficient appliances. They are similarly less able to afford to buy 'Green' products because they are generally more expensive than other brands (Huby, 1998, p 152).

It is also now widely acknowledged that the experience of negative environmental impacts falls most frequently and heavily on the poorest (WHO, 1992). This is replicated on both a local and a national scale. Whereas the rich are able to move from problem areas, the poor often have to remain and suffer the consequences:

> "... they [the poor] in the end are the people who are going to suffer because the middle classes will always find a way of surviving." (Labour MP)

Therefore the poor not only bear the brunt of the damage to which they have contributed themselves, but they are also victims of the polluting activities of the rich (Huby, 1998).

Analysis of the questionnaire showed that 22 of the 27 Labour respondents thought that environmental concerns were relevant to income maintenance. This compared to only 3 out of 12 Conservative MPs. When asked whether the environment should address the issues surrounding poverty and redistribution only two of the 12 Conservative MPs agreed, this was compared to 20 out of 27 Labour respondents.

Local government and Europe

Another issue that was clearly identifiable among the transcripts was the role of local government. When asked what level of government could best protect the environment only one Labour MP did not place importance on the role of local government. This was, he argued, primarily due to local government's lack of political power:

> "I think it has got to be national government in the end because you can get all the pressure from outside but unless national government wants to influence something, they won't do it." (Labour MP)

At the Earth Summit in Rio in 1992 over 150 nations, including the UK, endorsed a 500-page document, Agenda 21, which set out how developed and developing countries could work towards sustainable development. Agenda 21 singles out local government as having a special role, with two thirds of the actions in Agenda 21 requiring the involvement of local authorities (LGMB, 1997). In June 1997, shortly after taking power, Tony Blair announced the target that all UK authorities will have a Local Agenda 21 in place by the year 2000. However, currently there are wide variations in its implementation and success throughout the country.

> "LA21, I think, has been very, very important and in some areas within my constituency they are influential, less so in others, and the LA21 project has been more or less paid lip service to in some but in others it has led to an awful lot of very good work...." (Labour MEP)

There is a sense that local authorities were directed by Parliament to deliver on Mr Blair's promise of having a Local Agenda 21 in place, or rather on paper, but without clear direction, and more importantly, sufficient resources to implement the strategy successfully.

> "... the drift of power in Britain is now away from local government to central government and this government is gradually taking away the powers of local authorities and doing everything at the centre." (Labour MP)

Two of the five politicians (both Labour: one national and one European), expressed the view that all levels of government, local, national and supranational were important:

> "... they are all essential, you need some world bodies to have things like Rio and the biodiversity convention and all that sort of thing for the whole world, the European Union is a very useful way of getting the same environmental legislation and standards across a continent. Member states do have the task of making national policies to carry

out those environmental objectives but we must not neglect the role of
local authorities and of individual people." (Labour MEP)

The Conservative MP was in favour of local governments having more
power but, not surprisingly, was against policy being formulated by Europe:

"I think that it is rather absurd for the European community to get
involved at all, and the further you get away from the problem the less
insight you can have as to how it operates. The government has to
have some role in housing but the primary issues ought to be dealt
with by local authorities." (Conservative MP)

The role of Europe is important to the debate because there are some
environmentalists who argue that environmental protection largely
depends on agreements reached at supranational level (Garner, 2000).
Indeed, protecting the environment is regarded by the EU as a particular
area of success and the EU reports that its two main priorities and objectives
in 1999 were taking the environment into account in other policies, and
climate change (European Communities General Report, 1999). Again,
however, environmental protection is still primarily concerned with the
traditional areas such as energy and pollution.

When asked in the questionnaire about the amount of relevance that
Europe should have over the UK's environmental policies only 3 out of
12 of the Conservative MPs believed that Europe should have a fairly
strong influence compared to 18 of the 27 Labour MPs. It is necessary to
note here that European policy already wields a strong influence over
national policy in some areas; for example, it would be illegal under
European law for Britain to ban the export of live animals. It is also
important to remember that many environmental problems require action
at a supranational level. For these reasons, Greens are not against European
directives, but Green radical thought places considerable emphasis on
decentralisation, local self-government and egalitarianism as the key
operating principles of the sustainable society (Garner, 2000, p 69). The
Green Party politician was consistent with this discourse:

"The Greening of the welfare state would devolve power. Local Agenda
21 has no teeth whatsoever, it's a talking shop. You need power to make
decisions locally but behind that statement there is a fundamental belief
in the majority of people to work for the good of the community."
(Green Party member, No 4)

Community

The role of communities and the belief that people will work for the good of their communities was one area that was conspicuous by its absence in the majority of the interviews. This omission was especially evident when the politicians were asked about sustainable development and Local Agenda 21. The three MPs and one MEP all spoke of sustainable development in terms of traditional environmental areas such as conservation of resources with no mention of social or community issues. This was despite the fact that, as the LA21 officer pointed out, there is now a duty on all local authorities to link social, economic and environmental development.

In fact, all the Labour interviewees expressed the view that the general public did not want to get involved with local politics:

> "Well realistically, most people don't want to be involved in local activity.
> I mean they want to watch their television, go to football matches...."
> (Labour MP)

The cause of this lack of commitment to local activity and community involvement was attributed mainly to the busy individualistic lifestyles that most people lead.

Science and technology

All the interviewees, except for the Green Party politician who had a deep mistrust of science and technology, adopted a techno-centric approach to the environmental problem and thought that science and technology had a major role to play in achieving environmental sustainability. Therefore, they argued that national governments should formulate environmental policy relying heavily on advice from their scientific advisors. Environmental pressure groups, such as Friends of the Earth and Greenpeace were singled out for praise for their ability to present scientific evidence that could be incorporated into the environmental debate.

How then do these topics relate to the differing discourse surrounding ecological modernisation, sustainable development and Green social welfare?

Figure 11.1: Discourses – identifying intersecting areas of rapprochement and diversity

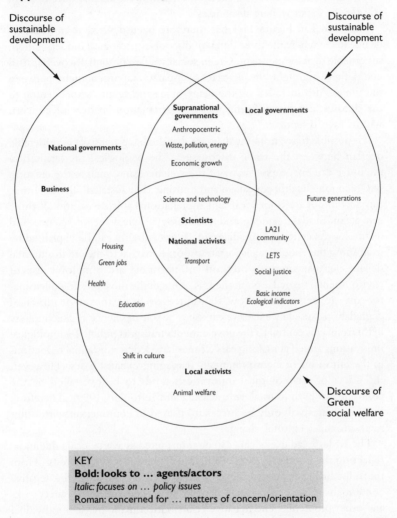

Discourse of sustainable development

Discourse of sustainable development

Supranational governments

Anthropocentric

Waste, pollution, energy

Economic growth

Local governments

National governments

Business

Science and technology

Scientists

National activists

Transport

Future generations

LA21 community

LETS

Social justice

Basic income
Ecological indicators

Housing

Green jobs

Health

Education

Shift in culture

Local activists

Animal welfare

Discourse of Green social welfare

KEY
Bold: looks to ... agents/actors
Italic: focuses on ... policy issues
Roman: concerned for ... matters of concern/orientation

Intersecting discourses

From analysis of the interviews and questionnaires it was possible to identify how the above topics were expressed discursively employing language from the debates surrounding ecological modernisation, sustainable development and Green social welfare. The next stage was to map these topics, or 'discursive instances' onto a diagrammatic representation of the ecological modernisation, sustainable development and Green social welfare discourses.

The model in Figure 11.1 has therefore been devised as an heuristic device to see where the three different discourses; ecological modernisation, sustainable development and Green social welfare potentially overlap, this could then highlight the degree of disparity/rapprochement between the three. Also included on the diagram are the agents/actors central to the debates and the differing focus of orientation/matters of concern within each discourse.

It is possible to see from the diagram that there is potentially considerable overlap between the three discourses. The ecological modernisation discourse can encompass many of the welfare issues, such as the creation of Green jobs, health, education and housing. The sustainability discourse can accommodate both local and supranational initiatives, and all three can accommodate science and technology. The issue of science and technology is central to the diagram. This centrality can be explained by examining the issue of transport: transport is crucial to the environmental debate because modern methods of transport are a major cause of environmental degradation in the UK. One of the most pressing dilemmas for any government is how to reduce or limit the environmental degradation caused by excessive car use. The role of science and technology in this respect is central to the government's transport policy. Technological innovations aimed at making cars cleaner have led to substantial reductions in the emissions of environmentally damaging exhaust gases. However, the effect of technological innovations tends to be overtaken by the continued growth in total car use (Steg and Tertoolen, 1999). Therefore, these measures will only be successful if used in conjunction with other methods and a cultural change.

The widespread use of cars can be interpreted as a large-scale dilemma, reflecting the conflict between individual and collective interests. From the individual's perspective, the advantages of car use outweigh the negative consequences, such as possible damage to the environment, safety risks and other problems. The negative contribution made by each individual to the sum total of environmental costs and risks seems negligible. Consequently the individual may doubt whether his or her contribution to reducing damage and risks really makes any significant difference (Steg and Tertoolen, 1999). The result is a classic problem of collective action: individuals tend not to feel responsible for collective problems because of the costs involved in attempting to solve them and the potential 'free-rider' issues that can result if an attempt is made. For this reason they tend to act out of self-interest and remain pessimistic about other people's willingness to change. It is therefore possible to interpret the current problem of car use as a summative consequence of the behaviour of many individual car users, each of whom is shifting off what are considered to be negligible costs onto society as a whole. Therefore reducing car dependency will involve not only providing a fully integrated transport system but also facilitating a shift in culture.

All those who were interviewed agreed that transport was one area that had the potential to unite social policy and environmentalism. The respondents also stated the need for a comprehensive integrated transport system to be put in place. However, for this to happen it appears that politicians will have to draw on the varying environmental discourses, including that of Green social welfare, which promotes a cultural shift in attitudes. This cultural shift would need to be promoted at the local level. The fuel crisis during the autumn of 2000 highlighted the fact that the public does not yet make a significant link between the current lifestyles predicated on car use and ownership and environmental damage. All those interviewed were critical of the government for not promoting environmental concerns during the crisis. One Labour MP was equally critical of the environmental movement for not voicing its concerns more loudly:

> "I mean they are very active, they are usually very loud and organised and yet it was deafening silence and one has to ask where they are. Do they see their campaign as attacking the government rather than promoting environmental arguments more widely?" (Labour MP)

The importance of transport, however, may be that government does not necessarily have to promote the environment for Green transport policies to be introduced. Green transport policies may evolve incrementally due to the nature of the problem. For example, if a fully integrated transport system was in place, more people would use it and culture may change. Or, equally possible, transport policy could be developed and promoted using a different justification. For example, if the most economically viable transport policies were those that involved the use of less polluting, renewable energy then these would inevitably also be Green policies. The first of these options involves 'stumbling' towards Greener policies (cf Jordan et al, 2000), and the second might entail achieving them by 'stealth'. Both of these options will be further explored at a latter stage of the research.

Conclusion

The purpose of this research has been to address the often-neglected debate surrounding the relevance of welfare systems to environmentalism, and vice versa. The author has argued that the ability to design and implement Green social policies that are both radical and feasible, and imaginative and consensual, will depend on obtaining a greater understanding of political attitudes towards environmental critiques. Environmentalism cannot be simply bolted on to social policy until we have some idea of which concept of sustainability we want to achieve in the long term.

The author began by examining some of the current Green approaches to sustainability. Analysis of recent government policy has indicated a commitment to a 'weak' form of sustainability, which continues to prioritise the needs of the economy over and above environmental concerns. In this concept existing institutions need only to be adapted, for example, become more energy efficient, if they are to be considered more sustainable. Social issues, while not totally neglected, are neither adequately addressed nor the connections between welfare and environmental issues made explicit enough, therefore offering little in the way of prescriptions of how welfare can be 'Greened'.

This research has shown that individual politicians do make connections between welfare and environmental issues: transport being a case in point. However, some politicians still find it difficult to reconcile a Green agenda with continued economic prosperity. The discourse of ecological modernisation is important in this respect because in its 'weak' version it allows economic imperatives to take the lead, preferring technological fixes and instrumentalist forms of policy making (Christoff, 1996), and is therefore compatible with current government policy. Of significance here is the fact that weak and strong ecological modernisation overlap to a certain extent (Christoff, 1996). So while those in favour of a discourse of Green social welfare may prefer a 'strong' form of ecological modernisation with a more ecological, deliberative, democratic approach, weak ecological modernisation may be a good place for the government to start. The author has also argued that it is possible for other environmental discourses to overlap and has offered a possible model to observe areas of rapprochement alongside those of diversity. A sustainable development discourse can bring the issue of social justice into the debate without necessarily being at odds with the goals of ecological modernisation. Likewise, a discourse of Green social welfare can allow more radical interpretations and prescriptions to be placed on the agenda.

Importantly, both 'sustainable development' and 'Green social welfare' have the ability to promote the quality of life argument. This in turn could facilitate a broadening of the current government concept of sustainability, which, at best, relates to Dobson's Conception A. The need to take into greater consideration those aspects of the environment whose loss would have a detrimental effect on both collective and individual welfare could lead to a reassessment of what it is that needs to be sustained and widen the debate to incorporate other issues including the intrinsic value of nature.

In conclusion, this research, though as yet incomplete, has dipped a tentative toe into the virtually uncharted waters between the disciplines of environmentalism and social policy and discovered pools of rapprochement alongside pockets of diversity. The issue of introducing Green social policies through 'stealth' or 'stumbling' has also been identified as an area worthy of greater exploration. Perhaps what is important for future progress is a process of institutional learning (Hajer, 1996) in a double sense: state welfare needs to learn from ecologism how to 'dematerialise' ideas about, and practices of, well being, while environmentalists need to engage with existing welfare institutions as an escapable feature of future social transformation (Fitzpatrick and Caldwell, 2001). In order to identify further potential areas around which this institutional learning may occur, a second round of interviews will take place to provide an 'audit' of existing political and environmental opinion towards the issues in the debate. This will give an empirical orientation to what is, at present, a fragmented set of ideas. If ecological issues are going to be essential to the future of the welfare state and if these preliminary findings are borne out, we may yet begin to see how Green ideas can be translated into an achievable social policy agenda.

References

Barry, J. (1999) *Environment and social theory*, London: Routledge.

Cahill, M. (1999) 'The environment and green social policy', in J. Baldock, N. Manning, S. Miller and S. Vickerstaff (eds) *Social policy*, Oxford: Oxford University Press, pp 199-221.

Christoff, P. (1996) 'Ecological modernisation, ecological modernities', *Environmental Politics*, vol 5, no 3, pp 476-500.

DETR (Department of the Environment, Transport and the Regions) (1999) *A better quality of life: A strategy for sustainable development for the UK*, London: DETR.

DETR (2001) *Sustainable development factsheets* (www.environment.detr.gov.uk/sustainable/factsheets/volun/index.htm).

Dobson, A. (1998) *Justice and the environment: Conceptions of environmental sustainability and theories of distributive justice*, Oxford: Oxford University Press.

Dryzek, J. (1997) *The politics of the earth*, Oxford: Oxford University Press.

European Communities General Report (1999) Chapter IV: The Community economic and social area, section 16: Environment (1/36).

Ferris, J. (1991) 'Green politics and the future of welfare', in N. Manning (ed) *Social Policy Review*, 1990-91, Essex: Longman, pp 24-42.

Fitzpatrick, T. (1998a) 'New welfare associations', in T. Jordan and A. Lent (eds) *Storming the millennium*, London: Lawrence and Wishart, pp 156-71.

Fitzpatrick, T. (1998b) 'The implications of ecological thought for the welfare state', *Critical Social Policy*, vol 18, no 1, pp 5-26.

Fitzpatrick, T. with Caldwell, C. (2001) 'Towards a theory of ecosocial welfare', *Environmental Politics*, vol 10, no 2, pp 43-67.

Garner, R. (2000) *Environmental politics*, (2nd edn), Basingstoke: Macmillan.

George, V. and Wilding, P. (1999) *British society and social welfare*, Basingstoke: Macmillan.

Guardian, The (25 October 2000) 'Blair calls for joint action on Green issues', J. Vidal, p 5.

Hajer, M. (1996) 'Ecological modernisation as cultural politics', in S. Lash, B. Szerszynski and B. Wynne (eds) *Risk, environment and modernity*, London: Sage Publications, pp 246-68.

Hayward, T. (1998) *Political theory and ecological values*, Cambridge: Polity Press.

Huby, M. (1998) *Social policy and the environment*, Buckingham: Open University Press.

Huby, M. (2002, forthcoming) 'The sustainable use of resources: domestic energy and water', in T. Fitzpatrick and M. Cahill (eds) *Greening the welfare state*, London: Palgrave.

Jacobs, M. (1999) *Environmental modernisation: The New Labour agenda*, London: Fabian Society.

Jordan, B., Agulink, P., Burbidge, D. and Duffin, S. (2000) *Stumbling towards basic income: The prospects for tax-benefit integration*, London: Citizens Income Study Centre.

Labour Party (1997) *New Labour because Britain deserves better*, London: Labour Party.

LGMB (Local Government Management Board) (1997) *Local Agenda 21 UK Review 1992-1997*, London: LGMB.

Martell, L. (1994) *Ecology and society*, Cambridge: Polity Press.

Meadows, D.H., Meadows, D.L. and Roberts, J. (1992) *Beyond the limits*, London: Earthscan Publications.

Meadows, D.H., Meadows, D.L., Randers, J. and Behrens, W. III (1972) *Limits to growth*, New York, NY: New American Library.

Mehta, R. and Sivadas, E. (1995) 'Comparing response rates and response content in mail versus electronic mail surveys', *Journal of the Market Research Society*, vol 41, no 4, pp 429-39.

Pepper, D. (1998) 'Sustainable development and ecological modernisation: a radical homocentric perspective', *Sustainable Development*, vol 6, pp 1-7.

Ross, A. (2000) '"Greening government" – tales from the new sustainability watchdog', *Journal of Environmental Law*, vol 12, no 2, pp 175-94.

Shaw, I. (1999) 'Resources for social policy', *Social Policy and Administration*, vol 33, no 4, pp 360-71.

Sneddon, C. (2000) 'Sustainability in ecological economics, ecology and livelihoods: a review', *Progress in Human Geography*, vol 24, no 4, pp 521-49.

Steg, L. and Tertoolen, G. (1999) 'Sustainable transport policy: the contribution from behavioural scientists', *Public Money & Management*, January-March, pp 63-9.

Toynbee, P. and Walker, D. (2001) *Did things get better?*, London: Penguin.

Tse, A. (1998) 'Comparing the response rate, response speed and response quality of two methods of sending questionnaires: e-mail vs. mail', *Journal of the Market Research Society*, vol 41, no 4, pp 429-39.

Van der Heijden, H. (1999) 'Environmental movements, ecological modernisation and political opportunity structures', in C. Rootes (ed) *Environmental movements: Local, national and global*, London: Frank Cass, pp 199-221.

Weale, A. (1992) *The new politics of pollution*, Manchester: Manchester University Press.

WHO (World Health Organisation) (1992) *Our planet, our health*, Report of the WHO Commission on Health and Environment, London: HMSO.

TWELVE

Using social capital in the policy context: challenging the orthodoxy

Martin Roche

Social capital and social policy in the UK

Social capital is one of those amorphous terms that appear to have the ability to cross the barriers of politics and academia and acquire a wider popular usage. Yet, to a large extent, the recent interest shown in the term in the UK merely reflects the longer-held fascination the concept has enjoyed among politicians and policy makers in North America. Indeed, the fact that social capital has enjoyed such a swift ascendancy into the political dialogue on this side of the Atlantic can be seen as in no small part due to the limited theoretical engagement there has been with the notion in academic circles here. Thus, when in 1996, and still only leader of the opposition, Tony Blair propounded the value of social capital within a speech to the CBI, he was paying lip service not to the work of a British academic but to that of the North American political polemicist Francis Fukuyama (King and Wickham-Jones, 1999, p 199). Even so, and although enthusiasm for this notion has been heavily influenced by trends in North American political circles, in the context of the UK the ideas of Anthony Giddens (1999) have undoubtedly provided at least some of the impetus behind engagement with the term. Particularly influential here have been Giddens' views on civic participation and its role in the reinvigoration of civil society (1999), which presaged the arrival of social capital into the political landscape of the UK. In fact, in many ways the notion of social capital has proved to be an ideal rhetorical tool for New Labour to operationalise the 'Third Way' project, which, in its most basic sense, refers to a process of socialisation, or the need to generate norms of behaviour of the type commentators have interpreted as the essence of social capital (Putnam, 1993, 2000; Fukuyama, 1995, 1999; Leonardi, 1995).

Moreover, following New Labour's 1997 election victory, and their more recent success at the polls, the social aspect of the Third Way agenda has found its home in the Social Exclusion Unit (SEU), a central focus of which has been the revitalisation of civic life within the UK (SEU, 1998, 1999). Within this policy culture, social capital has been ascribed a special role, that is as the very embodiment of the value of informal responses to addressing the various types of exclusion evident in modern society. The subsequent impact of social capital – or more specifically the approach it is seen to embody – in the UK policy sphere has been marked, with the term being embraced with such vigour that it now seems that almost every area of social policy, from health and crime to housing and education, is holding out the hope that social capital will provide the magic ingredient in the policy mix (Gillies, 1998; Saegert and Winkel, 1998; Leeder and Dominello, 1999; Hawe and Shiell, 2000).

However, at this juncture we come across a problem, namely that social capital is a notion which, at least in terms of practical application, is still very much in its infancy. Moreover, where it has been applied empirically a number of factors have limited its efficacy as a policy tool. One trend that has become increasingly evident in the policy-oriented literature is to interpret social capital as simply a new term for some well-established development ideas – a form of 'short-hand' for community-led responses to exclusion such as capacity building and self-help (Banks, 1997; Wall et al, 1998; Gamarnikow and Green, 1999). To an extent, this approach has resulted from the lack of any practical policy templates for practitioners to fall back on in relation to social capital. Yet it is also probably partly due to a degree of reticence among some within the policy community to engage constructively with what is, after all, a slippery notion.

Yet this is not to say empirical templates for realising social capital do not exist, with perhaps the most widely accepted and used of these being provided by two American political scientists, Robert Putnam and Francis Fukuyama. Their work has gained recognition at the highest levels of US government and, as already suggested, this reputation has recently been transferred to a UK context (Portes and Landolt, 1996; King and Wickham-Jones, 1999). Both these contributors adopt a similar approach to the problem of measuring social capital in practice, one which ostensibly involves using a combination of generic surveys on levels of trust, participation rates in various organisations (such as political parties) and time-use data. Indeed, the reputation of these two commentators is sufficient to have wielded considerable sway over the work of their peers – most notably in a UK context the work of Peter Hall (1999) – strongly informing political approaches to the notion (King and Wickham-Jones,

1999). Consequently, the idea that membership rates in voluntary organisations, participation in leisure activities and responses to generic survey prompts on trusting others, are useful means of measuring social capital has become common currency in both academic and political circles (King and Wickham-Jones, 1999). A number of dissenting voices, however, have suggested that the level of influence exerted by Putnam and Fukuyama in this respect is largely unwarranted (Fox, 1996; Levi, 1996; Morrow, 1999; Portes, 1999). Perhaps the most fundamental problem highlighted is the fact that data used by these two allows little scope for extrapolating aspects of social capital, such as trust, obligations, reciprocal relations and expectations, all of which the seminal theorists would highlight as pivotal to describing the notion (Bourdieu, 1996; Coleman, 1998, 1990). In tandem with this, such an approach produces a method that is inherently insensitive to the nuances of local populations – a characteristic which is again, directly attriubutable to a reliance upon forms of data not designed for the purpose of measuring something as nebulous as social capital (Sampson et al, 1993, p 638).

Another limitation of Putnam and Fukuyama's approach, and one with specific relevance for policy evaluations, is that the model it produces is input rather than output oriented. Consequently, little is said (or for that matter can be said) about the innate value the various processes of social capital it purports to describe have for deprived and excluded (in the various senses of these terms) communities.

To summarise, current orthodoxy concerning social capital and its applications in the field of policy suffer from two debilitating traits. The first of these relates to the high degree of theoretical naivety that characterises much of the current engagement with the term, while the second refers to the hegemony of inappropriate and dysfunctional methodologies in relation to the measurement of social capital. Consequently, there is a real danger that as the term social capital emerges into the vernacular of policy interpretations, much of the subtlety and innate value the notion possesses could be lost. In such a context there is therefore an urgent need to develop new and novel approaches to measuring social capital. A first step in this process involves revisiting the theory behind social capital and asking some fundamental questions, namely, just what is 'social capital' and what relevance (if any) does it have in terms of policy applications.

Unpacking the current orthodoxy: the theoretical origins of social capital

As suggested, in order to understand the fallibility of the current orthodoxy with regards the measurement of social capital it is important to examine the theoretical underpinnings of the notion. Complicating this task, though, is the fact that there are two schools of thought that can claim sovereignty over the notion; one grounded in the neo-classical school of the rationalists, the other in the postmodern tradition, and specifically the post-structuralists. The significance of this distinction is more than a semantic one. Naturally, the adoption of either approach for interpreting social capital could be seen as having distinct and far-reaching implications, not only in terms of how it is measured, but just what it is that gets measured. For its part, the rationalist interpretation has its roots in one of the debates that preoccupied economic theory in the 1960s and 1970s, namely the role of social structures in defining economic outcomes (Loury, 1977, 1981; Lin et al, 1981; Brubaker, 1985; Granovetter, 1985).

This question was perhaps the key influence on the work of the American sociologist James Coleman (1988), who used the term 'social capital' to describe the beneficial role of certain social processes in human behaviour. Furthermore, as a consequence of Coleman's analytical basis in rational choice theory, he defined social capital as embodying specific social processes, composed not only of certain social forms, but also the structures that these operated within – and even the motivational ideologies that they depended upon. All of these were seen as having a distinct and tangible value, or degree of capital, for the individuals or groups who engaged with them. Coleman viewed this process of engagement as the natural outcome of a decision-making process, based on risk assessment and evaluation, through which individuals made a rational decision as to the worth of taking part in certain social activities. One of the major consequences of this rational view is that social capital is seen in isolation, as a distinct process to itself. Moreover, Coleman enshrined the rational functionality of his interpretation by providing a ready typology of social capital (which included relations such as trust and obligations), together with specific social structures and altruistic ideologies (Coleman, 1988, 1990).

Contiguous with the rationalistic view of social capital there is another which interprets the concept as less process oriented, instead viewing it as one that is intimately bound up with a variety of other processes. This is where the work of the French sociologist Pierre Bourdieu comes to the fore, his interpretation of social capital owing a lot to post-structuralist interpretations of social and economic phenomena (Bourdieu, 1996). And while there are superficial similarities between these two interpretations, for instance, both Coleman and Bourdieu would situate social capital in various social forms and structures, Bourdieu departs from the rationalist's view in that social capital is seen as interdependent with other forms of capital within a societal context. Consequently, social forms of capital can only truly be understood if they are taken in tandem with other cultural, political and economic factors that influence the nature of social forms. The notion that social capital is a resource is defined within this interpretation by the extent to which external factors, whether chiefly political, economic or otherwise, facilitate access to those social structures which have the potential to prove beneficial. The post-structuralist definition of social capital, then, views it as not only manifest within specific forms and structures but equally within the mechanisms that facilitate and maintain access to such social processes.

However, although Bourdieu's interpretation seems to provide the answer to the atomistic view of social capital proffered by Coleman, his analysis has tended to be ignored. Ironically, it is the rationalism of the latter's approach, with its handy set typology of social capital, which has made it particularly attractive to both theorists and policy makers alike, regardless of concerns over its theoretical underpinnings, and has resulted in its adoption as the standard interpretation. As outlined in the previous section, however, this specific debt to Coleman's work in the current approaches has had distinct, and often negative, consequences. These are particularly evident in the work of political scientists such as Putnam and Fukuyama, who have developed methodologies that are largely insensitive to the role of external factors on the nature of social capital. Yet, if we accept that social capital is a far more complex and variegated notion than has to date been accepted within policy circles, there is a question of whether or not this new conceptualisation is, one: accessible in an empirical sense and, two: likely to be of practical use in the policy setting.

The favour with which social capital – as part of a more 'informal' answer to the 'inclusion' question – is currently viewed in political circles would seem to a large extent to negate the relevance of the second of these questions. Despite this political will though, little, if in fact anything, is actually known about how the precursors to such informal activity – such as, among others, trust, participation and altruism – actually influence one another to shape the success of collaborative action. This problem, at least in one sense, is where the value of social capital could come to the fore, insofar as the terminology of this complex notion offers a framework within which to assess how these various processes operate upon and affect one another. After all, there seems to be little point in encouraging participation-based regenerative policies if the relational foundations for such approaches, that is, social capital in its various guises, is not better understood. There is evidence to suggest that approaches such as self-help and the development of community capacity suffer from a lack of sensitivity, not only in respect to the extent to which social relations define outcomes, but also how they interact with other factors, particularly the political (Williams and Windebank, 2000). A failure to engage with a framework (theoretical or empirical), which is more accurately representative of social capital and its various constituents, is to perhaps miss a valuable opportunity. With this in mind, the following section elaborates one possible approach to this challenge.

Measuring social capital for social policy: an alternative theory-led approach

If social capital is to play a role in facilitating social policy, new and novel methods will need to be developed in order to transform this nebulous notion into a workable tool. The, not insubstantial, challenge this process poses is to measure a phenomenon which is typified by abstract human relations such as trust in a way which, while remaining true to the complexities of the notion, also reduces levels of abstraction sufficiently to allow a practical methodology to be developed. There are two distinct aspects to such an undertaking. First, there is the degree of theoretical robustness that can be employed for such a purpose, and second, there is the 'model' of policy prescription which social capital must adhere to. The latter factor can be seen as relating to a set of criteria that roughly fall into the categories of practicality and functionality. For its part, the other point relates largely to ensuring that any measures of social capital adhere, as far as possible, to the precepts concerning the theoretical manifestation of the phenomenon. The challenge is thus to develop a methodology which fulfils both of these criteria. In fact, an extremely useful starting point here is provided by the DETR's *Indices of deprivation* (DETR, 2000). The approach adopted in this case is to combine various measurable aspects of deprivation into a single overall measurement. The resultant indices incorporate domains such as: income; employment; health and disability; education, skills and training; housing; and access to services, to provide an inclusive, yet practical, means of measuring deprivation. Moreover, this approach appears to offer a particularly useful way forward in measuring social capital. It is possible to envisage adopting a similar approach to developing domains of social capital for the purposes of measuring it. The following is an example of one such derivative typology, adapted from a similar list constructed for the purpose of a study recently conducted in a number of metropolitan boroughs in the West Midlands:

- trust
- participation
- altruism
- sociability.

The domains chosen are far from arbitrary but reflect current understandings of social capital and adopt delineators that are both theoretically deduced and felt to be empirically accessible. In developing these, Onyx and Bullen's (2000) approach to quantifying social capital proved a particularly useful precedent (although it should also be added that they place little emphasis on the practicality of using social capital for policy purposes). The first of the above domains, trust, is recognised as the pivotal element in the development of social capital (Coleman, 1988; Fukuyama, 1995, 1999). Particularly important here is the manner in which this social form reduces what are termed 'transactional costs' and obviates risk factors in human interaction. Consequently, trust can be seen as a basic prerequisite in enabling the individual to acquire 'capital' from social 'situations'. In turn, if trust can be seen as fulfilling a facilitatory role within forms of social capital, then other types of social relation provide what can best be described as the motivational and structural elements to this picture, these being captured within the remaining three domains. For its part, participation is seen as the embodiment of the structural element of social capital, social networks being key signifiers of both potential and actual levels of social capital (Coleman, 1988; Putnam, 1993, 2000). In turn, the altruism domain attempts to encapsulate the 'public goods' aspect, which is key to explaining the motivational factors behind the decisions of individuals to engage with forms and structures of social capital, not only for their own benefit but also for that of others (Coleman, 1990). Lastly, the domain of sociability is intended to encapsulate a proclivity on the part of individuals to engage in informal types of activity, a dimension sociologists have recently begun to suggest is a key signifier of social capital (Portes, 1999).

If the development of such domains provides a strong theoretical foundation, then the next requirement of our novel methodology is that it be both implementable and functional as a tool of policy. In order to fit into existing local authority frameworks of practice the various domains could be investigated using a standard survey methodology. Moreover, while the domains of social capital developed here initially appear less tangible than those used in the case of the *Index of deprivation* used by the DETR, constructing indicators for them within an original questionnaire survey should not prove too difficult a task. For instance, in the case of the West Midlands study, a range of candidate indicators were used to provide a measurement for the sociability domain, including questions on who, as well as how often, respondents socialised with various groups and individuals, such as friends, relatives and workmates. The addition of a simple Likeart scaling system, providing various alternatives for respondents (for example, ranging from 'I benefit a great deal from this activity' to 'I get no benefit from this activity') also allowed the value of the forms of social capital to be gauged to some degree.

As highlighted earlier, a key element in making such a tool practically useful in policy terms is whether it can be easily replicated to enable assessment of changes in social capital over time. This is especially important in terms of gauging the success of policies targeted at increasing the stock of social capital in a locale. However, the cost of replicating such a survey methodology is likely to make longitudinal assessments prohibitive. One strategy in addressing this problem is to utilise the questionnaire survey suggested here as a foundational link to indicators that are more readily available to local authorities through existing means of consultation, as well as data collected for other administrative or statutory reasons. By validating the relationship between two sets of indicators – one theoretically derived and the other selected from the existing datasets on time-use and participation rates – within the initial questionnaire, a viable model of social capital which can be revisited longitudinally could be developed. While some ingenuity may be necessary to achieve lists of appropriate proxy indicators, in the case of domains such as participation, sociability and altruism, a variety of such indicators are likely to be available. For example:

Participation

- attendance at community consultation events run by the local council;
- voting in national and local elections;
- attendance at evening classes or other non-compulsory educational provision.

Altruism

- numbers of classroom assistants at local schools;

- numbers of Neighbourhood Watch (and similar) scheme coordinators;
- numbers of advocates for persons with disabilities.

Sociability

- numbers subscribing to sports facilities access schemes with local authorities;
- numbers using art galleries and museums;
- numbers attending after school events or activities.

However, for some indicators a more ingenious strategy may be required, as in the case of a domain such as trust. Given that it is unlikely that proxy indicators for something as nebulous as trust will be readily available (although some local crime surveys may include questions that touch on trusting people in the community), one approach is to impute levels of trust 'negatively'. This would entail the use of indicators such as those given below to develop an aggregate score of deficiencies in, say, levels of trust in a particular area:

Trust

- membership rates in Neighbourhood Watch schemes;
- levels of reported crime;
- sales of security equipment.

The composition of these separate fields of social capital allows the operationalisation of discrete aspects of the concept, which – when combined – act as a framework for a unitary model. Furthermore, while some of these domains necessarily remain relatively abstract, others could be linked more closely to real life scenarios in order to not only reinforce the practicality of the statistical relationships derived, but also to inform policy interventions. In this way, abstract (yet pivotal) notions such as trust could be related to the practical benefits of socialising and engaging in various modes of participatory activity. The context sensitivity that is inherent to the approach would also allow the definition of levels of social capital in relation to specific social groupings and geographically defined communities, thus defining the direction of future policy responses. Ultimately, the goal would be to replicate the most 'productive' (in a beneficial sense) modes of interaction more widely, or provide practical assistance to reduce barriers where such networks are already in existence.

While the approach proffered here could be used in a self-contained manner, it also has to be accepted that this self-styled, 'theory-led' methodology may only form part of a wider appraisal of social capital. This contention goes back to the earlier theoretical discussion. As already suggested, current interpretations of social capital owe a large debt to the work of James Coleman, whose functional account of social capital has provided a ready-made typology of the notion for both theorists and practitioners to draw upon. Indeed, the alternative account elucidated here is, to an extent, indebted to this approach. However, as already seen, there are limitations to this perspective, not least among these being the atomised view of social capital it produces. Although this caveat has been identified in theoretical terms, its impact on policy could prove particularly disruptive. This is because an atomised view of social capital fails to build in the range of other factors that can have a profound impact not only on levels of social capital itself, but on who gets to use it and who does not. It has also been recognised that one of the main mechanisms for these processes is likely to be the state and that, consequently, the state apparatus, whether at the local, regional or national level, has a key role in facilitating access for deprived groups to structures and agencies that may facilitate the development of social capital (Warner et al, 1999). In the first instance, this suggests a need to broaden the nature of any social capital oriented approach to include the issue of civic engagement. In particular, this relates to the factors which inhibit the ability of individuals and groups to gain access to, as well as value from, participatory structures, whether that activity be formal in nature (as in the case of local authority functions) or informal in nature (as in the case of voluntary grassroots activity). In the context of the policy environment, this is the most important lesson that can be learned from a post-structural perspective, namely that social capital cannot be understood and consequently manipulated if it is treated in isolation. But an embedded view of social capital also requires a more general acceptance of the myriad of social as well as economic phenomena that can impact upon it, as well as how social capital can be used as a tangible resource. However, while it is possible to envisage the incorporation of elements that seek to make cogent links between aspects such as culture and tradition and their impact upon social capital, it is also important to ensure that measuring the concept remains both a functional and practical aim within the local policy environment.

Conclusion: using social capital in the policy setting

Given the enthusiasm for social capital that local government is currently expressing in the UK, the need for more effective measures of this complex theoretical construct would appear to be a matter of pressing concern. Yet, as has been suggested here, the current orthodoxy in regard to this task would seem to hold little promise for practical purposes. Moreover, unless this situation is remedied, practical applications of the notion will continue to suffer from vague and insubstantial foundations, with potentially negative implications for the success of any resultant policies. In an attempt to provide some much needed direction in responding to this challenge, an alternative approach to the measurement of social capital has been outlined within this chapter – one which offers a tentative way forward for policy makers that is not only conceptually valid but also practically robust. Taking as its cue the DETR's approach to measuring the equally nebulous notion of deprivation, the first stage in this process involves 'unpacking' the concept of social capital into a workable typology based on a number of theoretically derived domains. Following this exercise, these domains are converted into a series of interview prompts that can then be applied to communities using the traditional mechanism of large-scale consultation, the questionnaire survey. However, given the strictures of the policy mechanism and community consultation, the replicability of such a process may be curtailed. The novel solution to this problem lies in the development of a series of proxy indicators that could be statistically linked to actual measures, therefore providing the scope to develop a longitudinal model of social capital. But there is also a more general point here regarding the ultimate objective of measuring social capital in the policy setting, namely the value of what is measured to the achievement of policy objectives, and there are a number of levels to this. As outlined at the beginning of this chapter, engendering social capital is increasingly being seen in policy circles as a 'good thing to do' and to a large extent this assumption is based on the findings of a number of studies which have suggested that informal activity can have positive impacts on things like economic prosperity, levels of malfeasance and social well being (Putnam, 1993). However, this work has been problematised in a number of ways, both for its flawed methodology and context dependency (Levi, 1996; Portes, 1999). Moreover, the assumption that social capital is an innate good is qualified by the fact that the structures and forms that it encompasses can be particularly useful in achieving some decidedly un-altruistic objectives, such as criminal activity. More generally, in some circumstances social capital could be seen as inherently exclusive, denying access to structures to individuals who do not hold ideals common to a dominant group (Portes and Landolt, 1996). There should therefore be a rejection of the notion of social capital as some sort of panacea, as an inherent good. This is where the methodology described in this chapter has a role, as a tool that can be used to assess both the value and nature of social capital to deprived communities. Applying such a methodology in a policy setting would be useful in three ways. First, as a means of characterising the resource, who possesses what forms of social capital and where? Second, there is the issue of the value of this social capital: do people see it as a useful thing and do they think it enhances their quality of life? Lastly, there is the more proactive dimension of this process, using the picture that emerges through the model to direct policies. For instance, if residents place a particular value on certain modes of participation in their local area this could be used as an effective means of disseminating information, whether about the availability of services or job opportunities. Yet, in the end, perhaps the main lesson to draw from the debates surrounding social capital and its application within policy circles, is the value of adopting a more nuanced approach to the phenomenon, one which strives to incorporate notions such as altruism, sociability and trust, and apply them in a practical framework. Only in this way can the value of social capital as an instrument of policy and, more importantly, as a weapon in the fight against social exclusion, be fully realised.

Acknowledgements

The ideas expressed in this chapter in part draw their inspiration from a research project recently undertaken by the Centre for Applied Social Research (University of Wolverhampton) on behalf of the Black Country Consortium's Health and Regeneration Steering Group, and funded by the NHS Executive (West Midlands). Copies of the final report are available from the author on request.

References

Banks, E. (1997) 'The social capital of self-help and mutual aid groups', *Social Policy*, vol 28, pp 30-8.

Blair, T. (1996) Speech to the Singapore business community, 8 January.

Bourdieu, P. (1996) 'The forms of capital', in A.H. Halsey (ed) *Education: Culture, economy, and society*, Oxford: Oxford University Press.

Brubaker, R. (1985) 'Rethinking classical theory: the sociological vision of Pierre Bourdieu', *Theory and Society*, vol 14, pp 745-75.

Coleman, J. (1988) 'The creation and destruction of social capital: implications for the law', *Journal of Law, Ethics and Public Policy*, vol 3, pp 375-404.

Coleman, J.S. (1990) *Foundations of social theory*, Cambridge, MA: Belnap Press.

DETR (Department of the Environment, Transport and the Regions) (2000) *Indices of deprivation 2000*, Regeneration Research Summary, no 31, London: DETR.

Fox, J. (1996) 'How does civil society thicken?: the political construction of social capital in rural Mexico', *World Development*, vol 24, pp 1089-103.

Fukuyama, F. (1995) *Trust: The social virtues and the creation of prosperity*, London: Hamish Hamilton.

Fukuyama, F. (1999) *The Great Disruption: Human nature and the reconstitution of social order*, London: Free Press.

Gamarnikow, E. and Green, A.G. (1999) 'The third way and social capital: education action zones and a new agenda for education, parents and community?', *International Studies in Sociology of Education*, vol 9, pp 3-22.

Giddens, A. (1998) *The third way: The renewal of social democracy*, Cambridge: Polity Press.

Gillies, P. (1998) 'Effectiveness of alliances and partnerships for health promotion', *Health Promotion International*, vol 13, pp 99-120.

Granovetter, M. (1985) 'Economic action and social structure: the problem of embeddedness', *American Journal of Sociology*, vol 91, pp 481-510.

Hall, P. (1999) 'Social capital in Britain', *British Journal of Political Science*, vol 29, pp 417-61.

Hawe, P. and Shiell, A. (2000) 'Social capital and health promotion: a review', *Social Science and Medicine*, vol 51, pp 871-85.

Home Office (1999) *Report of the policy action team on community self-help*, London: The Stationery Office.

King, D. and Wickham-Jones, M. (1999) 'Social capital, British social democracy and new labour', *Democratization*, vol 6, pp 181-213.

Leeder, S. and Dominello, A. (1999) 'Social capital and its relevance to health and family policy', *Australian and New Zealand Journal of Public Health*, vol 23, pp 424-9.

Leonardi, R. (1995) 'Regional development in Italy: social capital and the mezzogiorno', *Oxford Review of Economic Policy*, vol 11, pp 165-79.

Levi, M. (1996) 'Social and unsocial capital: a review essay of Robert Putnam's making democracy work', *Politics and Society*, vol 24, pp 45-55.

Lin, N., Ensel, W. and Vangh, J. (1981) 'Social resources and strength of ties: structural factors in occupational status attainment', *American Sociological Review*, vol 46, pp 393-405.

Loury, G. (1977) 'A dynamic theory of racial income differences', in P.A. Wallace and A. Le Mund (eds) *Women minorities and employment discrimination*, Lexington, MA: Lexington Books.

Loury, G. (1981) 'Intergenerational transfer and the distribution of earnings', *Econometrica*, vol 49, pp 843-67.

Morrow, V. (1999) 'Conceptualising social capital in relation to the well-being of children and young people: a critical review', *The Sociological Review*, vol 47, pp 744-65.

Onyx, J. and Bullen, P. (2000) 'Measuring social capital in five communities', *Journal of Behavioural Science*, vol 36, pp 23-42.

Pennington, M. and Rydin, Y. (2000) 'Researching social capital in local environment policy contexts', *Policy & Politics*, vol 28, pp 233-49.

Portes, A. (1999) 'Social capital: its origins and applications in modern sociology', *Annual Review of Sociology*, vol 24, pp 1-24.

Portes, A. and Landolt, P. (1996) 'The downside of social capital', *American Prospect*, vol 26, pp 18-21.

Putnam, R. (1993) 'The prosperous community: social capital and public life', *American Prospect*, vol 13, pp 35-42.

Putnam, R. (1995) 'Bowling alone: America's declining social capital', *Journal of Democracy*, vol 6, pp 64-78.

Putnam, R. (2000) *Bowling alone: the collapse and revival of American community*, New York: Simon & Schuster.

Saegert, S. and Winkel, G. (1998) 'Social capital and the revitalisation of New York City's distressed inner-city housing', *Housing Policy Debate*, vol 9, pp 17-60.

Sampson, R., Morenoff, J.D. and Earls, F. (1999) 'Beyond social capital: spatial dynamics of collective efficacy for children', *American Sociological Review*, vol 64, pp 633-60.

Schulman, M. and Anderson, C. (1999) 'The dark side of the force: a case study of restructuring and social capital', *Rural Sociology*, vol 64, pp 351-72.

SEU (Social Exclusion Unit) (1998) *Bringing Britain together: A national strategy for neighbourhood renewal*, London: SEU.

SEU (1999) *Annual Report*, London: SEU.

Steyeart, J. (2000) 'Local governments online and the role of the resident: government shop versus electronic community', *Social Science and Computer Review*, vol 18, pp 3-16.

Wall, E. (1998) 'Getting the goods on social capital', *Rural Sociology*, vol 63, pp 300-22.

Warner, M. (1999) 'Social capital construction and the role of the local state', *Rural Sociology*, vol 64, pp 373-93.

Williams, C. and Windebank, J. (2000) 'Self-help and mutual aid in deprived urban neighbourhoods: some lessons from Southampton', *Urban Studies*, vol 37, pp 127-47.

THIRTEEN

Participation and social policy: transformation, liberation or regulation?

Peter Beresford

This chapter aims to put participation in social policy in an ideological, historical and theoretical context. To do this, the chapter will identify the two dominant modern political discourses, which in the UK and beyond have provided the context for this discussion. It will also outline the development of counter discourses from social care and welfare service users[1], and explore the two key competing ideologies that have underpinned different models and understandings of participation, and examine the implications of these different approaches to participation, considering their regressive and liberatory potential. Finally, the chapter will also begin to examine the possibilities and problems now being highlighted for participation in social policy in theory and practice, taking the UK as a case study with wider implications.

The context of the discussion

One of the ironies of participation, which has so far largely passed without serious comment, is that while its conceptualisation and practice are ostensibly centrally concerned with involving and including people, in its own modern usage, it has generally tended to be abstracted and treated in isolation. There have been some discussions of the socio-economics, politics and ideology of participation, but these have been limited in number and range (for example, Pateman, 1970; Held, 1987). In contrast a much greater interest has developed in the 'technicalities' of participation, reflected in the production of a large and rapidly growing body of 'how to do it' manuals, courses and consultants (for example, Hanley et al, 2000; VSO, 2001). The emphasis is on techniques for and the findings from participation. There is even a national competition to identify the most 'successful' initiatives for public involvement run by *The Guardian* newspaper and Institute for Public Policy Research (Dean, 2000). This emphasis on empiricism is perhaps hardly surprising, bearing in mind the very limited achievements of provisions for participation to date and also the frequent failure of participatory schemes to challenge dominant discriminations and inequalities, particularly around 'race' and culture and disability in their own operation.

However, this phenomenon also raises broader questions and reflects broader issues relating to both participation and its policy/political context. Preoccupation with technicist approaches to policy and practice was first encouraged by the political New Right in public policy, particularly health and welfare policy, as it sought to discredit the value base of public provision and to challenge the power, competence, values and discretion of professionalised workers. The New Right tried to reduce their roles to bureaucratised 'competencies' and procedures subordinated to financial and state control. But can participation be encouraged, evaluated or even understood simply by reference to the techniques that are used in attempting to undertake it? Can we make sense of the strengths and shortcomings of participation or even particular approaches to participation in this way? Is it intelligible in isolation? This seems unlikely, given the inherently political and ideological nature of participation. Instead, the empirical emphasis may better be understood as a flight to safety – a search for a safe option, which helps divorce participation from its dangerous relations with power and ideology. Reminders of these relations can be expected to make the undertaking and analysis of participation more threatening and difficult and to challenge the cosiness that words like participation, 'user/consumer involvement' and related concepts like 'empowerment' and 'partnership' have come to have in recent times.

Ironically, this frequent failure to connect may also reflect the new significance that participation has in politics and policy both in the UK and internationally. Public, particularly social, policy has become permeated with requirements (some statutory) for user involvement in policy planning, management and provision. This stands in sharp contrast with the past. Welfare service users[2] have traditionally been excluded both from the construction of social policy and social policy debates (Campbell and Oliver, 1996; Oliver, 1996; Oliver and Barnes, 1998). Participation has now been put at the heart of health, social care, regeneration, housing and education policies. Provisions for participation extend from user involvement in Social Services Inspectorate/Audit Commission Joint Reviews of statutory social services, to new proposals for 'community representation' in 'local protection panels' to manage sex offenders (BBC TV, 2001). A number of senior social policy commentators now identify participation as a key issue for social policy in the UK (Becker, 2000). The same emphasis has been placed on participation by key international and European institutions like the World Bank, International Monetary Fund (IMF) and the EC Social Fund. This has been coupled with a search for and emphasis on new approaches to user involvement, like citizen panels and juries and the development of virtual and electronic approaches to participation.

There has never been so much political and policy interest expressed in participation, across so many fields. Yet equally there has probably never been so much ambiguity and uncertainty. Paradoxically now, when there is unprecedented pressure for involvement in policy practice and increasingly research, community, citizen and service user organisations seem to be increasingly wary of being involved. The talk is now increasingly of involvement 'overload', consultation 'fatigue' and of being 'all consulted out'. Service users and their organisations are increasingly highlighting the problems posed, at both personal and collective levels, by getting involved (Campbell, 1996, p 223; Beresford and Croft, 2001, pp 11-12). Such concerns also connect with broader debates about the regressive potential of 'participation' highlighted by development policies in the south (Cooke and Kothari, 2001). The gains of participation in many cases also seem limited. Thus, for example, in the UK, there has now long been a strong government emphasis on supporting 'user-led' services and independent social care service users' organisations. However, the two-year user controlled national research project initiated by the National Centre for Independent Living and the Centre for Disability Studies at Leeds University, reporting in 2001 on user controlled services, reveals a national picture of inadequately and insecurely funded organisations, greatly valued by their service users but struggling to maintain their activities and facing an uncertain future (Barnes et al, 2001). Even as government argues the importance of participation, it is reducing long-established provision for participation in land-use planning – where much of this discussion started in the 1960s (Hetherington, 2001; McCarthy, 2001; Vidal, 2001), and introducing ideas like 'user champions', which are being called into question by some service users as unaccountable and without mandate (Campbell, 2001).

The focus of this discussion

Even the most cursory situation report highlights fundamental and very evident contradictions in participation. As we have seen, there seems to be political interest, but public dissatisfaction; official priority, but very limited achievements and resourcing. While interest in participation has steadily mounted over the last 30 to 40 years, this has tended to be a recurring scenario, with participatory initiatives conspicuously underachieving. The aim of this discussion is to try to make more sense of this situation, specifically by considering the ideological, political and economic relations of participation as both conceptual framework and practice, and with particular reference to social policy. The concern here is to explore the role that participation, has played, does play and may play in the future, in relation to the social production and social relations of welfare and social policy. This focus is overdue, both because of the concerns that are increasingly being raised by recipients of social policy and their organisations about the failings of policy and provision which does not involve them and, as we have already heard, because of the increased political priority that participation now commands in social policy. The intention is to try and make some connections with participation and to consider the implications broader ideas, values and structures may have for its operation and potential and what part they may play in its limited effectiveness to date. These broader issues may or may not be the reason for participation's qualified progress, but they are likely to offer some insights into it. The assumption underlying this analysis is that participation cannot helpfully be understood or progressed in isolation and that if we seek to be serious in our examination of involvement and aspirations to advance it, then we will need to consider it in its broader context. The objective is to:

- put discussion of participation in ideological and historical context, taking account of shifts from pre-capitalist, to capitalist and postmodern society;
- briefly consider the two recent dominant political discourses, which in the UK specifically and frequently in European and Western societies more generally provide the context for this discussion;
- outline counter developments from social care and welfare service user movements;
- relate these developments to participation and different models and understandings of participation which have emerged.

Clearly only an initial exploration can be offered here, but hopefully this will provide a basis for and encourage further activity in this area.

As we have seen, the rhetoric of participation is now well advanced in social policy practice. However, so far, social policy as a *discipline* seems to have been much slower to address issues of participation in either its analysis or process. The signs are that the discipline has yet to prioritise either the perspectives of service users or their involvement and inclusion in its activities. Insofar as 'participation' has been identified as a focus for social policy interest, it has been much more as a subject of study rather than as a source of insight for social policy's own praxis. Thus the discipline still has fully to address the issues raised by service user organisations and movements, which as we shall see shortly, have played a central role in developing action and discussion on participation. So far, limited interest has been shown in these movements of welfare service users, their theories, discussions, proposals and their now large and growing body of published work. This was reflected in the findings of a review in 1997, based on looking at key current and recent social policy texts; recent social policy conferences and journal content. There is little sign that this overall situation has changed in any fundamental way since this review was undertaken (Beresford, 1997; Beresford and Holden, 2000). Most social policy texts, national and international, still do not discuss the user movements and their role in the development of social policy or include their perspectives (for example, Mullard and Spicker, 1998; Watson and Doyal, 1999; Gough, 2000; Alcock et al, 2001; Alcock and Craig, 2001; Harris and Rochester, 2001; Lavalette and Pratt, 2001; Taylor-Gooby, 2001; Yeates, 2001). Only a very few have started to do this (for example, Clarke et al, 2000; Drake, 2001). As yet, for example, participation has not yet been identified by the Social Policy Association as a priority for its own activities. The dominant conception of service users as a data source continues. More recently they have also come to be seen as a form of 'social capital' to serve social policy (Montgomery and Inkeles, 2001).

However, the signs are that this is going to have to change, both because of internal pressures (from an interested minority of the social policy 'community') and external political pressures. The latter are notably embodied in increasing government interest in participation in social policy and practice and because of the rapidly growing interest of both statutory and non-statutory funding organisations in 'user involvement' in research and analysis. We should also not forget the impact of welfare service user organisations and movements, of which more later. The inclusion of this chapter in this collection is perhaps another minor signifier of this shift. For this reason, if no other, it is essential that *critical* discussion of the idea and practice of participation and those agents involved in its development is taken forward within the discipline of social policy, so that its response to participation can be as well informed and well judged as possible. It would be regrettable if the discipline of social policy added itself to the long list of organisations and institutions that have approached participation in an uninformed and uncritical way.

This chapter's perspective

It is also helpful to locate this discussion itself. It may most accurately be described as coming from a 'service user's' perspective. The author writes as someone actively involved in the mental health service users/survivors movement, the broader disabled people's movement and welfare user movements more generally. Traditionally the relation of social policy commentators to social policy did not generally seem to be seen as significant and was often not articulated. From the 1970s, this was challenged by Black, feminist and gay, lesbian and bisexual critiques of social policy, whose proponents argued that their perspectives had tended to be ignored, obscured or misinterpreted by mainstream discussions, which reflected dominant identities, interests, understandings and objectives. A similar challenge has also emerged from the movements of welfare service users.

By such movements the author means those of people who identify as having been on the receiving end, long-term, of 'heavy end' social policy practices and provisions, and where this has played a central role in shaping their identity and/or their understandings of social policy. In the author's case, this means long-term use of income support and statutory mental health services. The movements (and we will come to these shortly) that have developed this discussion are particularly associated with long-term use of health and social care services. In developing their own discourses, they have highlighted the differences that have developed between discussions from service users' perspectives – where direct and explicit experience of such social policies is centrally involved – and those (dominant discussions) where this has not been the case. They therefore argue that people's status and role in relation to the use of such services is both relevant and important in understanding the values, beliefs and ideas that they bring to it. This continues to be a contentious issue and one that needs to be addressed in any detailed consideration of participation.

Dominant philosophical traditions in social policy

Two philosophical traditions have dominated the modern history of social policy. Indeed it could be said that since social policy as both a discipline and explicit practice had its major beginnings in the 19th century that they have dominated *all* its history. These traditions are those of Fabianism and Marxism. Both are concerned with change and reform (albeit one posits revolutionary change). Both are more or less committed to a planned economy. Both are concerned with societal change, but are also centrally associated with social policy. Popular and expert understandings of social policy have both been fundamentally affected by them. They are both complex, multifaceted and certainly not monolithic, so it is very difficult to do justice to their complexity in a short discussion. Both now tend to be seen as marginal and in retreat. Yet both have significance for our understanding of participation in social policy and for the role (or lack of a role) that participation has played in its history so far. It may also be argued that their inheritance continues to be much more powerful than is often acknowledged.

Fabianism and social policy

Fabianism can be seen as a 19th/early 20th century political philosophy, which had its fullest flowering in the UK after the Second World War with the creation of the welfare state. Two strands can be identified in its origins, reflecting its competing commitments to socialism and social democracy. These include its indebtedness to the utilitarianism that generated the New Poor Law, through the founding influence of the Charity Organisation Society, and to ethical and Christian socialism, embodied in the Webbs and Tawney (Tawney, 1931; Sullivan, 1998). Fabianism has become synonymous with state welfare and a commitment to collective provision, but in the UK context it was always actually associated with a mixed economy of welfare, with continuing significant roles played by both voluntary/charitable and private/for-profit provision. However there were several principles with which it was strongly and consistently associated. These included commitment to and reliance on:

• 'experts' having the central role in planning and shaping policy, including social policy, located in government – both central and local state – and acting as official advisers;
• specialist administrators who would make possible the better administration of state welfare. The state and its officials were thus seen as the politically neutral administrative arm of government. In this form of collectivism, Fabianism conceived that "the rules ... would be guaranteed, and if necessary enforced, by [these administrators acting as] a set of neutral umpires". Thus "experts would shape [social policy] and administrators would implement it" (Sullivan, 1998, p 71);

- the use of 'expert' and academic knowledge and research on social problems like poverty, to develop policy and to create pressure on the state to introduce welfare reforms through a 'public' 'educated' by its 'experts';
- the development of education for practice (as social services workers) and the professionalisation of welfare roles.

The Fabians saw the achievement of social equality and the abolition of poverty as possible within capitalism through social policy measures.

> For them the welfare state is built around redistributive taxation and universal benefits in partnership with municipal services delivered by competent professionals and administrators, regulated and financed to ensure an acceptable uniformity across the country. (Ginsburg, 1998, p 83)

Marxism and social policy

While for the social democratic Fabians, the welfare state or state welfare represented a solution to the problems of capitalism, for Marxists, particularly early Marxists, it was part of the problem. "Social policy decision-making was seen as subordinate to the requirements of capitalism. Social policy decision-making is inevitably limited to a role supporting or helping to legitimise the capitalist order" (Hill, 1998, p 137). In the Marxist analysis, welfare failed to replace the exploitative relationships of the labour market. Marxists argued that the welfare state failed to resolve the social problems of people experiencing poverty and of the broader working class, and that in reality it operated to *support* capitalism rather than to *challenge* it (Ginsburg, 1979, p 79). For such Marxists the state must play the major if not the exclusive role in the provision of social (and indeed economic and other) policy. However, as commentators like Pete Alcock argue, social policy developments have also transformed capitalist society (Alcock, 1996, p 147). In his discussion of the political economy of the welfare state, Ian Gough highlighted the contradictory nature of welfare states in advanced capitalist societies; that is to say the way in which they can at the same time serve to support capital accumulation and also provide social benefits for 'those in need' (Gough, 1979). At the same time, Ginsburg (1979) discussed the way in which welfare states controlled and oppressed service users as well as providing for them.

Fabianism, Marxism and participation

During the 20th century, neither Fabianism nor Marxism seemed to encourage the advancement of either the consideration or practice of participation in mainstream modern social policy. This appears to relate both to some shared characteristics and to some distinct differences between the two. Perhaps one thing which distinguished them was that proponents of Fabianism did not seem (certainly during its dominant years) to have given the issue of participation serious consideration, while among Marxists, participation was perhaps taken for granted, but not necessarily with any justification. The effect in both cases was to discourage broad-based or popular participation in the analysis, construction and operation of social policy

Both philosophies (despite Fabianism's preoccupation with empiricism) can be seen to be based on grand theories, operating primarily at the macro level. Both have a particular interest in the state as the planning, implementing and providing agent for welfare. Critics of each philosophy highlight fundamental problems that this latter issue may pose. Fabianism's focus on state welfare under capitalism is problematic for all (not only Marxists) who do not see the state's interests as necessarily synonymous with those of welfare service users and other citizens, or the state as necessarily representing or including such interests. Similar problems are posed for those who question assumptions that state socialism or Marxist regimes necessarily embody, or provide a basis for embodying the interests and perspectives of all citizens.

Fabian approaches to social policy can be seen as based essentially on notions of elite 'expertise'; committed to empirical investigation to identify need and social policy responses and a model of 'public education', to seek popular support and legitimation for their proposals and reforms. Fabian social policy was essentially 'top-down' in both its approach and process. There was little or no role for people who used or might use welfare services in conceiving, shaping, managing or critiquing its provision or proposals. They were confined to a passive position as data sources for its empirical investigation. Interpretation of their experience was seen by Fabians as a task for its experts and researchers. Fabianism can be seen as offering an inherently paternalistic approach to social policy analysis and formation, with its own preset proposals and programmes.

Marxist perspectives have been concerned with the ultimate inclusion and participation of people. Such participation clearly featured in Marxism's founding thinking (Marx and Engels, 1848/1998; Lenin, 1979).

However, unresolved problems remained of how to reconcile state and leader control with control by individuals and collectivities within societies. With its framework of class struggle, Marxism provided a basis by which participation might be understood, but there was frequently a failure to look beyond the need for 'popular' and revolutionary struggles to explore how these might truly be inclusive, anti-discriminatory, *participatory* and progressive in class terms. Marxism's originating emphasis on people conceived as workers (both within and outside welfare) had important implications for understanding in social policy and highlighted existing divisions. Many of the groups liable to be on the receiving end of welfare, for example, unemployed and casual workers, poor people, disabled people, mental health service users and so on, were among those negatively identified by Marx as *lumenproletariat*. Workers in the welfare system have often been experienced as oppressive by welfare service users, and their interests and those advanced by their trades unions would by no means be seen as consistent with those of service users. With some important exceptions (for example, Phillipson, 1982), the neo-Marxist critiques and those framed in terms of political economy of the 1970s and early 1980s, which focused on welfare and social services in general, did not address issues of participation or the perspectives of people on the receiving end of welfare (for example, Bailey and Brake, 1975; Corrigan and Leonard, 1978; Ginsburg, 1979; Gough, 1979).

It would be wrong to leave this discussion of Marxist thinking and social policy without taking account of one strand of action and thinking that had strong roots in leftist and Marxist ideology and a concern with advancing participation. Two of the best-known publications and activities associated with it were *In and against the state* and *Beyond the fragments* (London Edinburgh Weekend Return Group, 1979; Rowbotham et al, 1979). Both initiatives were linked with grassroots campaigning as well as producing best-selling pamphlets and books. Both were concerned with reconciling the interests of public service users and workers, of engaging with and involving the perspectives of service users and of advancing participation. Both originated with political and trades union activists concerned with challenging the controlling and negative aspects of state welfare and committed to working in more participatory and egalitarian ways. We will shortly also return to another key link with Marxist approaches to social policy by considering the development of the welfare service user movements.

New Right, 'Third Way' and social policy

The failure of traditional dominant political and social philosophies to advance participation can also be seen as the context and starting point for the emergence of two new modern political philosophies, which also have major ramifications for participation. These are the political New Right and the Third Way. Between them, they have fundamentally reshaped social policy in the West and beyond.

The proponents of the New Right or neo-liberalism came to political prominence in the US and UK in the late 1970s and early 1980s. They rejected a planned economy and favoured a competitive market economy. They argued that such a market economy was an essential basis for democracy and that the powers of government should be limited by constitutional law. They prioritised monetary policy, fiscal constraint and privatisation. They advocated individual freedom, unconstrained by state 'interference'. At a time when the authority of Fabianism was weakening, they attacked state welfare, arguing that it undermined the market economy. They attacked state intervention on the grounds of cost, inefficiency and the creation of 'dependency'. They emphasised instead individual responsibility for welfare, the purchase of health and welfare services and the restriction of the state's role to the provision of a safety net service.

The Third Way came to prominence with Britain's New Labour, but also reflects a more general development in modern European and Western politics and social policy (Giddens, 1998). It is presented in terms of a changed balance of state and market approaches to public policy and welfare. The Third Way emphasises the benefits of the private sector. Critics raise concerns over its ambiguity about redistribution (Lister, 2001), the possible shift away from universalism and its increased emphasis on managerialism and privatisation, reliance on means-testing and a more residual role for state welfare (Drake, 2001, p 158; Lister, 2001). New Labour social policy in the UK has been characterised by ambiguity and contradiction. There is little agreement about it. Some commentators highlight its effectiveness (for example, Glennerster, 2001; Oppenheim, 2001). Others stress its instrumental populism and narrow pragmatism (Lister, 2001); its tendencies to authoritarianism and 'scapegoating' (Butler and Drakeford, 2001); and its preoccupation with participation in the labour market (Levitas, 1998).

Some social policy analysts have highlighted the similarities between the political New Right and Third Way, suggesting that the latter simply represents Labour's adoption of right wing policies. However, the Third

Way and New Labour social policy can also be seen, and present themselves, as different in kind from both New Right and Old Labour. Indeed, a more interesting, but less often made connection, is between Third Way social policy and the shift to the right in Fabian social policy that began to develop in the late 1970s, associated with the Social Democratic Party (SDP) under headings like 'welfare pluralism' and the 'mixed economy of welfare', with a new emphasis on voluntarism, 'informal aid' and the marketplace (Beresford and Croft, 1984). This shift in Fabian consensus to the right can be seen as Fabianism's attempt at adaptation to meet the crisis then facing it. It may also be seen as laying the foundations for New Labour social policy, providing a model that was subsequently developed and embodied by it. To this extent, we should perhaps see Fabianism's influence as connecting with current government social policy, except that the 'expert administrator' and social planning are now replaced by managerialism and 'public private partnerships'. Perhaps what the Third Way comes closest to being is some kind of amalgam of right wing, Fabian and New Right social policy.

New Right, 'Third Way' and participation

These two political philosophies, the political New Right and Third Way, do have one other important feature in common, which also distinguishes them from their predecessors. Both place great emphasis on *participation*. In the UK, both political New Right Conservative administrations and New Labour 'Third Way' governments have prioritised participation and related concepts of 'partnership' and 'empowerment'. Arguably, it is in their commitment to a market-led and managerialist rhetoric and terminology of participation that these two political philosophies have come closest together. If anything New Labour has extended interest in participation highlighting it as a necessary feature, not only of policy and practice, but also of politics, with its rhetoric of participatory democracy and commitment to devolution, subsidiarity, parliamentary and local government reform.

The dominant modern model of participation, the consumerist approach, originates with the New Right. Increasingly overlaid with the goals and techniques of managerialism under New Labour, it might now be best to think of it as a *consumerist/managerialist* approach to participation. Associated with a retreat from state welfare and increasing emphasis on the market and individual responsibility, this approach to participation is closely linked with the philosophy and rhetoric of consumerism, including purchase of services and ideas of 'consumer/customer choice', 'voice'/

involvement' and 'exit' (Beresford and Croft, 1986; Winkler, 1987). It reflects the broader interest, associated with the market, of maximising profitability and effectiveness and the tendency to equate the latter with the former. It was originally presented in terms of advancing the 'three Es' in public policy, highlighted by Conservative administrations: efficiency, economy and effectiveness. It highlights all the ambiguities of consumerist approaches, with their emphasis on individual rights and choice coexisting with the imperatives of profitability and the market. Framed mainly in market research terms of improving goods and services through market testing and feedback, the consumerist approach has so far mainly been based on consultative and data collection methods of involvement. These have become increasingly sophisticated and innovative. As the clear equivalent of the market testing and focus groups associated with mainstream commercial goods and services, its role in improving provision on the basis of 'consumer' or 'customer' intelligence gathering can be readily understood. Prioritising the perspectives and the interests of the state, market and welfare service system, there is no commitment to the redistribution of power or control.

Welfare service user movements and participation

However, it has not only been these two dominant strands in modern political and social policy ideology, the New Right and the Third Way, which have prioritised participation or been influential in its conceptualisation. The same has also been true of the welfare service user movements, which have developed and come to prominence over a corresponding period. These movements, of disabled people, psychiatric system survivors, older people and other recipients and users of health, social care and income maintenance services, have become increasingly powerful and influential, with their own democratically constituted local, national and international organisations and groupings. These movements, and the organisations operating within them, have developed their own cultures, arts, ways of self organising, knowledges, theories, principles, strategies and demands (Campbell, 1996; Campbell and Oliver, 1996; Morris, 1996; Oliver and Barnes, 1998; Barnes et al, 1999; Beresford, 1999; Lindow, 2001). It is also important to note that Marxist analysis and leftist critiques played a significant part in the development of the thinking of these movements (see for example, Oliver, 1990; Shakespeare, 1998).

The welfare service user movements have developed their own model of participation – a *democratic* model. Service users' interest in participation has been part of broader political and social philosophies, which prioritise people's inclusion, autonomy, agency, independence and the achievement of their human and civil rights. This approach to participation is primarily concerned with people having more say in the political process; institutions, organisations and agencies which impact upon them, and being able to exert more control over their own lives. The democratic model of participation is rooted in people's lives and their aspirations to improve the nature and conditions of their lives. Participation has been one expression of a commitment to 'self-advocacy'; of people being able to speak and act on their own behalf. This has been framed primarily in terms of involvement through collective action in independent disabled people's and social care service users' organisations (Campbell, 1996; Campbell and Oliver, 1996; Oliver, 1996).

The democratic approach to involvement is explicitly political. Unlike the consumerist/managerialist approach, it highlights issues of power and the (re)distribution of power. The disabled people's movement, for example, bases its approach to participation on the social model of disability, using both parliamentary and direct action to achieve change. It prioritised the introduction of civil rights legislation and the provision of adequate support for organisations controlled by disabled people themselves, establishing the 'independent living' movement to ensure that disabled people can maintain control over their personal support through direct payments and self-run personal assistance schemes. The movements' democratic model of participation is liberational in purpose, committed to social change and personal and political empowerment.

The potential of participation

The development of these two different and in many ways opposed conceptions of participation, highlights the importance of considering participation in its broader ideological, political and socio-economic contexts. Participation may have many meanings and expressions. While there may be overlaps between consumerist/managerialist and democratic approaches to participation, the significant differences between them can be traced to their different origins, values and aims. Both approaches may be concerned with bringing about change. However, in the consumerist approach, the search is for external input which the initiating institution – state, market, service system or policy maker – *itself* decides what to do with. Control and the distribution of power remain unchanged. The democratic approach is concerned with ensuring that welfare service users and other citizens have the direct capacity and opportunity to make change.

While the logic of the democratic approach is for 'bottom-up' political process and 'user-led' and 'user-controlled' services; a consumerist/managerialist approach is clearly compatible with the retention of a top-down, provider-led approach to politics, policy and provision. While the democratic approach is explicitly political (and can expect to come in for criticism for this reason), the consumerist/managerialist approach tends to be abstracted and treated as if it were unrelated to any broader ideology or philosophy – although it is, of course, implicitly. Perhaps this highlights a more general problem that exists for managerialist/consumerist approaches to participation: the tension that there is when arrangements for participatory or direct democracy exist in a political structure based primarily on a system of representative democracy.

This draws us to two important and related issues that participation raises for social policy. What is its potential for liberation and transformation in social policy? What difference can it actually make and what kind of participation would be required? What impact can it actually have on social policy? Its liberatory potential concerns its capacity to advance people's rights and interests, particularly as subjects of social policy. Its transformatory potential relates to its capacity to support social policy capable of achieving such aims. The capacity of the two approaches to participation that we have been discussing – consumerist/managerialist and democratic – to achieve such objectives, seem to be markedly different.

While participation is generally presented in positive and progressive terms, it also has a regressive potential. Participatory initiatives frequently serve to obstruct rather than increase people's involvement, being used to tokenise and coopt people, delay decisions and actions and to legitimate predetermined agendas and decisions. This seems to have been particularly true of consumerist approaches to participation, where data collection rather than empowerment is the primary aim. To date it has been this approach to participation which has predominated and this may help account for the widespread distrust of and disillusion with participation that has developed. The commitment of the consumerist/managerialist model to exchange relationships, its reliance on hierarchical managerialism and its lack of attention to power relationships, suggest that it is as likely to reinforce the status quo as challenge it. In the UK context, this is highlighted by the extension of relationships with the market (with which this model of participation is most closely associated) through the development of 'private public partnerships' (PPP) and 'private finance initiatives' (PFI). These expose service users' 'voice' to new risks of being subordinated and marginalised by more powerful partners and interests, regardless of the concurrent rhetoric of involvement and empowerment.

In contrast, the democratic approach to participation does offer the promise of liberation and transformation. Indeed, its advocates can argue that the legislation with which it is already associated, like disability discrimination and direct payments legislation, has already begun this process. Its emphasis on the redistribution of power, the personal and political empowerment of people as citizens, workers and service users, the equalisation of relationships in public policy and user controlled support and services all have transformative implications for social policy. So does its commitment to service users' liberation, through the achievement of their human and civil rights and the support it has from grassroots mass movements as part of their broader ideologies.

While a managerialist/consumerist approach to participation may be written off as a dead end, tied to the status quo, it is difficult to see how any social policy that is committed to advancing the rights and needs of service users can ignore the democratic model. It may offer a basis for transforming social policy. This makes it essential to explore this model more carefully. It also makes it all the more important to be able to distinguish between these two models of participation and not confuse one with the other. Thus it is no longer good enough to offer general arguments for or against participation in social policy. These need to be related both to specific models of participation and the ideologies underpinning social policies. If there is one lesson to be learned from attempting to put participation into context, it is that social policy can no longer be considered in isolation from it or the welfare service user movements, which have been centrally involved in its development.

Key questions for social policy

The democratic approach to participation raises and encourages us to address some major issues and questions in analysing and developing social policy as both discipline and practice. These include:

- how social policy should be produced;
- the nature of knowledge formation and knowledge claims in social policy;
- the purpose and nature of social policy practice;
- how social policy workers should be socialised (educated and trained for their roles) and by whom;
- the nature of recruitment and employment policies for social policy;
- what and whose knowledge social policy should be informed by (Beresford, 2000);

- who shapes and controls social policy and its institutions;
- how it is researched and evaluated and by whom.

These questions apply, of course, to all approaches to and forms of social policy. The democratic model of participation, however, raises them with some intensity because it prioritises the role of service users in all these areas. Its advocates highlight the absence of service users in the past and offer powerful political, moral and practical arguments for their inclusion in social policy formation now. This approach to participation presents a challenge, which social policy as both discipline and practice has yet to address.

However, all approaches to participation still need to be located in two additional contexts. These are the contexts of globalisation and difference.

Participation and globalisation

Globalisation has been described as:

> ... the idea that the world has become more integrated, economically, politically and culturally. In *economic* terms, it refers to the internationalisation of production and trade and the increased mobility of capital. *Politically* this is seen to have placed constraints on national policy making, although it may also lead to new supra-national forms of governance. (Holden, 2000)

The dominant discourse on globalisation presents it as a rationale for accepting that social policies should be subordinated to narrow economic constraints. This discourse, tied initially to the ideology and politics of the New Right, takes as its starting point the freeing of the market from traditional controls and regulation. Social policies that are premised on low tax levels and budget restraints reduce the resources available for social services. Deterministic accounts of globalisation present the state as powerless and therefore imply major constraints on the influence that people can exert through participation in public policy and provision. In fact the state has been a powerful agent of change, playing an important role in the UK, for example, in "transmitting the global market discipline throughout the economy, transferring large sums to the private sector through subsidised privatisations and creating an infrastructure for the private sector to trade with through various forms of contracting out" (Dominelli and Hoogvelt, 1996, p 48). In the context of participation, the interactions of states with globalisation need to be considered more critically (Deacon, 1997; Beresford and Holden, 2000). Participation needs to be related to globalisation and globalisation needs to be related to the discourses of welfare service user movements. So far, few attempts have been made to do this, but it is an essential task if the ideas and practice of participation are to be critiqued and developed in social policy with any success (Beresford and Holden, 2000; Holden and Beresford, 2002).

Participation and difference

Participation implies active involvement in the social sphere and refers to a range of involvements which individuals and groups may have in organisations, institutions and decisions affecting them and others. While participation is generally associated with the public sphere, what is less often discussed, is that it is also affected by people's circumstances and responsibilities in the *personal* sphere. These can limit the participation of many groups, notably women and disabled people. The ways in which obligations imposed on women as mothers, 'carers' and wives/partners inhibit the social spheres of employment and citizenship is well documented (for example, Williams, 1989, 1997; Lister, 1997). The traditional failure to provide adequate and appropriate support to enable disabled people to live independently and to be included in and integrated into mainstream society on equal terms is equally well established (for example, Morris, 1993; Oliver, 1996). An approach to participation that does not take account of issues of identity and the operation of such constraints is likely to mirror dominant discriminations and exclusions (Mayo, 2000).

Any serious discussion of participation must address and take into account different and related social divisions and discriminations, which may impose restrictions of the capacity of and opportunities available to groups to participate in the social sphere. Two components are essential if people are to have a realistic chance of participating and all groups are to have equal opportunities to participate. These are *access* and *support*. These reflect the need for both the personal and structural conditions for participation; and are set out in detail elsewhere (Beresford and Croft, 1993; Croft and Beresford, 1993). Both are essential. The concern of welfare service user movements with both personal and political empowerment is consistent with this requirement. Experience indicates that without suitable support, only the most confident, well resourced and advantaged people and groups are likely to become involved, while without access, efforts to become involved are likely to be arduous and ineffective. Access includes equal access to the political structure at both central and local state levels and to the decision-making process of other organisations and institutions that affect people's lives. Support includes increasing people's expectations and confidence; extending their skills; offering practical support like childcare, information, advocacy and transport; enabling people to get together in groups; and ensuring that minority ethnic groups and others facing discrimination can be involved on equal terms.

Conclusion: reconnecting social policy and participation

This is an important time to explore the role of service user involvement in, and its implications for, social policy. Social policy and participation are both at complex and difficult times in their histories. Both face doubt and uncertainty. Participation is no longer necessarily seen simply as 'a good thing'. Welfare service users no longer receive offers of participation as a gift. There is a growing sense from citizens' and service users' organisations that those inviting participation should either 'put up or shut up'. Low levels of political participation – in terms of turnout for the 2001 general election and for local and regional mayoral elections, as well as declining membership of major political parties – suggest broader distrust and disillusion. This is happening even as governments seek to 'modernise' voting systems and increase provisions for political participation (Ashley, 2002). As for social policy, New Labour's shift to the market has not generally been welcomed by the public. Its whole approach to social policy was based on radical reform, but now New Labour has itself been driven to 'think the unthinkable' and suggest that raising taxation may be the only way to 'save' the National Health Service (Elliott and White, 2001).

Both participation and social policy urgently require review. However, what is perhaps most important now is for their *relationship* to be subjected to critical consideration and development.

There is no doubt that there are strong political and organisational pressures to limit the effectiveness of welfare service users' participation; to coopt and incorporate it. But current developments in the UK suggest that existing ambiguities and contradictions may also offer opportunities. The interventions of the welfare service user movements (rather than the consumerist participation they have been offered) *have* made a difference. They have resulted in changes in legislation, policy and in some cases even the ideological basis of practice and provision. For example, while both the Disability Discrimination Act and the Disability Rights Commission fall short of the demands of the disabled people's movement, they now provide a framework for highlighting and protecting the rights of disabled people. Service users are represented in the new bodies and structures established by government to regulate and monitor social care, like the National Care Standards Commissions and the General Social Care Council. A disability activist has been appointed chair of the new Social Care Institute for Excellence, which has responsibility for developing the knowledge base of social care.

In a complex situation of ambiguity and uncertainty, a democratic model of participation does seem to offer the potential for change in social policy. There is now a need for a systematic examination of what:

- the pressures for and against such participation in social policy are in the UK and other settings;
- policy provisions need to be in place to support it;
- requirements there are for participation to be effective (for example, support for service user organisations, developmental work);
- implications participation may have for the process and focus of social policy as both discipline and practice.

These are issues which the social policy community must now address seriously. If this is to be done, then it should be in a way that is consistent with the liberatory ethos of participation. Such an initiative should reflect a commitment to real and effective participation in its own construction and operation. This must mean that it is developed in close and equal partnership with user controlled organisations and service user analysts and researchers. Then perhaps people's participation may become a key constituent for transforming social policy, instead of, as now, an increasingly devalued byway in policy discussion and development.

Notes

[1] This chapter draws on a Symposium paper, 'Der Klient als Produzent – Perspectiven der Demokratisierung Sozialier Arbiet', jointly presented by Peter Beresford and Suzy Croft at the 4th Bundeskongress Soziale Arbeit, 22 September 2001, University of Mainz.

[2] The terms 'service user' and 'welfare service user' are used in this discussion to describe people who receive or are eligible to receive social care, health and welfare services, particularly over a longer period. This embraces people included in a wide range of categories, including mental health service users/survivors, lone parents, people living with HIV/AIDS, children and young people in state 'care'

or who are fostered or adopted, disabled people, older people, people living on low income, low wages and/or receiving or entitled to state benefits or tax credits, people with learning difficulties, people with addictions to alcohol and proscribed drugs, and so on. People may receive welfare and social care services voluntarily or involuntarily. The term 'service users' is problematic, because it conceives of people primarily in terms of their use of services, which may well not be how they would define themselves. However, there is no other umbrella term that can helpfully be used to include all these overlapping groups. For example, some may include themselves as and be included as disabled, but others would not. Therefore the term 'service user' is used here, recognising its inadequacies, as a shorthand to describe the subjects of welfare and social care, without seeking to impose any other meanings or interpretations on it or them.

References

Alcock, P. (1996) *Social policy in Britain: Themes and issues*, Basingstoke: Macmillan.

Alcock, P. and Craig, G. (eds) (2001) *International social policy*, Basingstoke: Palgrave.

Alcock, P., Glennerster, H., Oakley, A. and Sinfield, A. (eds) (2001) *Welfare and wellbeing: Richard Titmuss's contribution to social policy*, Bristol: The Policy Press.

Anderson, V., Beresford, P., Croft, S., Dawe, S., Hebditch, S., Hodgson, G., Mullin, C. and Hain, P. (1982) *The realignment of the Right: The real face of the SDP*, London: Labour Coordinating Committee.

Ashley, J. (2002) 'Cook plans to make UK first to vote on internet', *The Guardian*, 7 January, p 1.

Bailey, R. and Brake, M. (1975) *Radical social work*, London: Edward Arnold.

Barnes, C., Mercer, G. and Shakespeare, T. (1999) *Exploring disability: A sociological introduction*, Cambridge: Polity Press.

Barnes, C., Morgan, H. and Mercer, G. (2001) *Creating independent futures: An evaluation of services led by disabled people*, Stage Three Report, Leeds: Disability Press.

BBC TV (2001) *National News*, 16 January.

Becker, S. (ed) (2000) 'Forward thinking', *SPA News*, February/March, Social Policy Association, pp 15-29.

Beresford, P. (1997) 'The last social division?: Revisiting the relationship between social policy, its producers and consumers', in M. May, E. Brunsdon and G. Craig (eds) *Social policy review 9*, London: Social Policy Association, pp 203-26.

Beresford, P. (1999) 'Making participation possible: movements of disabled people and psychiatric system survivors', in T. Jordan and A. Lent (eds) *Storming the millennium: The new politics of change*, London: Lawrence and Wishart, pp 34-50.

Beresford, P. (2000) 'Service users' knowledges and social work theory: conflict or collaboration', *British Journal of Social Work*, vol 30, no 4, pp 489-504.

Beresford, P. and Croft, S. (1984) 'Welfare pluralism: the new face of Fabianism', *Critical Social Policy*, Issue 9, Spring, pp 19-39.

Beresford, P. and Croft, S. (1986) *Whose welfare? Private care or public services*, Brighton: Lewis Cohen Urban Studies Centre, Brighton University.

Beresford, P. and Croft, S. (1993) *Citizen involvement: A practical guide for change*, Basingstoke: Macmillan.

Beresford, P. and Croft, S. (2001) 'Mental health policy: a suitable case for treatment', in C. Newnes, G. Holmes and C. Dunn (eds) *This is madness too: Critical perspectives on mental health services*, Ross-on-Wye: PCCS Books, pp 11-22.

Beresford, P. and Holden, C. (2000) 'We have choices: globalisation and welfare user movements', *Disability and Society*, vol 15, no 7, pp 973-89.

Butler, I. and Drakeford, M. (2001) 'Which Blair project: communitarianism, social authoritarianism and social work', *Journal of Social Work*, vol 1, no 1, April, pp 7-19.

Campbell, J. and Oliver, M. (1996) *Disability politics: Understanding our past, changing our future*, Basingstoke: Macmillan.

Campbell, P. (1996) 'The history of the user movement in the United Kingdom', in T. Heller, J. Reynolds, R. Gomm, R. Muston and S. Pattison (eds) *Mental health matters*, Basingstoke: Macmillan, pp 218-25.

Campbell, P. (2001) The Richard Sutton Memorial Lecture, Bromley Psychosocial Rehabilitation Forum, 23 November.

Clarke, J., Gewirtz, S. and McLaughlin, E. (eds) (2000) *New managerialism, new welfare?*, London: Sage Publications/Open University.

Cooke, B. and Kothari, U. (eds) (2001) *Participation: The new tyranny?*, London: Zed Books.

Corrigan, P. and Leonard, P. (1978) *Social work practice under capitalism*, Basingstoke: Macmillan.

Croft, S. and Beresford, P. (1993) *Getting involved: A practical manual*, London: Open Services Project/Joseph Rowntree Foundation.

Deacon, B. (1997) 'Social policy in a shrinking world', in P. Alcock, A. Erskine and M. May (eds) *The student's companion to social policy*, Oxford: Blackwell, pp 128-35.

Dean, M. (2000) 'Creating an inclusion zone', *Guardian Society, The Guardian*, November 1, pp 10-11.

Dominelli, L. and Hoogvelt, A. (1996) 'Globalization and the technocratization of social work', *Critical Social Policy*, vol 16, no 2, issue 47, May, pp 45-62.

Drake, R.F. (2001) *The principles of social policy*, Basingstoke: Palgrave.

Elliott, L. and White, M. (2001) 'Brown's pledge on the NHS – and now for the tax rises', *The Guardian*, 28 November, p 1.

George, V. and Wilding, P. (1999) *British society and social welfare: Towards a sustainable society*, Basingstoke: Macmillan.

Giddens, A. (1998) *The third way: The renewal of social democracy*, Cambridge: Polity Press.

Ginsburg, N. (1979) *Class, capital and social policy*, Basingstoke: Macmillan.

Ginsburg, N. (1998) 'The socialist perspective', in P. Alcock, A. Erskine and M. May (eds) *The student's companion to social policy*, Oxford: Blackwell, pp 78-84.

Glennerster, H. (2001) 'Social policy', in A. Seldon (ed) *The Blair effect: The Blair government 1997-2001*, London: Little Brown, pp 383-403.

Gough, I. (1979) *The political economy of the welfare state*, Basingstoke: Macmillan.

Gough, I. (2000) *Global capital, human needs and social policies*, Basingstoke: Palgrave.

Hanley, B., Bradburn, J., Gorin, S., Barnes, M., Evans, C., Goodare, H., Kelson, M., Kent, A., Oliver, S. and Wallcraft, J. (2000) *Involving consumers in research and development in the NHS: Briefing notes for researchers*, Winchester: Consumers in NHS Research Support Unit.

Harris, M. and Rochester, C. (eds) (2001) *Voluntary organisations and social policy in Britain: Perspectives on change and choice*, Basingstoke: Palgrave.

Held, D. (1987) *Models of democracy*, Cambridge: Polity Press.

Hetherington, P. (2001) 'Green belt fears over Byers reform plans', *The Guardian*, 13 December, p 12.

Hill, M. (1998) 'Social policy and the political process', in P. Alcock, A. Erskine and M. May (eds) *The student's companion to social policy*, Oxford: Blackwell, pp 136-41.

Holden, C. and Beresford, P. (2002) 'Globalisation and disability', in C. Barnes, L. Barton and M. Oliver (eds) *The sociology of disability*, Cambridge: Polity Press.

Holden, M. (2000) 'Globalization and social work', in M. Davies (ed) *The Blackwell encyclopaedia of social work*, Oxford: Blackwell, p 147.

Lavalette, M. and Pratt, A. (eds) (2001) *Social policy: A conceptual and theoretical introduction* (2nd edn), London: Sage Publications.

Lenin, V.I. (1979) *On participation of the people in government*, Moscow: Progress Publishers.

Levitas, R. (1998) *The inclusive society?: Social exclusion and New Labour*, Basingstoke: Macmillan.

Lindow, V. (2001) 'Survivor research', in C. Newnes, G. Holmes and C. Dunn (eds) *This is madness too: Critical perspectives on mental health services*, Ross-on-Wye: PCCS Books, pp 135-46.

Lister, R. (1997) *Citizenship: Feminist perspectives*, Basingstoke, Macmillan.

Lister, R. (2001) 'New Labour: a study in ambiguity from a position of ambivalence', *Critical Social Policy*, vol 21, no 4, issue 69, pp 425-47.

London Edinburgh Weekend Return Group (1979) *In and against the state*, London: Pluto.

Marx, K. and Engels, F. (1848/1998) *The manifesto of the Communist Party*, (Communist Manifesto), in *Marx and Engels classics in politics*, London: ElecBook.

Mayo, M. (2000) *Culture, communities, identities: Cultural strategies for participation and empowerment*, Basingstoke: Palgrave.

McCarthy, M. (2001) 'MPs given new power in planning shake-up', *The Independent*, 7 November, p 14.

Montgomery, J.D. and Inkeles, A. (ed) (2001) *Social capital as a policy resource*, Dordrecht, Netherlands: Kluiver Academic Publishers.

Morris, J. (1993) *Independent lives: Community care and disabled people*, Basingstoke: Macmillan.

Morris, J. (ed) (1996) *Feminism and disability*, London: Women's Press.

Mullard, M. and Spicker, P. (1998) *Social policy in a changing society*, London: Routledge.

Oliver, M. (1990) *The politics of disablement*, Basingstoke: Macmillan.

Oliver, M. (1996) *Understanding disability: From theory to practice*, Basingstoke: Macmillan.

Oliver, M. and Barnes, C. (1998) *Disabled people and social policy: From exclusion to inclusion*, London: Longman.

Oppenheim, C. (2001) 'Enabling participation?: New Labour's welfare-to-work policies', in S. White (ed) *New Labour: The progressive future?*, Basingstoke: Palgrave, pp 77-92.

Pateman, C. (1970) *Participation and democratic theory*, Cambridge: Cambridge University Press.

Phillipson, C. (1982) *Capitalism and the construction of old age*, Basingstoke: Macmillan.

Rowbotham, S., Segal, L. and Wainwright, H. (1979) *Beyond the fragments*, London: Merlin Press.

Shakespeare, T. (ed) (1998) *The disability reader: Social science perspectives*, London: Cassell.

Sullivan, M. (1998) 'The social democratic perspective', in P. Alcock, A. Erskine and M. May (eds) *The student's companion to social policy*, Oxford: Blackwell, pp 71-7.

Tawney, R.H. (1931) *Equality*, London: Allen and Unwin.

Taylor-Gooby, P. (ed) (2001) *Welfare states under pressure*, London: Sage Publications.

Vidal, J. (2001) 'Startling new developments: big business on the one hand, and community groups on the other, are watching the overhaul of the planning process with interest', *The Guardian*, 11 December, p 13.

VSO (Voluntary Service Overseas) (2001) *Mobilising disadvantaged communities: A global perspective on participatory approaches*, International Conference, 29 October, London:VSO.

Watson, S. and Doyal, L. (eds) (1999) *Engendering social policy*, Buckingham: Open University Press.

Williams, F. (1997) 'Women and community', in J. Bornat, J. Johnson, C. Pereira, D. Pilgrim and F. Williams (eds) *Community care: A reader*, Basingstoke: Macmillan/Open University, pp 34-44.

Williams, J. (1989) *Social policy: A critical introduction*, Cambridge: Polity Press.

Winkler, F. (1987) 'Consumerism in health care: beyond the supermarket model', *Policy & Politics*, vol 15, no 1, pp 1-8.

Yeates, N. (2001) *Globalization and social policy*, London: Sage Publications.

Index

working conditions 177-8, 179,
186-7
and migration 164-5, 178
for people with learning difficulties
96
policies for globalised world 109
Employment Relations Act (1999)
119
environmental justice 236-7
environmental movement 134
see also Green social policy
equality issues and EU
Charter of Fundamental Rights
183-7
equal treatment principle 178-9
Ericson, R. 212
Esping-Andersen, Gøsta 108, 109, 111
ethnic minorities
attitudes towards 5-6
people with learning difficulties 95
see also asylum seekers; migration
policy
European Public Procurement
Directive (EPPD) 116
European Union (EU)
acquis communautaire 172, 177-9,
193-4
and care provision 116
Charter of Fundamental Rights 173,
182-8, 189
and environmental protection
policy 238-9
equal treatment principle 178-9
and migration policy 154-5, 178
non-discrimination policy 178-9,
183-5
social policy developments 7, 106,
171-90
focus on employment 171, 176-9,
186-7
health services 181-2, 186
social protection measures 179-82,
185-6
treaty background 172-7
European Women's Lobby 184
evidence-based policy and crime 201,
217
extinction of species 227

F

Fabianism 270-2, 273, 275, 276
family carers
consultation on Learning
Disabilities Strategy 86, 87-8
disregard for role of 89-90
recognition of contribution 90-1
support for 95
family reunion conditions for
migrants 155, 156
Feeley, Malcolm 210-11
feminisation of migration 153
Ferris, J. 225
Field, Frank 181
Fitzpatrick, T. 225
'fortress Europe' 154
Foucault, Michel 195, 199, 200,
202-3, 210-12, 213, 214, 217
France: immigration policy 152
Fukuyama, Francis 249, 250-1, 253

G

G8 organisation 6-7
Garret, Geoffrey 9
GDP and public expenditure 68-70
General Agreement on Trade in
Services (GATS) 116
General Municipal and Boilermakers
(GMB) union 117
general practitioners (GPs) *see*
Primary Care Groups and Trusts
Geneva Convention 155, 157, 167n
Genoa anti-globalisation protests 134,
135
geo-demographics 8, 9, 11
George, V. 109
Giddens, Anthony 9, 111, 114, 249
Ginsburg, Norman 272
globalisation
anti-globalisation movements 6-7,
105-6, 127-45
effect on migration 153
effect on welfare state 9, 105, 107-23
and participation 281-2
and social policy 105, 112-13,
139-44
theory on 8, 9, 108, 109, 122